IN PURSUIT OF EXCELLENCE
MISSOURI SOUTHERN STATE COLLEGE
1937–1992

IN PURSUIT OF EXCELLENCE
MISSOURI SOUTHERN STATE COLLEGE

1937–1992

BY G. K. RENNER

To Dave Tate —
Many thanks for your
support. Hope you will
find many reminders
of your years at
MSSC in the
book.

G. K. Renner

A study in how well-groomed freshmen of that era dressed, 1940–1941 freshman class officers are shown strolling down the staircase. From left: Albert Stewart, president; Margaret Bull, secretary; and Roy Lee Daniel, vice president.

THE
DONNING COMPANY
PUBLISHERS

DEDICATION

To my children, William and Carolyn, and the many other students whose studies at Missouri Southern have opened new vistas of excellence for them.

(Photo page 2) This aerial view, looking eastward, shows the Missouri Southern campus as it appeared in the fall of 1992. Omitted from the photograph is that portion of the campus located north of Newman Road, encompassing the residential complex and the Anderson Police Academy. In the immediate left foreground is the Ummel Technology Building, which anchors the western end of the campus. In the center is Matthews Hall, the largest structure on campus. Hughes Stadium, upper center, occupies the easternmost extension of the campus. The Taylor Education and Psychology Hall, partially visible to the upper right, marks the southern edge of the campus. The new Webster Communications and Social Science Hall appears in the upper left.

The Donning Company/Publishers
184 Business Park Drive, Suite 106
Virginia Beach, VA 23462

Steve Mull, General Manager
Richard A. Horwege, Editor
Mary Eliza Midgett, Designer
Nancy Schneiderheinze, Project Director
Laura D. Hill, Director of Research
Elizabeth B. Bobbitt, Production Editor

Library of Congress Cataloging in Publication Data:
Renner, G. K. (Gail K.), 1924–
    In pursuit of excellence : Missouri Southern State College, 1937–1992 / by G. K. Renner.
        p. cm.
    Includes bibliographical references (p.) and index.
    ISBN 0-89865-876-4 (alk. paper)
    1. Missouri Southern State College—History. I. Title.
LD3500.R46 1993   93-29631
    378.778'72—dc20   CIP
Printed in the United States of America

CONTENTS

Coach William N. "Bill" Collins is shown addressing his football team during halftime at Junge Stadium in the fall of 1940. A popular coach, Collins is remembered for making eloquent pep talks to his teams at game time. Uncertainty about the future of wartime college athletics led Collins to resign in December 1942 in favor of a job in industry, but he later returned to physical education with a position at the University of Missouri. Collins died in 1961.

FOREWORD

The Missouri Southern State College that we know today didn't spring into being overnight. Its building actually was a process of evolution stretching over forty years and involved the dedicated efforts of scores of Jasper County citizens.

Its roots can be traced to the founding of the Joplin Junior College authorized by the Joplin Board of Education in 1937. This institution served the local educational system well for a period of twenty-seven years and many of its graduates carried high academic standards while completing their education at other four-year institutions.

In the early 1960s during the Christmas holidays, a comparative handful of citizens gathered in the old Joplin Board of Education building on Pearl Street. Their talk was about the need for a four-year college which would provide a complete college education in this area and make it unnecessary for the junior college graduates to go out of state, as many of them were, to finish their degrees. Their thoughts and efforts were to become known as "the impossible dream" because of the long odds against achieving their objective.

MSSC founders were aware of the efforts of Flint, Michigan citizens who were successful in persuading the governing board of the University of Michigan to fund two additional years on top of the Flint Junior College, thus providing a full four-year institution. Local supporters were hopeful of accomplishing something similar in Jasper County.

A bill introduced in the Missouri legislature called for a four-year institution in Jasper County and to be a part of the University of Missouri system. Surprisingly it passed on the first try, only to be vetoed by the governor because the University was already acquiring two new campuses in Kansas City and St. Louis.

Meanwhile local voters created the Junior College District of Jasper County. This action took place in April 1964 and provided for the school to have its own tax base including all of Jasper County and parts of Newton, Lawrence, and Barton and to be governed by a six-member board of trustees. The institution was named the Jasper County Junior College.

On land lying east of Joplin and formerly occupied by Mission Hills Farm where registered Hereford cattle were raised, a new campus was established. The land was paid for entirely by local donors and the new buildings by a combination of federal government funds and local taxes.

House Bill 210, passed by the Missouri legislature in July 1965, provided for the establishment of a two-year senior college in Jasper County funded by the state and to be operated in conjunction with the junior college. The college now became known as Missouri Southern College with the first two years still supported by local taxes.

The final legislative act providing for the Missouri Southern State College which exists today was passed as Senate Bill 114 and was signed on the college campus by Governor Kit Bond on June 26, 1975. It called for the state to provide funds for the operation of the entire four years.

Thus ended over ten years of effort on the part of Jasper County citizens and legislators to bring into being a four-year college which took its place among earlier established state institutions of higher learning.

The "impossible dream" had become a reality.

Fred G. Hughes

PREFACE

Serious interest in writing a book-length history of Missouri Southern State College dates from 1987 and the institution's golden anniversary. The Fiftieth Anniversary Committee, formed to plan activities for that milestone, came to realize that no adequate, comprehensive account of the college's history existed. Accounts that existed were either piecemeal renderings of particular happenings or were tabulations of important events that, while covering a span of years, offered little insight, depth of analysis, or sense of continuity.

In Pursuit of Excellence attempts to fulfill that need. Its writing has been made especially difficult by the lack of earlier, comprehensive accounts of the college's development. Research has involved digging through masses of original sources to find interesting material that is significant and that casts light on the overall development of the college. The task has been a demanding one that has gone on intermittently over a period of five years. Hopefully those with an attachment to Southern, including the approximately fifteen thousand alumni and those with family, business, or community ties to the college, will find in the book's pages a sense of enlightenment and much that is familiar and interesting.

Activities connected with Southern's fiftieth anniversary have had the effect of reviving interest in the institution's junior college origins. Junior college alumni, of whom there are many, have always defended its importance, but the later generation of baccalaureate degree–holding alumni have tended to overlook MSSC's junior college roots and to treat them as a bygone era only vaguely connected with the senior college. In reality, some thirty of Southern's fifty-five years have been as a two-year junior college. This includes the Joplin Junior College, 1937–1964; the Jasper County Junior College, 1964–1965; and its continuation, 1965–1967, under the name of Missouri Southern College.

In a sense, the book is written on two levels. Its approximately three hundred photographs and their accompanying captions give a quick overview of the college's history, rich with meaning in that special way that only pictorial images can give. On the other hand, there is a comprehensive narrative history that traces the college's development, picking up not only important milestones, but also relating the steady growth of established functions such as sports, student clubs, social events, and especially quality academics. A common thread running through this account is that of the search for excellence in education which characterized the early junior college, much as it does today's greatly expanded senior institution.

(Opposite) Edith Lundien Mayes, a native of Carl Junction, was JJC's first "College Queen." She is shown with her attendants Mary Laird (left) and Joan Epperson (right). The ceremony was part of the college's first prom, held in the spring of 1938 at the Sagmount Inn, near Joplin.

Members of the 1942–1943 basketball team pictured are, from left, front row: Bill Weaver, Al Pearson, Bob Rousselot, and Bob Close. Second row: Jim O'Hara, Dick Gambill, Lee McNeill, and Francis Roderique. Back row: Coach Clay Cooper, Charles Frisby, Bob Warden, Jack Thompson, and Darrell Smith. Rapidly disintegrating due to a loss of players to the armed forces, the basketball team was discontinued for the next year.

In the spring of 1943, Bill (Dennis) Weaver, active in football and track as well as basketball, was called up for service in the Navy Air Corps, where he spent the next twenty-seven months. He never completed his sophomore year at JJC. After the war, Weaver graduated from the University of Oklahoma and then moved to New York City where he began his illustrious career as a stage, movie, and television actor.

Years later, reminiscing about JJC, Weaver recounted how, as a financially strapped student, he accidentally burned a hole in his pants, leaving him with only one pair. The incident led him to set up a clothing fund for deserving MSSC Athletes. He also established two $500 annual scholarships for Southern students.

ACKNOWLEDGMENTS

Many individuals and organizations have helped with writing, *In Pursuit of Excellence*. Their aid has added immeasurably to the richness and accuracy of the book. Any errors, however, are my own.

The Fiftieth Anniversary Committee initiated this project. Though the committee no longer functions, it played an important role in getting the work under way. Richard Massa, Chairman; Jean Campbell, Staff Assistant; and several other members, have continued to promote completion of the project. Other members of the committee were: Sue Billingsly, Judy Conboy, Beverly Culwell, Glenn Dolence, Kreta Gladden, Robert Higgins, Richard Humphrey, Gwen Hunt, Jim Maupin, John Messick, and Val Williams.

The Missouri Southern Foundation deserves special credit for underwriting publication of the book. Without their timely support, issuance of the book would have been greatly complicated. Members of the committee in the 1992–1993 academic year are: Roy Mayes, President; Dr. Lance Beshore; James Bracht; Joy Cragin; Dr. Donald Crockett; Douglas Davis; Jack Dawson; Ray Grace; Fred Hughes; Lawrence Kloeppel; Robert Lamb; Dr. Julio Leon; Allen McReynolds; Gilbert Roper; Jim Spicer; Jim Spradling; Hubert Van Fleet; Jerry Wells; Gene Wild; and Glenn Wilson.

The more recently formed Pictorial History Book Committee is in charge of promotion and sales of the book. Members of the committee have spent many hours planning promotion and sales campaigns as well as expediting these activities. Members of the committee are: Fred Hughes, Chairman; Benton Whitaker, Vice-Chairman; Jean Campbell, Liaison; Richard Massa; Gwen Hunt; Kreta Gladden; and Sue Billingsly.

Many people have been especially helpful in researching and writing *In Pursuit of Excellence*. These include Jean Campbell who, as adviser to the *Crossroads* as well as being staff assistant and liaison for both the earlier Fiftieth Anniversary Committee and the Pictorial History Book Committee, has spent many hours gathering research materials, negotiating with publishers and organizing sales of the book.

Gwen Hunt, Director of Public Information, has been unfailingly helpful in providing information and photographs dealing with the history of MSSC as well as arranging press releases and radio and television appearances to promote the book. Mrs. Hunt, a JJC graduate, has also provided valuable information about the college's early years.

Larry Meacham, writer and photographer for the Public Information Office and another JJC graduate, has also been generously helpful in providing historical photographs as well as relating his knowledge of important college events.

Charles Nodler, College Archivist, has been very patient and cooperative during the untold hours I have spent culling through the Archives' extensive holdings of MSSC memorabilia. Nodler, a Southern graduate, has also drawn on his wonderful knowledge of sports and college personnel to help clarify my understanding of many events.

Richard Massa, has been of inestimable help initiating and expediting the history book project through his roles on the Fiftieth Anniversary and Pictorial History Book committees. He has also lent his expertise in editing and publishing by serving as reader of the finished copy.

After JJC's first year, the college moved to this building at Fourth and Byers, which became its home for the next twenty years. The main structure was built in 1896 with an expansion added in 1907 to the south. An exterior of Carthage cut stone for the first floor and red brick for the upper stories gave the building a massive appearance that masked its serious structural weaknesses. Home to Joplin High School from 1897 to 1918, the structure then served various purposes until the school district began remodeling it for the junior college (a 1938 marker above the main Fourth Street entrance identified this project).

Kreta Gladden, Director of Alumni Affairs, has been unstintingly helpful in expediting the history book project through her membership on both the Fiftieth Anniversary and the Pictorial History Book committees. A Southern alumnus herself, as well as being Director of Alumni Affairs, Dr. Gladden has been cheerfully helpful in providing photographs and information about alumni activities.

Dennis Slusher, Director of the Sports Information Center, has been unhesitatingly helpful in drawing on his extensive files of sports statistics, games, and players, as well as photographs, to help in highlighting significant activities in MSSC athletics.

Much credit is due Mike Gullett, a professional photographer, for reproducing most of the photographs used in this book. The consistently high quality of his work relieved the author of many potentially nettlesome problems.

Though numerous people have been interviewed in writing this book, lengthy conferences with some have given extensive insights into certain aspects of the college's history. Among these people is Fred Hughes, whose long service as President of the Boards of Trustees and Regents has provided unparalleled insights into the transition from a junior to a senior college. Also his generous service as Chairman of the Pictorial History Book Committee and his making the Fred Hughes Papers available for research have added immeasurably to the project.

Sue Billingsly deserves special credit for her steady support of the history book project. Always cooperative, she has devoted much time to the undertaking through her service on the Fiftieth Anniversary and the Pictorial History Book committees as well as through her role as Director of the Missouri Southern Foundation. Also, as widow of the late President Leon Billingsly, she has patiently shared her knowledge of little-known events in the formation of the four-year college.

Special recognition is due Mrs. Bernice Gockel, widow of longtime professor and MSSC benefactor Harry Gockel, for her staunch support of Southern as well as for sharing her many memories of the college's early years.

Many thanks are due to Dr. Paul Shipman, retired Vice President for Business Affairs, for so generously sharing his knowledge of the formative years of the senior college, years in which he played a major role.

Special thanks go to Mrs. Jacqueline Potter for sharing her wonderful knowledge of the Mission Hills estate. A niece of the late Mrs. Juanita Wallower, Mrs. Potter, as a young girl, became very familiar with life at Mission Hills, and her knowledge of the Wallower family, as well as her extensive collection of photographs, is unparalleled.

James Maupin, with his unfailing memory and long tenure as a professor and as a dean, is always a prime source of information on Southern's development. He has been especially helpful in casting new light on the transition from a junior to a senior college and on developments in the School of Technology.

Cleetis Headlee, a retired professor of English, has been of great help in explaining events and personalities of the junior college era, in reminiscing about her role as adviser to *The Chart*, and her experiences in developing the curriculum for a four-year college.

Howard Dugan, retired Director of Physical Plant, has been a fountain of information on little-known facts relating to the building of the campus.

The late Dudley Stegge, Douglas Landrith, Sallie Beard, and James Frazier have generously provided invaluable information on the development of Southern's sports program.

Other individuals who have provided important information include Carolyn Billingsley, Robert Brown, William Caldwell, Judith Conboy, Glenn Dolence, Edward Farmer, Conrad Gubera, Tom Holman, Larry Martin, Mary Laird McClintock, Nancy Messick, John Messick, Val Williams, and Donald Youst.

Much praise and many thanks are due to my wife Nickey, not only for her patience during the seemingly endless task of writing this book, but also for her work in keyboarding the manuscript and for attending to such mundane chores as spell-checking and entering the many alterations and corrections needed into the manuscript.

Most photographs used in this book have come from sources within the college. The *Crossroads* has been the major single source with a few coming from MSSC's other leading publication, *The Chart*. Other leading sources have been the Archives, the Public Information Office, and the Sports Information Center, with the Alumni Affairs Office and the Theatre Department being other important sources. Also, photographs have come from independent contributors, some within the college, and are individually credited to the person or organization supplying them.

"Nurses" was a semi-official school organization that grew out of a cooperative wartime program, beginning in 1943–1944, between JJC and St. John's Hospital School of Nursing. The girls took required academic courses at the college while all clinical training was completed at the hospital. Shown in this 1945–1946 photograph are, from left, front row: Alice Pryor, Betty Robbins, Jessie Hodson, Margaret Fullmer, and Virginia Garbacz. Back row: Sultana Farris, Delores Allen, Betty Jean Lofton, Brownie Sizemore, and Marietta Cullver.

CHAPTER I
HIGHER EDUCATION COMES TO JOPLIN

Joplin grew rapidly in the last three decades of the nineteenth century, but its large transient population and its mining boomtown atmosphere did not encourage the development of higher education. Lead and zinc mining required college-trained engineers, geologists, and other professionals, but this need was met by graduates of universities who came into the Tri-State mining area to put their expertise to profitable use. Thus, advanced education developed slowly and, by the turn of the century, even high school enrollment was only about 250. Yet the census showed Joplin had a population of 26,023 and was Missouri's fifth largest city.

Colleges then tended to be associated with a tranquil environment that would stimulate intellectual growth and were often located in rural towns. Joplin's boisterous atmosphere did not fit in well with this setting. This tendency was reflected in the experience of neighboring towns. Springfield had Drury College, established in 1873 and, in 1905, the state founded a college that, in time, became Southwest Missouri State University. Pittsburg, Kansas, only twenty-five miles from Joplin, underwent a similar development with the establishment of what became Pittsburg State University. A few miles to the southwest, at Miami, Oklahoma, a state school evolved into Northeastern Oklahoma A & M Junior College. Small private colleges established in the nearby towns of Carthage, Neosho, and Webb City lasted for a few years early in the twentieth century. Also, junior colleges formed in a number of eastern Kansas towns and in Monett, Missouri, all within a hundred miles of Joplin.

Yet, as Joplin advanced into the twentieth century, its young people graduating from high school benefitted only from trade schools. Various business and secretarial schools existed such as the Joplin Business College and the Joplin Trade School. Also, functioning at times were schools of cosmotology, barbering, music, and dancing. Most young people, particularly in the manual trades, simply learned on the job. Those aspiring to enter the professions, and in need of formal college training, had to leave Joplin.

By the 1920s, Joplin's image began to change. Though still the business, cultural, and residential heart of the Tri-State district, large-scale mining now centered in the new mine fields of Picher and Commerce, Oklahoma, and adjacent areas in Kansas. Joplin took on a more settled, urban appearance. The large, floating population had moved on and the rows of miners' shacks were being torn down. Though many miners still lived in Joplin, they resided in substantial homes and commuted back and forth to work by automobile or on the district's splendid interurban railway system. New national highways were making Joplin a growing center for retail and wholesale trade. Businessmen began to speak of a Four-State district as Joplin's trade territory expanded into Northwest Arkansas. The city's excellent public school system and the growing cultural refinement of the population pointed the way toward a growing demand for a college.

By the late 1920s, Joplin seemed to be moving slowly toward establishing some kind of an institution of higher learning, but the Great Depression provided the real catalyst. Civic, business, and educational groups began to look seriously at the establishment of a college as one way to alleviate the city's economic woes. A junior college seemed the realistic solution. These institutions had come into vogue early in the twentieth century as a way to provide

(Opposite) Harry E. Blaine, the first dean of Joplin Junior College, is fondly remembered by students of that era for his personal interest in them and for his role in making the college a constructive force in their lives. He well understood the transitional role a junior college can play in helping young people adjust to college. Veteran faculty praised his leadership in selecting effective classroom teachers, in building high academic standards, and in providing a wide variety of extracurricular activities for students; all of which assured that the institution would be more than a "glorified high school."

Blaine was in many ways an old-fashioned, nineteenth-century gentleman. Longtime teacher Harry Gockel often recounted the story of how Blaine would stand at the head of the stairs shaking hands with students and greeting them by name on their arrival for morning classes.

Born in Pennsylvania in 1872, Blaine received his master's degree from the University of Chicago. He served as principal of Joplin High School from 1912 until he joined the junior college in 1937. It is interesting that, at the age of sixty-five, he retired from one career as a high school administrator and began another as a college dean, continuing in that role until he retired in 1947 at the age of seventy-five.

publicly supported vocational training for those who wished to enter a trade, and the first two years of arts and sciences courses for those who wished to complete a baccalaureate degree. Missouri statutes permitted public school districts to set up junior colleges, but left their financing largely to the district. Already over twenty-five existed or were being formed.

The idea struck a responsive chord in Joplin and, in the fall of 1932, parent-teacher groups established a committee to study the proposal. In an address to the Joplin Kiwanis Club, local attorney Norman Cox outlined the basic arguments in favor of establishing a junior college. He stated that Joplin, as the leader of the Four-State district, had an obligation to provide higher education facilities for area youngsters to the extent that it was "feasible and practicable." Cox also dwelt on the economic benefits. He estimated that 150 boys and girls left Joplin each year to attend college and that an equal number also left from area communities. From $700 to $1,000 per year was spent on the educational costs of each of these 300 young people. Essentially this money was lost to the district and if these students could attend college in Joplin it would markedly stimulate business. Furthermore, Cox pointed out that many families of modest means could not afford to send their sons and daughters away to college. Also, he explained that many boys and girls, just graduating from high school, are too immature to leave home and need to start their college training under parental supervision. In conclusion, the Joplin attorney urged civic organizations to support the junior college proposal but only if school officials could implement it without additional taxes.

Responding to the ground swell of popular support, E. A. Elliott, Joplin superintendent of schools, arranged for O. G. Sandford, assistant state superintendent of schools, to make a survey. When Sandford visited Joplin in February 1933, he was favorably impressed with the need for a junior college and advocated establishing one if it could be done without undermining the quality of the elementary and secondary school programs. He pointed out that a junior college would be more expensive to operate than a high school. Obviously the whole plan, while desirable, was contingent on raising additional revenues. The Joplin School Board realized that with the city's depressed economy and severe unemployment, they could not ask for an increase in property taxes and the whole junior college issue was then deferred to a time when the financial outlook would be more favorable.

Though stalled by the depressed economy, local parent-teacher groups continued to actively champion the junior college idea. By 1937, the outlook had brightened considerably. The economy was much improved over the dark days of 1932–1933, thanks in part to massive infusions of federal aid under the New Deal programs.

The problem of funding a junior college no longer seemed so dismal. Up to this time, public school districts had been supported largely by local property taxes but, goaded in part by the financial plight of local school districts, the state legislature established Missouri's first sales tax in 1935 and in 1937 doubled it from 1 percent to 2 percent. One-third of the state's revenues were earmarked to support public schools, as for the first time the state began to help fund public schools in an important way. The Joplin Public School District benefitted handsomely from this largess. State funding for the fiscal year 1935–1936 amounted to $75,613.58 and the next fiscal year it increased to $95,706.24. With revenues pouring in from the new two percent sales tax, it appeared the local district would receive more than $60,000.00 in additional revenues for the year 1937–1938. Suddenly, a junior college, which in 1933 had been a hopeless prospect, now seemed possible, and particularly so since state funding would also apply to junior college enrollment.

E. A. Elliott, superintendent of Joplin Public Schools, became the first president of Joplin Junior College when it was founded. Elliott had been superintendent since 1930 and played a key role in establishing the junior college.

In December 1943, he resigned to accept a captaincy in the U.S. Army's military government division. Assigned to Germany, he worked at reorganizing the school system of Bavaria after the war, rising to the rank of major.

Public sentiment favored establishing a junior college. Most members of the Board of Education favored the move with some reservations, but Board President S. A. Harris was an especially strong supporter as was Superintendent of Schools E. A. Elliott.

In early May 1937, the Board directed Elliott to draw up a prospectus for the proposed junior college. Elliott, presenting his plan at the May 18, 1937 board meeting, noted that he had sent a questionnaire to the parents of six hundred graduates of Joplin High School and seventy-five indicated they would send their youngsters to the proposed junior college. He felt there might be a struggle the first year or two, but the new institution would succeed. Elliott calculated that costs for the first year would total $66,450, a substantial portion of which could be raised through student fees, but an additional property tax levy would probably be necessary. The Board and Elliott favored housing the new college in the old school building at Fourth and Byers, which they optimistically estimated could be renovated for $19,000. But the Board, feeling the matter needed more public input, postponed further action on Elliott's prospectus.

During the next two weeks, a considerable public debate developed over the issue. Individual Board members appeared before various civic groups. William Markwardt, local civic leader, called a public meeting for the evening of June 3, 1937, to further air the issue. Though the parent-teacher organizations had long been behind the movement, powerful support also developed from other quarters. Just before the meeting, the Board of Education received a letter from Elmer Ellis, chairman of the Accrediting Committee of the University of Missouri, praising them for their efforts and promising his cooperation. A *Joplin Globe* editorial lent support as did many business organizations and various clubs.

An estimated 150 to 200 people attended Markwardt's third of June meeting. Superintendent Elliott told the assemblage that though the Board felt the junior college would be a valuable asset for the community, they had no desire to proceed with the plans unless it was clear the public really wanted such an institution. By this time, the estimated costs had been revised upward entailing an even higher property tax increase.

In the general discussion that followed, all the old arguments aired in 1933 were reiterated. Though the crowd seemed overwhelmingly in favor of the proposed college, reservationists soon gave a negative tone to the proceedings.

Joplin Junior College's first faculty appear in this 1937 photograph. From left, standing: E. O. Humphrey, football coach; Armel Dyer, English and Speech; Eugene Henning, Spanish and dean of men; T. Frank Coulter, Music; C. J. Sommerville, Chemistry. Seated: Ada Coffey, English; Martha McCormick, Mathematics; Edna Drummond, Zoology, Botany, and dean of women; H. E. Blaine, dean. Some taught part-time that first year, dividing their time between the college and the high school or other activities.

Dyer taught only three years at JJC. A captain in the Army Reserves, he was called to active duty with the approach of war.

Henning served as the college's first dean of men and as its first foreign language instructor until the end of the 1947–1948 school year, except for four years of military service during World War II. The post of dean of men was discontinued after his departure.

Coulter, as director of music education for the public schools, initiated the college's Music program, but he was never more than partially involved in JJC's musical activities. Coulter died in 1973.

Sommerville, a Chemistry teacher, left JJC in 1941 to join the Eagle-Picher research staff. There he died tragically during World War II while taking part in research. The experiment he was conducting unexpectedly produced poisonous arsine gas which he inhaled with fatal results.

Ada Coffey, shown here; Edna Drummond; and Martha McCormick were undoubtedly the most significant teachers of that first staff of 1937–1938. Coffey, who held a master's degree from the University of Kansas, transferred from the Joplin high school to the new junior college as a teacher of English and Literature. She died in August 1963. Some 850 books from her private collection were bequeathed to the college library.

Ex-students remember Coffey most vividly for her enthusiasm, she made literature come alive and instilled in students a love of the subject and a desire to read more on their own. She was also a strong spokesman for teachers' interests and a leader in local and statewide teacher organizations.

Martha A. McCormick was one of the junior college's master teachers who emerged from the original teaching staff of 1937–1938. She served on into the senior college era, retiring in 1972 as an emeritus professor. From 1963 on she was the sole remainder of the original staff of 1937. McCormick died in 1987 at the age of eighty-four.

A native of Carthage, and with a master's degree from the University of Chicago, she taught at Ozark Wesleyan College, finally losing her job because of the college's bankruptcy. In 1937, Dean Blaine, needing a mathematics teacher with a master's degree, hired her to teach part-time for $75 per month.

McCormick established a strong rapport with her students, and years later many remembered her patience and understanding; she steered many of her majors toward careers in engineering.

Some objected to the property tax increase. Others feared the college would erode the quality of Joplin's elementary and secondary schools by siphoning off revenues. Some felt the action was too hasty and that there should be more study and planning. At this point, Mrs. Cora M. Clay, a widow, turned the meeting around with an emotional appeal for the college. She described the struggle to put her four sons through college after their father's death. Joplin, she noted, had many "poor and disadvantaged parents" who could not afford to send their children away to college. This appeal for a junior college "for all the people" awakened the assemblage from their lethargy, and they voted overwhelmingly to establish a standing committee to work with the Board of Education on the college issue. Markwardt was named permanent chairman.

As Joplin entered the early summer of 1937, the Board of Education realized they needed to take a new approach. Establishing the college in its own quarters would at least require a special election to vote a bond issue entailing a tax increase and they did not have enough time for this. Public sentiment seemed overwhelmingly favorable, still an election campaign would give that important group who were lukewarm toward the college a specific issue around which to coalesce and they might succeed in defeating it. More time was needed in which to organize and build public support. Furthermore, it would take time to prepare the new quarters.

Fortunately there was an alternative. For some time, the Extension Division of the University of Missouri had offered college work at the local high school on a course by course basis. If this program could be expanded, Joplin would have an embryo junior college. The Board authorized Superintendent Elliott to consult with the university on this basis and how the credits could be handled. Plans to remodel the Fourth and Byers building were dropped in favor of crowding the classes into the high school. The Board had concluded that they needed to start with a modest program, one that involved minimal expense and that avoided a complex administrative structure. They wanted a tentative junior college, an experiment, to see what the enrollment would be and how favorably the public would react to it. At the August 3, 1937 board meeting, Elliott reported on his negotiations with the Extension Division. The university could offer the courses at a cost of $6.00 per credit hour, but if the school district provided its own teachers, $4.00 could be deducted from this hourly charge. Fortunately Joplin High School had a strong teaching staff with a number of the faculty qualified to teach on the college level; the university insisted on instructors with a master's degree in their respective subject matter fields. Realizing they could provide the necessary teachers and bear the $2.00 per credit hour charge without additional taxes, the Board moved to put the program into operation. Thus, did Joplin's first junior college come into being.

With the college scheduled to open on September 7, the administration had only five weeks in which to establish a curriculum, assign or hire faculty, recruit students and attend to the other seemingly endless details of making the college operational. H. E. Blaine, veteran principal of the high school, was put in charge. Finding a suitable mathematics teacher presented the greatest difficulty since none of the high school staff in that area had a master's degree. Finally, Martha Ann McCormick was hired on a part-time basis.

Enrollment proceeded slowly and was extended for several weeks into the fall semester. Officials were pleased that they were getting enrollees from Neosho, Webb City, Carthage, and other nearby towns. The superintendent reported to the Board, two weeks after classes began, that total enrollment then stood at 80. Enrollment was fluid. University of Missouri records show that 114 eventually enrolled, and this figure is confirmed by the 1938 yearbook, but enrollment at any given time seems to have ranged between 80 and 90. Twenty-one new students entered for the spring semester.

At this stage, the new junior college could have become submerged in the high school routine, but the director, H. E. Blaine, was determined to give it an identity of its own. Classes were concentrated, where possible, on the upper floor and steps were taken to involve the students in as many college-level, extracurricular activities as possible. Fraternities, sororities, and academic clubs needed to be organized and social gatherings arranged. Programs were needed in dramatics and music. A yearbook and newspaper seemed desirable. Steps were taken to select the college colors and song, to adopt a mascot, and to select class officers. A complete sports program of football, basketball, and track needed to be implemented. Students that first year had a rare opportunity to establish a number of the college's enduring traditions. As Joan Epperson Giles commented, on the college's fiftieth anniversary, "We were not so talented but we were there."

Paul R. Stevick joined the junior college's staff in the fall of 1938, having last taught at the defunct Ozark Wesleyan College in Carthage. Stevick, who taught primarily Philosophy and Sociology, was unique among the early junior college instructors in that he was a Methodist minister and in that he had a doctor of philosophy degree from the University of Iowa. He was the only member of JJC's teaching staff to have a doctorate during his fourteen-year tenure.

A published author, Stevick died in 1952 just short of his sixty-fourth birthday.

Edna Drummond often remarked, "My work is my life." With a master's degree from George Peabody College, Drummond served as principal of the Bentonville, Arkansas high school for a number of years before coming to the Joplin high school in 1930 as a teacher. In 1937, she joined JJC's original staff, serving as dean of women and teaching Botany and Zoology until her retirement.

Many students were so inspired by her insightful teaching that they took her courses as electives. Immature students often learned from her the rudiments of disciplined study. Decades later, many looked back on Drummond as the junior college's finest instructor at a time when the institution had a number of truly outstanding teachers.

A tall, yet graceful and dignified figure, Drummond was also somewhat eccentric. She wore an engagement ring on her right hand, but curious students never learned the story behind it. She was a very private person.

Drummond also had a phobia of germs, constantly washing her hands, taking handkerchiefs to doorknobs, and heating student's test papers in an oven before grading them. Drummond retired from JJC in 1955 at the age of seventy and returned to Bentonville to live with her sister, Mamie. She died in February 1966, leaving a bequest of $43,187 to Missouri Southern to fund scholarships for science students.

Alpha Kappa Mu was Joplin Junior College's first social sorority. This 1938–1939 photograph shows its second-year membership. From left, first row: Mary Laird, Betty Barlow, June Van Pelt, Dorothy Lee Wilkins, Irene Reynolds, Betty Patterson, Ellen Beasley, and Joan Epperson. Second row: Dorothy Lee Bloomer, Betty Meese, Irene Fleming, Edna King, Irene Corn, Alice Magoon, Martha Jean Miller, Imo Jean Aggus, Mary Bartlow, Kathleen Moyer, and Sponsor Martha McCormick. Third row: Victoria Hakan, Betty Mae Winter, Mary Louise Farrar, Florence Wyatt, Evalyn Martin, Evelyn Eggerman, Ruth McReynolds, Jean Hendrichs, Margaret McGregor, Geraldine Marshall, and Jane Fletcher.

The large membership indicates the initial enthusiasm of JJC's student body for participating in extracurricular activities. This sorority was discontinued after the 1953–1954 school year due to a lack of student interest.

Members of Alpha Theta Chi gathered for this photograph during the 1937–1938 school year. From left, first row: Elby Butcher, J. R. Graue, Robert Fontaine, Emerson Jackson, Bill Fogg, Jim Corl, Chet Wilson, and Sponsor C. J. Sommerville. Second row: Joe Van Pool, Jack Swope, Parker Rogers, Paul Garlock, Dale Palmer, Wilbur Byers, Mack Clarke, and Raymond Fly. Third row: Bob Glenn, Gordon Silliman, Edwin Boucher, Ray Palmer, Frank Fogg, Leonard Duncan, and Beverly Setser.

Alpha Theta Chi counted among its membership some of the college's most capable young men. A number became officers during World War II and Beverly Setser was killed in action.

The last, as well as being the first, of JJC's social fraternities, ATC collapsed in the early post–World War II era due to a lack of interest. There would be no more in the junior college era.

ALMA MATER

Words by Mary Laird,
Class of '39

Music by Emerson Jackson,
Class of '39

Our Al - ma Ma - ter, we ho - nor thee.

shap - ing and guid - ing our de - sti - ny.

Af - ter we have part - ed as the years roll by;

we'll keep each me - mo - ry hail, hail to thee.

Joplin Junior College's "Alma Mater" was drafted during the school's second year by a group that included Mary Laird, Joan Epperson, Enos Currey, Ellen Beasley, and Emerson Jackson. Laird was principally responsible for the lyrics while Jackson set it to music. It was first sung during a Class-Day program in 1939.

Members of the first Student Senate proudly pose in this early photograph. From left, standing: Jack Cooper, vice president; and Enos Currey. Seated: Mary Laird; Kathleen Moyer, president; and Joan Epperson, secretary.

All five of these Senate members were very active in student organizations. Currey, became the initial JJC graduate to receive a degree by virtue of being first on the alphabetical list.

Founded in the 1937–1938 school year, the Senate was one of Joplin Junior College's first student organizations and its most durable, coming down to the present as a strong institution.

Joplin Junior College's first play, The Patsy, *a comedy, was initially shown on December 20, 1937, and proved so popular that it was repeated a month later.*

Pictured are, from left: Mary Laird, Emerson Jackson, and Ellen Beasley who played leading roles. Other members of the cast were: Joan Epperson, Raymond Fly, J. R. Graue, Enos Currey, Lola Houk, and Bob Fontaine.

Joplin Junior College's first football team was hastily formed in the fall of 1937. Shown from the left, front row, are: Tom Prince; Leonard Duncan, Jim Attebury; Bert Spencer, Jack Cooper, and Bayred Vermillion. Back row: Coach E. O. Humphrey, Raymond Fly, Bob Lawson, J. R. Graue, Bob Fontaine, Delmer Strait, Frank Hamilton, Bill Snow, Bob Howard, and Assistant Coach, Sgt. C. E. Treager.

The team lost all five of its games in this initial season. In the first game, halfback James "J. R." Graue of Carterville took the initial snap of the ball from center Bayred Vermillion.

Humphrey, a former high school football coach, was director of athletics for the public schools at this time and coached the Lions for only one season. Later, the E. O. Humphrey Award in athletics was established in his memory.

Seven of the eight members of the junior college's first basketball team in 1937–1938 are pictured here with their coach. From left: Delmer Strait, Bayred Vermillion, Shelby Slinker, Don Russell, Leonard Duncan, Jim Attebury, Bert Spencer, and Coach Walter Wheeler.

Coach Wheeler was physical director of the YMCA and the team both practiced and played their home games at the "Y." More successful than their football counterparts, the basketball Lions won eight games out of fifteen. Shelby Slinker was team captain.

College colors were chosen at the beginning of the football season. Joan Epperson and Mary Laird, who were close friends, made this selection. Red and green and black and gold were the colors of the Joplin and Neosho high schools, respectively. Since Joan was from Neosho and Mary from Joplin, the two friends agreed to combine Joplin's green and Neosho's gold. As early as October, newspapers were referring to the new football team as the "Green and Gold."

Also, at this time, the lion was picked as mascot for the athletic teams. Bayred Vermillion, J. R. Graue, and some of their fellow players on the first sports teams made this selection. The name *Lions* did not appear in the first yearbook, but was used the following year.

Other activities involved publication of a yearbook supplement, establishment of a Student Senate, presentation of a play, and the organization of a chorus.

Much effort went into developing an athletic program for the new college. While the track program remained only rudimentary, effective teams were developed for football and basketball. E. O. Humphrey, an experienced coach and respected member of the high school staff, coached the football team. With about twenty players, experienced but light in weight, Humphrey arranged a tough schedule, playing the neighboring junior college teams of Miami, Coffeyville, and Monett, and the "B" teams from the four-year state colleges at Pittsburg and Springfield. The team was plagued by injuries, and halfback J. R. Graue later recalled that in the last game of the season against Coffeyville, a top-rated junior college team, they were down to eight players by the last quarter and the opposing team offered to loan them men, but they refused. Graue played the backfield by himself. At the end of the game, which the Joplinites lost 0–45, the crowd applauded them for their courage.

The new JJC athletes proved more successful in the basketball season. Under Coach Walter Wheeler, the basketball Lions played mostly local club teams with few junior college games. By avoiding the heavy competition which so damaged the football team, they ended the season with a creditable record, winning over half their games.

At the end of the first year, students, administrators, and the public could look back with satisfaction, as could University of Missouri extension officials who had supervised the program. Though tentative, the first year had proven its worth. Students were impressed with the quality of the academic program and especially with the high caliber of instruction. The rush to establish extracurricular programs had provided the students with an enriched college life and given them an identity separate from the swarms of high school students on the lower floors. Patterns and traditions were established that would carry on even after the infant college expanded into an institution that few could imagine at that time.

The college had proved itself and the general consensus was that it should be continued. Superintendent Elliott, noting that 150 members of the current high school graduating class had indicated they would attend the junior college, said, "It is no longer a question of whether we can afford a junior college and a well-equipped vocational training school. The question is, can we afford to be without it?"

The new Joplin Junior College had to be given more of an identity of its own. The first step was to break its ties with the University of Missouri Extension Division.

Art instructor Arthur W. Boles came to JJC in its second year and retired in 1968, completing a thirty-year tenure. He specialized in children's sculpture in graduate school and this abstract Norwegian dragon, *located in his yard, is a fine example of Boles' art work.*

Boles encouraged art students to express their own perceptions freely. He believed there was no bad art as long as it was genuinely creative, and he found merit in even the crudest of creations. Casual students sometimes called his classes "fun" courses, but many talented individuals found inspiration in his approach.

Boles built his own house and after he and his wife died, his property was left to the college. He died in 1972.

Founded in 1939, the junior college band appears in this 1940–1941 photograph with its members resplendent in their new uniforms. They are listed, by section of instruments, Bass: Jack Snyder. Percussion: Harold Shepman. Clarinet: Leonard Montgomery, Cameron Jackson, Wayne James, Erwin Nommenson, Winnie Lou Carter, and Dick Wardlow. Horn: Ruth Garlock and Bill Hastings. Bassoon: Estelle Cookerly. Coronet: V. A. Leverett, Maurice Bellis, Richard Snyder, Bob Wagner, Bob Hayes, Carl Saft, and Ivan Shug. Trombone: Jack Holden, Glenn Sheppard, and Al Stewart. Baritone: Roy Lee Daniel, Burleigh DeTar, and Lloyd Cantrell.

The band marched in parades, played at football and basketball games, and at the annual music festival.

Never more than a temporary arrangement, this posed no problem though accreditation of JJC's academic program continued to be through the university for another decade. The most serious problem was that of quarters. Elliott ruled out continuing the classes in the high school because of overcrowding.

By this time, only the Fourth and Byers location was seriously being considered as a home for the new college. It offered a quick and affordable solution to the problem. Though remodeling this building would entail a tax increase and an election, the very issues that had stalled the same move the previous year, this time the success of the college seemed to make it more acceptable. The Board approved submitting a $100,000 bond issue in a special election on May 10, 1938. The proposal called for $50,000 to rehabilitate the Fourth and Byers building and another $50,000 for additions to the Eagle-Picher and Lincoln schools. The Board hoped that combining the two issues would broaden support. They also pointed out that though the proposal would increase property taxes by two cents on the hundred dollars valuation, no additional taxes would be needed to operate the college.

Once again, powerful groups who wanted a junior college supported the bond issue and it carried by a resounding vote of 3,411 to 720. This almost five-to-one margin of victory indicated the tremendous community support for a college, a support that has continued through the years with an enthusiasm that few institutions of higher learning enjoy.

The work of remodeling the new college quarters went on through the summer of 1938 with the school district utilizing a force of carpenters, WPA laborers, and contractors. The remodeling, plus the all-new equipment that was installed, gave the interior the appearance of a new building. The ground floor was largely reserved for vocational training on both the high school and junior college levels. It contained automotive, carpentry, and electrical shops. The *Joplin Globe* hailed the structure as "one of the finest and most modern junior colleges in the southwest." Actually it was a modest edifice, but it must have seemed splendid to the students, and the community was immensely proud. Finally Joplin had a real college.

The Joplin Junior College that opened in the fall of 1938 was a greatly expanded institution over that of the previous year. Enrollment exceeded the most optimistic expectations, totaling 314 with 75 being from outside the

Joplin School District. Faculty consisted of twenty-three full-time and part-time instructors. New terminal programs were added in Carpentry, Automobile Mechanics, and Business. The Arts and Sciences curricula was expanded, particularly with the addition of French and German, and a Teachers' Training program was instituted. The first catalog was issued and scholarships were set up in an effort to attract out-of-town enrollment. The extensive program of student activities, started in 1937–1938, was continued and expanded upon. Social activities began in September with the YMCA-YWCA mixer, which became something of a JJC tradition.

Joplin Junior College tended to attract a type of student body that has characterized the college ever since. Many commuted back and forth from their homes and a sizeable number had to work to finance their education. Joan Epperson Giles, reminiscing fifty years later, remembered that she rode back and forth from her home in Neosho by bus the first year and in a car pool of five the second year. Many students drew aid through the National Youth Administration

Members of Pi Rho Phi, a newly formed forensic fraternity are shown in this 1939 photograph. Left to right: Marion Barnhart; Edward G. Farmer, Jr.; Merlin Stratton, president; and Charles Lewis. PRP was the college's first nationally chartered, honorary academic fraternity. Barnhart earned a doctorate from the University of Missouri and later taught physiology at Wayne University, Detroit, Michigan. After serving in World War II, Farmer completed a law degree at Wayne University. A longtime Joplin lawyer, and former state legislator, he was Republican candidate for governor of Missouri in 1960 and held the state post of director of insurance, 1973–1975.

The junior college's first sophomore class officers appear in this 1938–1939 photograph. From left, Emerson Jackson, president; Irene Reynolds, vice president; Mary Laird, reporter; Duke Wallace, treasurer; and Joan Epperson, secretary.

This class, both as freshmen and sophomores, had been unusually active in extracurricular projects. Commenting on the small class's remarkable diligence, the first Crossroads *noted, "The work of the class is done. Soon it will be graduated and make way for other classes to come. As the years pass by, the members of this class will be proud to look back and say, 'We were the pioneers'."*

THE CHART

VOL. I   JOPLIN JUNIOR COLLEGE, JOPLIN, MISSOURI, NOVEMBER 10, 1939   PRICE 3c   NO. 1

J. J. C. Team To Be Honored By Banquet Tonight

Group Will Attend High School Game At Stadium After Dinner

Nov. 10—A banquet honoring members of the football team is to be given tonight at Roberts Cafeteria by the Spinx Club, in cooperation with other fraternities and sororities of Joplin Junior College.

Gayety will prevail in the appropriately decorated dining room where more than one hundred students are expected to gather at 5:30 for dinner. A short program will be presented between courses.

After the banquet the group will attend the Joplin-Miami high school football game at Junge's Stadium.

A dance at the college will be given after the game with members of the Carthage and Joplin teams as guests.

MIXER FOR STUDENTS OPENS SOCIAL YEAR

The Y.W.C.A and Y.M.C.A started the 1939-40 college social year by giving the annual "Joe and Judy" mixer at the Y.M.C.A in September. Faculty and students alike joined in the games—a shaving contest, ice holding, and a balloon race. Dancing provided the central entertainment. Refreshments were served in the lobby.

Delegates Attend Y. W. C. A. Meet

The Kansas Junior College Y.W.C.A. conference in Coffeyville, Oct. 27, 28 and 29 was attended by Jeanne Keith, Mary Louise Knell, Dorothy Friend, Helen Claire Prigg, Eugenia Hatfield, Bonnie Farneman, Frances Secrest, Lorraine Cole, Miss Vera Steininger, Miss Dorothy Stone, and Mrs. Margaret Witcosky. Frances Secrest was elected recording secretary of the 1940 conference to be held in Parsons.

Drama Is Selected

Miss Jetta Carleton has announced that the first major production of the dramatics department, "The Importance of Being Earnest" (Oscar Wilde) will be presented December 15. Tryouts, which will be open to the entire student body, will be announced on the bulletin board.

College Sponsors Program On Radio

For the second year the college is sponsoring a program each Tuesday night on radio station W M·B H The debate program, directed by Mr. Armel Dyer, and inaugurated last year, alternates with a drama skit under the supervision of Miss Jetta Carleton.

The series began October 17 with a discussion by Bill Owen, Ed Farmer, Paul Morrison and Merlin Stratton about the arms embargo and neutrality.

"Alias Smackout," a drama was presented the second week with Jeanne Kersting, Ed Farmer, Lonny Chapman, Bob Hatley, Paul Morrison and Norman Mauldin.

"Should the United State enact the Senate Neutrality Bill?" was the subject of the third program, debated by Ed Farmer and Paul Morrison.

On November 7, Betty Wicks and Betty Ingram upheld the question, "Resolved: That There are Too Many College Students," opposed by Merlin Stratton and Lawrence Ray.

Rev. Titus Speaks At J. J. C. Assembly

Nov. 8—Rev. Cliff Titus was the principal speaker at the regular assembly this morning. His talk pertained to the National Education Week observance.

Carol Yonker sang two solos and the Junior College Orchestra played several numbers.

Football queen candidates and their managers were introduced by Dorothy Friend, editor of "The Crossroads" which is sponsoring the contest. The candidates with their managers are as follows: Jane Jackson, Herbert McColgin; Lynn Cragin, Gibson Wolfe; Billye Grattis, Ed Farmer; Mary Louise Hutchinson, J. R. Graue. The queen will be chosen by the sale of tickets to the Miami-Joplin football game, Thursday, November 17.

Inspectors At College

Nov. 2—Classes were visited today, records inspected, and courses checked by four members of the Missouri university faculty. The college is inspected annually as a requirement of the American Association of Junior Colleges.

Those visiting were Herbert E. French, R. D. M. Baure, Dr. C. A. Phillips, and Harold Y. Moffet (coauthor of the English grammar text used by the college.)

KING, QUEEN OF FROLIC CHOSEN

Auditorium, Oct. 31—At the Trojan sponsored Halloween Fun Festival tonight, Mary Helen Hayes was crowned Queen Festoonia and Bob (Leo) Galbraith, King Frolic, by Hank Gibson, last year's King Frolic. The King and Queen were chosen by a faculty committee as the masked and costumed couples joined the grand march.

The decorations, dominated by the name Trojans in large, orange letters on the stage curtain, abounded with cats, witches, and owls in the windows. Balloons and crepe streamers hung overhead.

Cider and cookies were served on the lower floor.

Sorority Entertains Guests On Hayride

Nov. 3—Members and guests of the Beta Beta Beta sorority went to Schermerhorn Park, near Galena, tonight for a hayride and steak fry. Games and singing formed the entertainment.

Also, tonight, the Pine Tree Patrol, a senior scouting organization, most of whose members are college students, accompanied by guests went on a hayride to Boy Scout Camp. The program consisted of singing, games, and the presentation of a charter to the organization.

The Sphinx Club and guests went hayriding to McClelland Park October 18.

SCHOOLS OBSERVE EDUCATION WEEK

Nov. 5—A program by the city education system on station WMBH this afternoon started Joplin's observance of American Education Week. Radio programs, in which the college takes a prominent part, school exhibits, and classroom visiting are the features of the week.

The nationwide observance has as its 1939 slogan, "Education for the American Way of Life."

College Y Starts Weekly Luncheons

Y. M. C. A., Nov. 7—The fourth weekly student luncheon of the college "Y" featured Mr. Jack Fleishaker, a young lawyer who spoke on the interests, difficulties and rewards of law.

Farmer Elected President Of Student Senate

Other Organizations Have Also Selected Officers

The governing Student Senate of the college has elected Ed Farmer, president; Everett Reniker, vice president; and Betty Wicks, secretary and treasurer.

Following are the officers of other college organizations: Alpha Theta Chi—Beverly Setser, president; J. R. Graue, councilor; Chet Wilson, secretary and Leonard Duncan, treasurer.

Trojans—Everett Reniker, president; Homer Brigance, vice president; Harold Cloud, secretary; Ed Wyrick, treasurer; and Lawrence Ray, pledge chairman.

Beta Beta Beta—Billye Grattis, president; Jeanne Keith, vice president; Mary Belle Edmondson, treasurer; Margaret Baughman, reporter; Margaret Morris, sergeant-of-arms; and Kay Buchanan, social chairman.

Spinx—Ed Farmer, president; Russell Holden, vice president; Paul Morrison, reporter; James Bastian, treasurer; and Ed Harris, pledgemaster.

Orchestra—Donald Gant, president; Raymond Kelley, vice president; Louise Davis, secretary; and Maurice Bellis, treasurer.

Y. W. C. A.—Jeanne Keith, president; Betty Wicks, vice president; Mary Reynolds, secretary; and Eugenia Hatfield, treasurer.

Y.M.C.A.—Ed Wyrick, president; Bill Tipping, vice president; Ed Farmer, secretary; and Paul Morrison, treasurer.

Cheering Squad—Bill Owen, Billye Grattis, Kay Buchanan, and J. R. Graue.

Freshman Class—David Remillard, president; Dick Rudolph, vice president; and Lillian Shaw, secretary.

Sophomore Class—Bill Owen, president; Everett Reniker, vice president; and Kay Buchanan, secretary.

Speech Institute Held

Oct. 28—A speech institute demonstrating public speaking forms was held at the college today. Teachers and students from other colleges and high schools participated.

(NYA) which paid them for working at the college in work-study programs. In 1938, to accommodate those employed in downtown stores during the Christmas shopping season, class schedules were altered and periods shortened so that the school day would end at 12:30 p.m.

In the spring of 1939, JJC graduated its first class. Of the original 114 who had enrolled two years before, only 23 graduated. Published lists of the time show 24 names though a check by the Registar's Office on the classes' twentieth anniversary showed a count of 23, and some of these may have received diplomas under the terminal programs. Baccalaureate services were held on Sunday, May 14, followed by graduation ceremonies the following Wednesday. The graduates wore blue caps and gowns. Forty of these had been ordered by the Board and were owned by the college for use by the graduates and by the chorus.

(Opposite page) The front page of The Chart's *first issue is shown here. With administrative support, it succeeded where* The Challenge *had failed the previous year. The name, suggested by the publication's first editor, H. Kenneth McCaleb, seemed appropriate because, as the 1940* Crossroads *pointed out, it aimed to present "a chart, no less, of the students' campus life."*

Events moved on for the graduates and the college. A survey one year later showed that of 21 who were tracked, 6 had enrolled in senior colleges, 5 were teaching in

The staff of the newly organized Crossroads *yearbook appear in this 1939 photograph. From left: Erma Jean Scott; Joan Epperson; Dorothy Lee Wilkins; Virginia Gibson; Virginia Warden; Dorothy Friend; Evelyn Eggerman; Mary Laird, editor; Edwin McReynolds, sponsor; Ada Coffey, sponsor; Paul Morrison; Ellen Beasley; Everett Reniker; William Magoon; Elby Butcher; and Jimmie James.*

In JJC's first year, a portion of the high school yearbook had been devoted to junior college activities, but the next year students were determined to have their own yearbook. The name Crossroads, *selected in a student contest, was originally proposed by Mary Laird, the yearbook's first editor. Laird chose the name for its double connotation. Joplin was popularly referred to as the "Crossroads of America" at that time and the junior college was seen as a crossroads in student life, connecting high school with senior college.*

Appearing here are members of the Baptist Student Union, newly formed during the 1940–1941 school year. From left, front row: Glenda Muhlenburg, president; Ruth Lawson; Lois Van Horn; Joy Bowles; and Elsia Potts. Back row: Nadine Hosp; Mildred Finley; Betty Jo Horn; Bob Wagner; Bill Gandy; Alberta Leach; Lucille Wray; and Hildred Beebe. The college's first religious student organization, the BSU collapsed after only two years and was not revived as an active organization until the 1967–1968 school year with the advent of a four-year college.

Joan Epperson, first Crossroads *Queen, promenades in regal splendor in this 1939 photograph taken in the junior college auditorium. The beginning of a durable tradition, the Crossroads Ball became the junior college's principal formal gala and lasted until 1978.*

rural schools, and the rest had found other jobs. The 1939 graduation ceremonies were followed by the college's first summer session. Some 76 students enrolled for the ten-week term; of these, 35 were working on teacher certification.

Enrollment in the fall of 1939 increased to 335 students, some 21 more than the previous year. The rate of increase was sharply down from the almost three-fold growth of the second year, but this reflected a leveling off. The college was nearing its potential enrollment limit, based on the district's population base and the limited number of high school graduates who then went on to college. Even so, it was Missouri's third largest junior college and in this sense reflected an impressive accomplishment for an institution just entering its third year. But this 1939 enrollment figure would not be equalled or surpassed for seven more years. The student count dropped slightly in the next two years, but declined drastically during World War II.

As classes began on September 5, 1939, war had just broken out in Europe. This development, and the growing concern that it might involve the United States and the students personally, is evident in articles that appeared in the college newspaper. *The Chart* conducted an opinion poll in February 1940 that showed JJC students were conservative and somewhat isolationist in their views. Some 97 percent were willing to fight for their country if invaded, but only 39 percent were willing to fight overseas. As to the military, 57 percent favored a strong military establishment and 80 percent believed in military programs such as the ROTC in schools and colleges. Only 38 percent favored a third term for President Roosevelt.

By its third year, JJC had a well-developed junior college program. It continued to be fully accredited by the University of Missouri. Admission was open to those who had completed at least fifteen units of accredited high school work. Tuition was free to all residents of the Joplin School District who were under twenty-one. Nonresidents, and residents aged twenty-one or over, paid a tuition of $20.00 per semester for full-time work. All full-time students paid an incidental fee of $12.00 plus a textbook and locker rental fee of $5.00 per semester. A grading system of ESMIF was used. Associate degrees (sixty-four credit hours) were offered in the Arts, Science, Education, and Music; later Business was added to this list. Diplomas were awarded to those following the Terminal (non-transferable) programs in Automobile Mechanics, Practical Electricity, Carpentry, General Business, Secretarial, or General Culture. School administrators were proud of the Terminal Division and 164 students enrolled in these courses in the fall of 1938. JJC's vocational program was one of the largest of any junior college in Missouri.

Some 75 students graduated in May 1940, a number more than triple that of the first graduating class and an indication of how rapidly the college was growing. This class had shown remarkable stability. Of the freshmen who entered in the fall of 1938, approximately 44 percent graduated, one of the highest retention rates ever recorded for JJC. Fortunately, the 1940 graduates entered an expanding job market as many new jobs opened up in defense industries. A growing military establishment also absorbed many young men, as the Great Depression's long grip on the nation began to weaken. Graduates continued to increase the next two years before beginning to drop as World War II affected enrollment.

The year 1941 marked the end of an era for the Joplin Junior College. A growing reputation for academic excellence was its most significant feature, and this reputation stemmed largely from the quality of its teachers. The Great Depression made it possible to build this impressive staff. During the long years of the economic slump, when jobs were scarce even for highly qualified people, the Joplin High School had assembled an excellent teaching staff. The administrators simply skimmed the cream off this staff and transferred them to the new junior college. But some came from other sources as well. The Ozark Wesleyan College in Carthage was a good example. That small Methodist college's bankruptcy provided the junior college with three of its finest teachers, Harry Gockel, Martha McCormick, and Paul Stevick.

Another factor in the academic success of the new college was the quality of its students. Years later, veteran teachers from that era recalled their dedication and eagerness to learn. Many were highly capable young people whom the Depression had robbed of an opportunity for a higher education until JJC opened up. Also, college students then were generally a more select group than some fifty years later. Studies of that period show that nationally only 12 percent of the youth of high school age ever entered college.

By the spring of 1941, Joplin Junior College seemed solidly established. Many of its traditions, though not yet deeply rooted, would prove to be lasting. Alumni left with fond memories that would linger on through their lives, and the new institution had the respect and support of the community. But World War II was already on the horizon and it would pose the greatest threat to the young college's existence.

Students who gathered for the fall semester in September 1941 were acutely aware of the spreading war that threatened to engulf the United States. After December 7, 1941, four years would lapse before the college experienced another peacetime semester. The stability of the new college was severely tested as enrollment dropped drastically, programs had to be modified, and activities sharply curtailed. But the war was immediately followed by a flood of veterans which inundated the modest institution at Fourth and Byers.

Enrollment figures for the fall 1942 semester show approximately 248. By this time, many young men were being drafted into the armed forces while other people of college age were moving away to where defense work was more plentiful. It set a pattern that continued throughout the war. By September 1943, the drop in enrollment had become alarming. Only 129 regular students were enrolled, little more than the college's first year. Attrition was severe; some 49 students dropped at the end of the fall 1943–1944 semester alone. Figures for the years 1942 through 1945 show that less than 30 percent of those entering

Dorothy A. Stone, who came to JJC in 1939, was another of the illustrious instructors whose careers bridged the junior and senior college eras. Primarily a teacher of accounting and secretarial courses, she was a pioneer figure in establishing the college's Business Administration curriculum. Stone retired in 1975 with the title of emeritus professor. A native of Columbia where she earned her bachelor's and master's degrees, Stone returned there after her retirement.

Harry C. Gockel, one of the college's most memorable instructors, came to JJC in 1939 and retired in 1972 with the title of emeritus professor. He had master's degrees from both Washington University and the University of Wisconsin. Born in St. Louis, Gockel died in 1984 at the age of eighty-two. Like his colleagues Martha McCormick and Paul Stevick, he came to JJC after the collapse of Ozark Wesleyan College in Carthage left him unemployed. It was in one of his classes at Ozark Wesleyan that he met his future wife, Bernice. Primarily a teacher of Economics, History, and Geography, Gockel also held various administrative posts and he became the first chairman of the new Social Science Division of the four-year college.

Gockel is best remembered as an excellent teacher. He was a strict disciplinarian and held students to high academic standards. His seemingly fierce demeanor in the classroom sometimes frightened newcomers to his classes, but it belied a kind and gracious nature that students better understood as they became more familiar with him. Many alumni have fond memories of Gockel and consider him one of the master teachers of the college's early history.

(Top) Dean Blaine is shown greeting 1940–1941 Student Senate President Kenton Slankard. An Air Force pilot during World War II, Slankard earned a law degree at the University of Missouri after the war and became a lawyer in Springfield.

(Bottom) Roi S. Wood, the second and last president of Joplin Junior College, became superintendent of the Joplin Public Schools in February 1944. A native Missourian, Wood earned his master's degree from the University of Missouri. His 25-year tenure encompassed one of the longest and most successful superintendencies in the history of the Joplin school system. Though a strong champion of JJC, in the end Wood worked to sever it from the public school system because it was growing too large for the local school district to support.

completed their degrees. As more and more young men were drafted into the armed forces, it left a college population composed mostly of girls and boys waiting to be called into service. Girls averaged about two-thirds of the student enrollment throughout the war years; at times, the ratio ranged much higher.

Roi Wood, who became superintendent of Joplin public schools and president of the college on February 15, 1944, recalled that JJC's enrollment then consisted of 79 girls and 11 boys. Some members of the School Board wanted to close the college at the end of the spring semester, but Wood urged them to postpone the decision and authorize him to hire a field secretary to work at soliciting students. That summer Wood employed Leah Robinson, an English teacher, for the recruitment drive. While the effort did not produce spectacular results, it at least stabilized the enrollment. Student population increased slightly, reaching 135 in the fall of 1944 and 143 the following fall.

The junior college's drop in enrollment was not unusual. Other colleges experienced a similar phenomena as students moved into the armed forces. At the University of Missouri, enrollment dropped from a prewar peak of 5,212 to approximately 1,500 in 1943. At Southwest Missouri State Teachers College, girls outnumbered boys eight to one by 1943.

The war caused changes in the faculty, but left the staff largely intact; though the drastic drop in enrollment meant that the whole faculty was just barely holding on. Six teachers were laid off at the beginning of the 1943–1944 school year. Salaries, though increased, did not keep pace with the rising cost of living. By 1944, yearly salaries ranged in the $1,800 to $2,100 bracket, whereas in 1939 they had approximated $1,500 to $1,800. Some JJC instructors, hard pressed to support their families, took side jobs and one even drove a taxi. Superintendent Roi Wood was hired in 1944 at a salary of $4,800.

On the other hand, the overall job picture for teachers was optimistic. Public school teachers—and most of the college staff were certified to teach on that level—were in strong demand. Women, in particular, gained status at this time. In 1942 the Joplin Board of Education suspended the rule against hiring married women as teachers. A traditional policy common to most public schools, the rule had not been rigidly enforced against the junior college. Lillian Baker Spangler, foreign language teacher, had married in 1941. In 1943, Mrs. Alta Dale replaced her husband, William, when he was drafted, but prior to that she had tutored students in applied music on a part-time basis.

The junior college's curriculum underwent some modifications to accommodate the needs of wartime. Basic Arts and Sciences courses were continued, but the number of sections offered were cut back. Specialized military courses, as in the aviation field, were added. The Vocational program was vastly expanded to accommodate the need for trained workers in the defense industries. JJC cooperated with St. John's Hospital in the Nurse Cadet Corps training program. To expedite the training of young people, the "All Year Plan" was adopted under which regular semesters were lengthened to eighteen weeks and summer sessions to twelve weeks so that students could complete an associate degree with one school year and two summers of work. High school seniors in the upper one third of their class could enroll at the college for the spring semester and, if successful, they would be excused from the last semester of their high school work.

College activities continued on as normal a basis as possible considering the sharp drop in enrollment and the shortage of male enrollees. But the war could never be far from the students' minds as their friends, one by one, dropped out to enter the armed forces. On Monday, December 8, 1941, students gathered in the auditorium to listen to President Franklin Roosevelt's declaration of war speech. Early in 1942 classes were dismissed to enable the faculty to help with sugar rationing registration. At the time of the D-Day landings in France, June 6, 1944, classes were dismissed and the student body went to church to attend prayer services for the success of the invasion.

Though many student organizations collapsed during the war, students still found it possible to participate in a rich social life. The wartime college was small enough so that all students knew one another. A friendly atmosphere prevailed with much camaraderie. Many recreational opportunities were available in the community. The Joplin Symphony Orchestra held concerts in Schifferdecker Park, the city had six motion picture theaters, and "name" dance bands appeared regularly in Joplin. Some girls joined the Girls Service Organization, a branch of the United Service Organization (USO), whose function was to entertain soldiers at the Joplin USO and to attend USO dances at nearby Camp Crowder. As the shortage of young men deepened, groups began to organize "harem parties" in which boys vied with one another in bringing the largest number of girls to the parties. In one instance, an enterprising young man won a prize for bringing eleven girls to a party.

An important tradition-setting development, that occurred during the war, was the organization of a standing alumni association. On May 18, 1945, alumni gathered for the first of what came to be termed the alumni-student banquets and to set up the new association. Martha McCormick was the first sponsor.

After the struggle of starting an athletic program the first year, JJC maintained modest teams from 1938–1939 through the 1946–1947 school year. One head coach, with part-time assistance from the high school staff, was responsible for all the varsity sports, basketball, football, and a minor program that included at various times track, golf, and tennis. Women's teams played intermural games in connection with their physical education classes and occasionally an informal game with a team from another college. William N. "Bill" Collins became head coach in the fall of 1938 and continued in that position until December 1942. Clay Cooper replaced Collins for the 1942–1943 basketball season, but Cooper resigned in May 1943. From Cooper's resignation to the end of the war, the college had no head coach. The three basketball teams fielded in that period were coached by part-time staffs. In the fall of 1946, with the resumption of full varsity competition, Linn Stair became head coach and continued in that position through that and the following year.

Of the college's two major varsity sports, basketball and football, the latter faired the worst. In the ten years 1937 through 1946, the football teams enjoyed only two winning seasons, those of 1939 and 1942. At

The 1946 Crossroads *was dedicated to these twenty-four gold star Joplin Junior College students who gave their lives in World War II.*

We Dedicate —
this book to those who make
the new world, with peace,
possible — they gave
their lives!

JOHN NICHOLS	FLOYD LYON
WALTER E. TONNIES	RICHARD McWILLIAMS
FRANKLIN F. SIEBENTHALER	ALBERT STEWART
BOB GALBRAITH	JAMES LACY
VENCIL JESSEE	BOB LISCH
LLOYD HEMPHILL	LEONARD DUNCAN
ROBERT PECK	MORTON RADFORD
JOHN BROCK, JR.	CLAY JAMES
HOWARD MYER	BOB O'BERT
BILLY EPPERSON	JOE KOLKMEYER
ERNEST DIGBY	IVAN C. SCHUG
BEVERLY SETSER	ROBERT RICE

This 1944–1945 wartime photograph of the Dramatics Club suggests there might have been a problem finding enough boys to fill the male roles in plays. Members pictured are, from left, front row: Janet Switzer; Vonna Dell Elmore; Ruby Granger; Anna Jean Elliot; Betty Ann Harner, president; Bob Patrick; Doris Isenmann; and Margaret Rawson. Second row: Bobbie Lowe; Virginia Garrison; Jean McGregor; Virginia Southard; Betty Ann Sebring; Rose Ann Williams; Wilma Hardin; Mary Virginia Hollman; and Peggy Davison. Back row: Joe Beattie; Bill Thompson; Don Newby; Bill Claybourn; Helen Ummel; Emma Jean Hinkle; Doris Caler; Jean Alice Cain; and Stan Maret. The Dramatics Club, one of the college's oldest organizations, was formally organized in 1938–1939 as the College Players and was known only briefly as the Dramatics Club.

El Club Panamericano, new in 1944, was the college's first foreign language organization. Two years later it was renamed the Modern Language Club. Appearing in this 1945 photograph are, from left, front row: Richard Sayers; Mary Virginia Hollman; Janet Switzer; Virginia Mallet; Walter Walker, president; Vonna Dell Elmore; Ruby Granger; and Betty Dale Russell. Second row: Jean Cutright; Doris Caler; Patricia Bethel; Shirley Brunkhorst; Kathleen Thomas; Helen Ummel; Virginia DeGraff; Patricia Murphy; Betty Ann Parker; Carolyn Johnson; and Lillian Spangler, sponsor. Back row: Dorothy Cearnal; Patty Flanery; Lu Ann Lane; Gloria Doty; Barbara Caskey; Betty Boswell; Doris Isenmann; Wilma Hardin; and Margaret Ann Rawson. Lillian (Baker) Spangler taught foreign languages at Southern for thirty years, 1938–1968. Late in 1941, Miss Baker, defying tradition, became the first woman on JJC's regular teaching staff to marry. She died in 1987 at the age of eighty-four.

the Homecoming game of 1942 against Fort Scott, the last home game played until after the war, the ball used in the game was auctioned off to the bidder who pledged to buy the largest amount of war bonds. R. W. Baker secured the ball for his son, Bobby, by pledging $400. No football games were played in the three years 1943 through 1945.

The basketball Lions established a much better record, partly because they played a number of local independent teams as well as the more competitive junior colleges. Primarily, basketball's success was due to the fact that the teams could draw on a larger reservoir of local talent from small, rural high schools which often did not maintain football teams, but were competitive in basketball. The basketball Lions did not suffer a single losing season before World War II. After a wartime lapse of one season in 1943–1944, they continued to win through the 1946–1947 season.

The war years also brought on a decline in the number of graduates from JJC that paralleled the overall drop in enrollment. The ninety-three who graduated in the spring of 1941 marked a high for the prewar period and a figure that would not be exceeded for seven years. By 1943, wartime attrition had cut heavily into the sophomore class as only fifty-

In this photograph, Head Coach Bill Collins (left) and Line Coach Ferrel Anderson (right) confer during the 1939 football season with Team Captain Lloyd Shafer (center), the squad's outstanding ball carrier. Looking on is sophomore Billye Grattis, popular cheerleader and 1940 Crossroads Queen.

Lined up for a formal group photograph are members of the 1940 football team. From left, front row: Virgil Schmidt, Gordon Waldrop, Earl Robinson, Reuben Mills, Richard Gibbs, Robert Wagner, Max Brown, Bill Hartley, Howard Dale, Don Fitzwater, and Jack Carlisle. Second row: Art Gondles, Ed Wyrick, Tommy Bell, Paul Camfield, Gene Moore, Reeford Smith, Clarence Shields, Captain Charles Crampton, Gordon Calhoun, Willie Corder, James Shaw, and Pete King. Back row: Junior Harchas, Ervin Helton, Forrest Bishop, Bill Warren, Bill Campbell, Robert Hoofnagle, Arrell Gibson, David Rowland, Raymond Carlisle, Jack Robinson, Delmar Armstrong, and Lewis Pearcy.

Arrell Gibson (No. 90) later became a nationally prominent Indian and Western historian at the University of Oklahoma; he wrote twenty-five books and over one hundred articles. A recipient of Southern's Outstanding Alumnus award for 1973, Gibson died in 1987 and was buried in Joplin.

one graduated. The ceremony included reading the names of forty-three class members who had dropped out to enter the armed services. In 1944, the full impact of the war held the graduating class to twenty-nine. Other than the first year of 1939, this figure still stands as an all-time low for the college. The next year, with the college population stabilized by a heavy preponderance of girls, thirty-six graduated; of these, only five were boys and three of them immediately entered the service. In 1946, even though the war had ended, graduating sophomores still reflected wartime enrollment patterns and only thirty-nine received degrees, of whom eleven were boys.

The brightest spot in Joplin Junior College's wartime programs was the summer school. There enrollment remained relatively stable as opposed to the precipitous drop during the regular school years. By 1941, summer school registration had risen to ninty-four and the figure held at near one hundred through the war years.

A primary reason for the strong wartime summer school enrollment was the growing teacher shortage. The war created a major crisis as teachers, traditionally underpaid, left the classrooms for higher paying jobs in industry or to join the armed services. Locally the shortage reached such proportions that then Superintendent Roi Wood later recalled how one year he drove six thousand miles looking for prospects to fill 112 vacancies. Many schools turned to hiring married women. There was a considerable reservoir of women ex-teachers who had been forced out of the profession because they married. Now they were gladly accepted back. However, state rules required six hours of refresher courses for renewal of their certificates. Many of these people met the requirement by attending the JJC summer sessions. In addition, there were others who were working on their sixty-hour elementary certificates. These trainees found ready employment in nearby small town and rural schools at an average salary of $115 per month for a nine-month session.

With the war over, the junior college did an about face as it struggled to accommodate an influx of returning veterans. The war ended too late in 1945 for many to enroll that fall, but it was evident the college would soon be flooded with ex-servicemen. Many veterans had had their plans for higher education delayed by the war, but more importantly, veteran's benefits made it attractive for them to attend college. Under the G.I. Bill of Rights, single veterans received $65 per month; if married the figure increased to $90. In addition, all fees, books, and supplies were paid for. Public Law 16 provided for disabled veterans to draw even more.

The real tidal wave of veterans struck in the fall of 1946 when enrollment topped out at a record-breaking 484. The college, with a faculty of only twenty-one full-time teachers, was not really prepared for this massive influx. Though five teachers had been added to the skeletonized wartime staff of the previous year, it

With leather helmet strapped on and shoulder padding in place, Don Fitzwater is ready to throw the football during the 1940 season. Players were not then as well protected from injury as in later years.

was hardly sufficient for an enrollment that had more than tripled. Teachers were swamped. Some 398 of these enrollees were freshmen and, reversing the wartime trend, boys outnumbered the girls by approximately three to one. Many of these young men were nontraditional students, much more mature than the prewar beginning freshmen.

The flash flood of entering veterans crested in the fall of 1946 and then began to subside, though enrollment remained high for the next three years. In the fall of 1947, entering freshmen dropped to 284. Buoyed up by large returning sophomore classes, total enrollment peaked at 501 in the fall semesters of both 1948 and 1949, figures that would not be exceeded for another five years. Meanwhile, as the number of new enrollees slowly ebbed, the freshmen classes took on a younger cast, the ratio of boys to girls began to even out, and the school returned to a more normal peacetime pattern.

The veterans had brought a broader geographical background to the student population and the college began to take on a more regional tone. In the prewar period, 1938-1941, nearly 67 percent of the entering freshmen came from the Joplin school district, but in the postwar years, 1946-1952, this figure dropped to approximately 53 percent.

The returning veterans were a new type of college student, more mature and more worldly wise than the 18-to-20-year-olds that junior college instructors were used to dealing with. Most were in the 21-to-24-year age bracket, but their wartime experiences, in many cases, had made them serious beyond their years. A no-nonsense atmosphere prevailed. Motivated to further their educations, they tended to take courses that would aid them in transferring to four-year colleges and universities. Many instructors found the veterans a delight to teach because of their willingness to learn, their insights, and their sophistication. Because of the core of outstanding teachers, the veterans were not generally disappointed in their decision to attend JJC. Many recalled years later that when they moved on to four-year colleges they found themselves as well or better prepared than their new classmates who had started there on the freshman level.

The 1946-1947 school year marked Joplin Junior College's tenth anniversary. During the decade since its founding, JJC had emerged from its initial organizational problems to become a strong institution that had grown faster than originally anticipated. One of Missouri's larger junior colleges in 1941, it had almost collapsed during World War II only to be severely strained by the record enrollment of veterans at the end of the war. By the spring of 1947, though overcrowded and understaffed, that crisis was on the way to being controlled.

(Top) The first "Pigskin Princess," Victoria Evans, from Carthage, is shown at festivities after her selection by the football squad in the fall of 1940.

A significant new development at this time was the initiation of Homecoming festivities for the alumni, but the merging of the football queen ceremonies with Homecoming activities had to await the post–World War II era and the organizing of a formal alumni association.

(Bottom) The basketball Lions returned for the 1944–1945 season after a wartime lapse of one year due to a shortage of players and to transportation problems. Pictured are, from left: Don Testerman, Robert Myers, Richard Hadden, Bill Vaughn, Robert Mann, Richard Queen, Bill Claybourn, and Bob Patrick. Testerman became JJC's head basketball coach in 1952. Due to wartime conditions, the Lions played only the junior colleges of Bolivar, Miami, and Wentworth, plus some local independent teams.

35

Beta Beta Beta, founded in the 1938–1939 college year, was the second sorority organized at JJC and the longest lived. Girl's organizations, unlike boy's clubs, remained comparatively strong during World War II. Members shown in this 1942–1943 photograph are, from left, front row: Betsy Ross Pogue, Marjorie Hampton, Shirley Cox, Betsy Balsley, Catherine Schellack, Gerry Goodrich, and Martha Jean Brown. Second row: Winifred English, Nadine Wade, Mary Lou Marlatt, Vera Goodwin, Mary Stevens, Mary Margaret Cater, Shirley English, and Beulah Marshall. Third row: Martha Lee Troutman, Donna Foshay, Imogene Craig, Jan Walker, Quanita Morrison, and Mignon Henley. Back row: Magie Hinds, Betty Brotherton, Marilyn Kost, Nancy Sanders, Mary Catherine Randall, Lisbeth Day, Llwellyn White, Mary Lou Farmer, Frankee Guthals, Claudine Duvaney, Maty Burt, Jean Wommack, Mary Rice, Hazel Farneman, Jean Davis, Virginia Lankford, Ada Coffey (sponsor), and Gerry Stowell.

Gerry Stowell later became the wife of Bill (Dennis) Weaver. The couple met at the YMCA-YWCA Mixer at the beginning of Weaver's sophomore year. Spotting her on the floor, Weaver asked a mutual friend to dance her over and introduce them. In a sly reference to their expertise as dancers, the "We'll Always Remember:" column in the 1943 Crossroads noted, "How a certain couple Weaved across the dance floor and almost always Stowell the show."

Stowell and Weaver were married at the end of World War II, on October 20, 1945. They have three sons. After forty-seven years of successful marriage, the Weavers make their home in Malibu, California.

It was time for new leadership to cope with the college's postwar problems. Dean Blaine had led the college through all these difficult years, now he was stepping down. In his decade at the helm of JJC, he had served a longer tenure than would any of his five successors. At the annual alumni-student banquet in May 1947, he was presented with a billfold containing $277 as a token of appreciation from the alumni, students, faculty, and friends. Blaine deserves much credit for his role in making JJC into the solidly established institution it had become. Already the college was acquiring a regional reputation as one of the better junior colleges to be found in its immediate four-state trade area and in the state of Missouri.

After a wartime absence of three years, the junior college resumed football competition in the fall of 1948, suffering a 4–5 losing season. Members of the 1948 team pictured are, from left, front row: Floyd Belk, Truman Holden, Bob Jester, Jack Tabler, Jerry Lacey, George Landreth, Leo Turnbull, Richard Covey, Howard Belk and Bud Passley. Second row: James Neblet, Alan Johnson, Truman Jeffcott, Joe Keys, Richard Renick, Gerry Brown, Rex Fraley, Neal Williams, Bill Cutbirth, Wayne Muhlenburg, Bill Garrison and Bill Hood. Back row: Coach Linn Stair, Leonard Laird, Harley Ballenger, Bob Cash, Bill Shaner, Bob Todd, James Perry, Tom Grim, Jesse Reed, Robert Woods, Bill Stipp, Don Gregory, George DeTar, and Bill Hurd.

Belk, co-captain of the team, later became an administrator at the college and held the position of vice-president of Academic Affairs from 1974 until his retirement in 1990.

Housing for the heavy influx of ex-servicemen after World War II became a problem for JJC, with the shortage of apartments for married veterans being most critical. To alleviate the problem, the Federal Housing Authority provided six surplus military barracks buildings, with four apartments in each, at government expense. These were set up at Thirteenth and Murphy, just west of Junge Stadium. Opened for the spring semester of 1947, the units were soon full. Commonly referred to as "G.I. City," wits jokingly termed the settlement as "Fertile Acres" because of the number of children there. The units were later torn down.

A crowd of students and faculty gathered on November 1, 1946, to witness this dedication of Blaine Hall. The name, overwhelmingly chosen by student ballot, honored the popular Dean Harry E. Blaine who retired the following spring. The building, a house located immediately south of the college, provided badly needed space for the burgeoning college enrollment. The main floor featured a cafeteria—the college's first—while a student lounge, the Lion's Den—borrowing a name earlier used by a nearby lunch counter—occupied the basement.

TRIBUTE TO HARRY E. BLAINE

Dean Blaine has been one of my dearest friends since 1937. Our friendship did not end with his death this year. One does not lose a friend whose kindness has cut so sharply across one's life.

I worked for two years as a student in his office. My respect for him and his dear wife grew with each day. There were so many acts of kindness . . .

> very practical acts such as giving money from his own pocket to financially distressed students . . .

> or paying for meals for the football team when there was no money in the college budget . . .

> or graciously entertaining the sophomores in his home on Class Day . . .

> or less tangible acts such as following us after graduation with news of better jobs than we could have found for ourselves . . .

Mr. Blaine had the rare gift of understanding. I think it was because he listened so well. I see him yet, seated at his desk slowly pushing a pencil between his fingers as he listened to a student. His keen mind sensed unspoken thoughts, needs, and hopes.

This large, deliberate man had white hair and rounded shoulders. He met the challenge of establishing the junior college at an age when many men have retired. Yet we never missed his slow-moving figure at a football game, or a track meet, a pep rally, or a class play. His very age had given him the patience to cope with his job, a great wisdom to share with his students, and a deep faith in young people.

He never forgot a face, rarely a name. He "kept track of his people" until his death. I have the feeling he is still "keeping track" of us. Remembering him gives us a warm sense of being cared for. Greatness never dies. Sometimes it lives on in music, statues, paintings or words. Dean Harry E. Blaine's greatness lives on in the lives of his students.

Mary Laird McClintock
Editor, 1939 Crossroads

This moving tribute to Harry E. Blaine by Mary Laird McClintock, 1939 alumnus, appeared in the 1957 Crossroads. *Blaine died February 20, 1957, in Marshfield, Missouri.*

CHAPTER II
AN EXCELLENT JUNIOR COLLEGE

A s the flood of World War II veterans began to subside in the late 1940s, student enrollment at the junior college returned to near the prewar levels and remained there until the mid-1950s. It was a time of stability, an era in which academic excellence held priority over physical growth. Programs were broadened and strengthened and a number of outstanding new teachers were brought in. From 1954 on, steady growth set in, but not to the extent that it upset the stability of the college, and JJC continued to gain in recognition as a leading junior college.

On August 1, 1947, F. Harlan Bryant succeeded the retired Harry E. Blaine as dean of JJC. In hiring Bryant, President Wood's principal charge to him was to gain accreditation for the junior college from the North Central Association of Colleges and Secondary Schools. Ten years had passed since the founding of the college and it was not yet a fully accredited institution. Though University of Missouri officials recertified JJC yearly and its credits were fully accepted by the university and the Missouri state system of colleges, as well as by most other institutions of higher learning, some schools rejected its credits, and this hurt the junior college's prestige. An earlier attempt at gaining certification had failed because of insufficient student records and an inadequate library.

Bryant immediately tackled these problems. The recordkeeping shortcoming had already been resolved by setting up a registrar's office on September 1, 1946, with Theo Hart as the first registrar. The library problem stemmed, in part, from a lack of room for more books and an expanded study area. Steps were already underway to resolve the overcrowding. G.I. City had been set up to provide housing for married veterans and Blaine Hall had been opened up as an annex for student services, but the vocational education shops needed to be moved out of the main Fourth and Byers building to provide more space. Work was already well advanced on a new building for the school district's Franklin Technical School and its completion in early 1948 made it possible to remove the shops for automobile repairs, carpentry, electricity, and engineering drawing from the college building. With this move, the old building received its final renovation to provide more classrooms and an expanded library.

With these changes underway, Dean Bryant initiated the involved process of submitting the college to a North Central review. Success crowned his efforts and on March 30, 1949, the college received accreditation. It was a milestone in JJC's development; now the little college joined the national family of colleges and universities with full reciprocity of its credits. Not only that, but the North Central report was generally favorable. Though the institution was criticized for tying its curriculum too closely to the general education requirements of the University of Missouri and not providing sufficiently for local educational needs, it noted that steps were underway to resolve these problems. In summary, the report noted: "The quality of instruction appears to be very good. . . .The instructors are excellent classroom teachers. . . . Evidences are available to indicate that Joplin students who transfer to other institutions are well prepared to do the work. . . .The financial position of Joplin Junior College is sound . . . and the community is solidly behind it." The report vindicated the efforts of the staff of dedicated teachers who had long worked to improve the college. It also solidified the college's

(Opposite) Cheerleader Trinket Plumb congratulates football tackles Skip Drouin No. 65, and Hank Urbanowicz, No. 66, after the Lion's 26–14 victory over the Fort Scott Greyhounds in the 1965 Homecoming game. Plumb was later named Basketball Queen for the 1965–1966 season. Sharon Campbell was Homecoming Queen for that school year.

reputation as one of the state's best junior colleges, a reputation that would grow as JJC advanced through the decade of the 1950s.

With the passage of the 1940s, veterans ceased to be a significant factor in JJC enrollment. The student count for the fall of 1950 semester totaled 362 and enrollment remained near this level until the fall of 1954. Enrollment for these four years, 1950–1954, averaged 338, comparing closely with the immediate prewar years, 1938–1942, which averaged out at 327.

The heavy enrollment of veterans had merely masked the fact that the war years had brought no significant strengthening of the junior college's demographic or economic base. War industries and military bases, like Camp Crowder at Neosho, were soon either eliminated or greatly curtailed. More significantly, the mining industry, which had been the leading sector in the Tri-State District's industrial economy for seventy-five years, neared a state of collapse by the early 1950s. The Korean War brought some important new industries to Joplin that helped stabilize the population count, but several small towns and rural areas in the Tri-State District suffered severe population losses. Many families left the area looking for brighter economic opportunities. Also, the count of young people was down. Those reaching college age in the 1948–1955 time period had been born in the depths of the Great Depression, a time when the birthrate was low. But for other factors that began to spark enrollment in the 1950s, JJC's student population might have dropped to even lower levels.

With the veterans gone, the composition of the student body tended to return to its traditional pattern. Most were young, in the eighteen to twenty-one age bracket, enrollment was about 60 percent boys, and the freshman class was almost double the size of the sophomore class. The Korean War that started in 1950, unlike World War II, tended to strengthen enrollment rather than weakening it. College students were able to get draft deferments if they ranked in the upper half of their class or if they passed a Selective Service Qualification Test.

JJC's enrollment reached a new plateau starting with the 1954–1955 school year. The student count for that fall totaled 509, almost 30 percent above the previous year; never again would enrollment drop below 500.

Several factors combined to bring about this new era of growth in spite of the area's rather static population base. The growing number of students coming from outside the immediate Joplin area was one factor. Though always important, this source had become more so starting with the influx of veterans and by 1955 approximately one-half of the students came from outside of Joplin. Also, a higher percentage of young people were going to college as they perceived the need for higher education to further their career opportunities. Furthermore, the enlarged programs, especially in business, plus an expanded offering of evening courses, opened up new educational opportunities, particularly to nontraditional students. Finally, the low cost was a continuing factor. Fees had risen only slightly since the founding of the college, and tuition remained free to residents of the Joplin School District though the age limit had been lowered from twenty-one to twenty years. The basic tuition rate for full-time students was thirty dollars per semester.

The year 1954 marked a milestone in JJC's development when, for the first time, blacks were admitted to the college. Only about two weeks after the Supreme Court's historic antisegregation ruling, *Brown v. Board of Education of Topeka*, the Joplin School Board considered the issue of admitting blacks to the junior college. Inquiries had already been made about attending that fall. The Board's attorney rendered an opinion that the court's ruling made admission of blacks mandatory. Joplin had long maintained a segregated school

(Top) F. Harlan Bryant became the second dean of the Joplin Junior College in the fall of 1947 replacing Harry E. Blaine. Bryant, in his brief tenure of two years, is remembered for gaining North Central accreditation for JJC, completing an expansion of the library, and for remodeling the college's quarters at Fourth and Byers.

Bryant, with a doctor of education degree from the University of Missouri, was the first dean of the college to have a doctorate, but all future deans would have them. He later became president of Western State College, Gunnison, Colorado.

(Bottom) Margaret Mitchell was the college's registrar from 1949 to 1968. A meticulous manager of student records, she replaced Theo Hart, the first registrar, who had served in that capacity for three years. An accounting teacher prior to becoming registrar, Mitchell died in 1993 at the age of ninety.

The Franklin Technical School was completed in March 1948 to house all of the public schools' vocational shop courses, including those that were moved out of the junior college. Located on Thirteenth Street between Wall and Pearl avenues, it occupied the site of the old Franklin Elementary School. The Federal Works Agency funded moving the surplus building from Camp Crowder near Neosho. JJC students took their shop courses here until near the end of the junior college era.

The Women's Athletic Association (WAA) promoted an interest in women's sports in the years 1945–1949. It sponsored intramural contests and sometimes the girls informally played rival teams from nearby colleges, but no college-sponsored varsity sports for women existed at this time.

Appearing in this 1949 photograph are, from left, front row: Jackie Olson; Marjorie Pflug; Jane Williams; Pat Greene; Patt True; Betty Jo Weber; Mary Walker; Maria Surgi; and Marilyn Greene. Second row: Loralie Robertson; Rayma Jean Rowland; Celia Braeckel; Mary Wright; Billye Talmadge; Patsy Ruth Miller; Wylene Kennedy; Genevieve Bauman; Ermanell Joslin; and Lucille Downer, sponsor. Third row: Nancy Frisinger; Shirley Merritt; Bettye Hoover; Stella Felkins; Mary Cole; Bobby Ann Hays; Helen Louise Hough; Janice Everhard; Jeanne Rataczyk; Jane Rothenbarger; Helen Ard; and Marilyn Land, president.

Kathleen Cearnal, a freshman from Joplin, was crowned the first Homecoming Queen in this November 1947 ceremony. Cearnal, in the foreground, was escorted by Student Senate President Jack Short. Behind are her attendants, from left, Ruth Lowe and Rosemary McIntire. Lowe's escort is Douglas Landrith, later a coach at the college.

Prior to this time, football queens had not been identified with Homecoming festivities. Known before World War II as "Pigskin Princesses," the 1946 queen, Mary Alice Dabbs, was identified simply as "Football Queen."

Nancy Moss, a sophomore, was crowned 1948 Crossroads Queen in a colorful ceremony at the Scottish Rite Temple, February 27, 1948. Her manager, Dick Sayers, escorted Moss to the throne.

In the spring of 1953, Moss married her classmate at JJC, Floyd Belk, who later became Southern's vice president of Academic Affairs. The Belks have two sons and are now retired.

system, as required by the state constitution. The Lincoln school provided education for black children, though some integration had long existed in the elementary schools. Considerable dissension was voiced that evening of June 1, 1954. One board member vigorously opposed the motion but finally, for the sake of unanimity, voted "yes under protest." Thus, by a unanimous vote of the five members present (one was absent), the Board moved to integrate the junior college. No immediate action was taken on integrating the high school and lower grades pending a clarification of state policy.

Integration of the junior college proceeded smoothly. Blacks had always accounted for only 2 to 3 percent of Joplin's population and, while there had been two bad mob actions at the turn of the century, race relations had been generally tranquil. Eight blacks entered JJC in the fall of 1954: two boys— Eugene Roscoe, Joplin, and Laverne Stewart, Baxter Springs; and six girls— Peggy Sue Crawford, Joplin; Elese Frazier, Carthage; Carroll Logue, Joplin; Helen Scott, Carthage; Anne Terry, Joplin; and Betty Marie Young, Baxter Springs. Blacks were accepted on campus without open dissension and soon they were involved in extracurricular activities, particularly in athletics.

The number of students graduating in the years 1948 to 1966 followed the trend in overall enrollment. The flood of veterans after World War II resulted in a graduating class of 103 in 1948, a record high that stood for eleven years. After that the numbers declined sharply, reaching a low of only 45 in 1953. From that point on, graduates grew steadily in number, once again reaching the 100 mark in 1958 and never again dropping below that point. The year 1958 marked the twentieth anniversary of graduating classes, and Margaret Mitchell, the registrar, calculated that 1,379 had graduated in those twenty years.

Joplin Junior College's curriculum had not fundamentally changed as the institution advanced into the 1950s. As before, it offered a variety of academic and vocational courses leading to either an associate degree or a diploma, but the program had been revised and expanded with more emphasis put on studies leading to associate degrees. Some 10 to 40 percent of the graduates normally received diplomas, the rest associate degrees.

With the growing emphasis on tailoring programs to the needs of students, some changes had been made in the associate degree offerings. To meet the growing demand, business education had been notably upgraded. Initially it had consisted largely of terminal courses in secretarial training, but by 1953 an associate of business degree was offered with a choice of two emphases: Distributive Education or General Business. Reflecting the general upgrading of academics, the General Culture curriculum had been changed from a diploma to an associate degree program, and an English placement test was instituted to identify those incoming freshmen who needed remedial work in that area. The associate in education degree was dropped at the end of

The saga of Jo Juco, the stuffed lion cub mascot with an inquisitive stare, has sporadically stimulated student interest throughout most of the college's history. Rescued from a storeroom in 1952, the mascot was named "Jo Juco" in a student contest.

Jo Juco captured the imagination of JJC students to an extent that few mascots ever do. The 1955 and 1959 Crossroads used Jo Juco as a theme and such phrases as "Jo Juco says" or "Jo Juco presents" were common in The Chart.

Sadly, the little lion faded away with the transition to a four-year college. No enthusiasm could be generated for giving Jo Juco a name more suitable for a senior college and, though moved to the new campus, he soon disappeared.

Jo Juco was symbolic of the Junior College. Young students, coming in daily contact with the mascot mounted in a trophy case, were fascinated; but the coming of the four-year college, with its more mature student body spread over a large campus, caused Jo Juco to lose his grip on the collegiate imagination.

Thomas H. Flood became the third dean of JJC in the fall of 1949, replacing Harlan Bryant. Flood, at twenty-eight, was the college's youngest dean. A native of Missouri and an Army veteran, he had a doctorate in education from Columbia University. Flood resigned in 1953 to enter the insurance business in Joplin.

the 1959–1960 school year because of the decline in demand for sixty-hour certified teachers. For a decade, most JJC students, intent of entering the teaching profession, had completed the associate of arts degree with a pre-education emphasis.

In the period 1947–1964, Vocational Education continued to be an important, but increasingly minor, part of JJC's curriculum. These programs, usually leading to a diploma, were not necessarily less rigorous than associate degree offerings, but were more job oriented and the specialized courses were not transferable except as they might apply to a similar program in another institution. As the college advanced into the 1950s, most diplomas were granted in the Secretarial Science area. Vocational shop courses had been very popular with the veterans, but in 1948 these courses were transferred to the school district's new Franklin Technical School. There JJC students received training in common with high school students and adults enrolled on a noncredit basis. The result was that fewer JJC students undertook the Vocational diploma curriculum when they could receive the same technical training on a noncredit basis.

JJC's program of evening classes underwent a series of modifications in the 1950s. In the early postwar years, evening offerings consisted of a few credit courses, but this program declined in popularity to the point where it was dropped in 1949. Starting in the fall of 1951, a new Division of Adult Education was set up to conduct noncredit vocational and nonvocational evening classes for career advancement or personal satisfaction. Tuition was five to seven dollars per course depending on the size of enrollment. This program proved to be reasonably popular until the late 1950s. Most of the courses were in the Business field or other vocational areas, though a number were personal interest courses such as Dressmaking, Square Dancing, or Model Airplane Building.

The late 1950s brought on another change of direction in the night program as a growing demand by adults, who were pursuing degrees, led to a revival of the program of evening credit courses. A few such courses were offered on a trial basis in 1957 and when some 235 students enrolled for evening courses that fall, the need became obvious. Seeing this need to provide a fuller educational opportunity to nontraditional, employed adult students, an expanded Evening Division was set up and in the fall of 1958, for the first time, JJC offered a full academic schedule of twenty evening credit courses that could lead to an associate degree. Tuition was set at six dollars per credit hour plus the usual book rental fee. The expanded Evening Division was an important factor in JJC's growing enrollment in the late

A typing class practices with their manual typewriters in this 1950 classroom scene. Supervising in the background is Vera Steininger, pioneer teacher of Typing and Shorthand at the college. Secretarial Training made up a major part of the Business curriculum in the college's early years. Dorothy Stone and Steininger laid the foundations of the Business Training program at JJC. Steininger retired in 1963, rounding out twenty-five years of full-time service at the college.

With lights ablaze, this view of the junior college's new roomier quarters at Eighth and Wall on a snowy evening in the winter of 1959–1960 symbolized JJC's growing Evening Division program. The expanded curriculum, which made it possible for nontraditional students employed full time in the day to complete an associate degree in the evenings, led to a substantial increase in the college's enrollment.

This interesting view of 1954–1955 Student Senate officers posing on the back of an old car includes, from left, bottom row: Wylene Waggener; Kay Roland; Tom Gerwert; and Bill Agan. Top row: Patty Deatherage, 1954 Crossroads *Queen; and Ruth McKinney.*

(Top) An example of the new academic clubs forming at JJC, the Distributive Education Club was organized in 1949 as an academic support group for the new Business curriculum area of Marketing. Appearing in this 1956 photograph are, from left: Vic Duncan; Ron Robson; Sandra Samples; James R. Stratton, sponsor; and Bob Braxton.

Robson later followed a career in radio and television, and once served as MSSC's public relations director, retiring in 1976. Stratton taught at JJC from 1951 to 1959.

(Bottom) Lloyd L. Dryer appears here in a typical role as a counselor of students. Coming to JJC in 1950, he was for many years the only teacher of Psychology. He also served as director of Guidance and Counseling and as a school psychologist.

A popular teacher, Dryer was for several years the only instructor with a doctor's degree. Known as "Doc" by his friends, students remember Dryer for his kindness, gentleness, and compassion. He retired in 1976 and died in 1984.

1950s and it enhanced the college's prestige as an excellent junior college. By the early 1960s, students were graduating who had taken all their courses in the evenings.

The summer program did not fare as well as other parts of JJC's curriculum, though it did experience a revival at the end of this time period. In the immediate postwar era, the summer sessions continued to offer a curriculum attractive to beginning freshmen and to elementary teachers, but by 1948 enrollment was dropping due to the decline in the numbers of veterans and a near collapse of the two-year Elementary Teacher Certification program. The summer of 1950 marked a termination of these sessions until the end of the decade.

Even after a lapse of eight years, difficulty was experienced in reviving summer sessions. The overall growth in student enrollment and the increased demands for more flexibility in offering courses indicated a need, but attempts to revive the program in 1959 and 1960 proved unsuccessful with enrollments of 77 and 61 respectively. In 1965, the summer school was successfully reinstated with 79 students enrolled. From that time on the summer program became continuous.

While important changes like the expanded evening school program stand out, there were minor changes that also enhanced the academic standing of JJC in the period 1947–1966. In 1950, a placement service was initiated to help students and graduates find jobs. Two years later a new competitive scholarship program was instituted for high school graduates. After being extensively renovated in 1947–1948, the library was steadily expanded and by 1961 book holdings reached a total of 11,500. In keeping with a general trend at this time, the ESMIFW grading system, used since the founding of the college, was changed to the ABCDFW format effective with the 1965–1966 school year.

Joplin Junior College, already noted for its fine staff of teachers, was able to reinforce its reputation for quality instruction throughout the period 1947 to 1966. The teaching staff grew slowly at this time, turnover was low and, as a result, the average years of tenure at the college grew. Where vacancies occurred, quality teachers tended to be recruited to take their place. Faculty salaries had increased significantly from the meager stipends paid in the prewar and World War II periods, but were still modest compared with state and national averages. In 1954, the nine instructors at the top of the pay scale received $4,550 each for the nine-month school year.

The faculty of the late 1940s, 1950s, and early 1960s was characterized by an extraordinary closeness. Observers often commented that they were like "one big family." Physical proximity was a factor in this closeness. The operations of the school, aside from shop courses and some athletic activities, were all encompassed in one building where teachers were in daily contact with one another. Another factor was the heavy preponderance of veteran faculty whose associations over a period of years tended to build respect and a compatibility for one another. Then, too, the absence of a merit system or professorial rank tended to mute rivalries while the peer pressure of professional pride kept them all working toward the common goal of excellent teaching. Also, social events like the annual faculty Christmas party and the alumni banquets tended to bring all the faculty together.

Though the junior college's academic program tended to be strengthened after World War II, the trend toward becoming more of a commuter college affected social cohesion and extracurricular activities. The increase in automobile ownership meant that more students coming from outlying areas were driving to and from school rather than finding lodging within the city. Though the small size of the student body assured a strong fellowship, commuter students were less interested in college activities outside the classroom. They came from and returned to their homes and jobs by automobile, spending a minimum of time on campus.

A further blow to student body cohesion came in 1960. In an effort to improve scheduling for the increasing enrollment and for students who worked, the universal free period was dropped. Since the beginning of the college, one free period a week had been set aside for the entire student body. This arrangement had provided a prime hour in which assemblies could be scheduled and in which members and sponsors could attend club meetings without missing classes. The change left student clubs facing a dilemma in finding suitable times for meetings, and it led to a further erosion in such organizations.

These changes in the orientation of the student body had a marked effect on organizations. Efforts in the college's early years had generated an overabundance of student organizations, but much of this structure had collapsed during the war years and the attrition continued in the postwar period. By the end of the junior college era, all social fraternities and sororities were gone. The largely social YMCA and YWCA organizations began to lose their popularity after the college moved away from Fourth and Byers. The YMCA faded in the late 1950s and the YWCA became extinct early in the next decade.

With the decline of on-campus social organizations, and the growing academic excellence of the college, it is not surprising that academic clubs and honorary scholastic societies multiplied. Academic clubs, open to general membership within a discipline, such as the Student National Education Association, became more popular in the 1950s. Also, such older academic clubs as the College Players, and the Modern

Members of the newly formed Phi Theta Kappa, honorary scholastic fraternity for junior colleges, gathered for this 1951 photograph. From left, front row: Mickey Bauer, Jack Gibson, Linda Haslett, Dick Henrickson, Phyllis Bogardus, Harold Connor, Geneva Huercamp, and Robert Eldridge. Back row: James Chaney, Lee Dew, Joe Harner, Leslie Pearson, Dean Gilstrap, Harold Zabsky, Eddy Vaughan, and Larry Dunham. The strongest of JJC's scholastic honor clubs, PTK lasted until 1977.

Leslie Pearson was editor-in-chief of The Chart *for the 1950–1951 school year. He later became assistant managing editor of the* St. Louis Globe-Democrat.

Larry Dunham, then president of the sophomore class, later taught English at Southern from 1962 to 1967.

Members of Theta Mu Gamma, an honorary scholastic music fraternity, appear in this 1956 photograph. From left, seated: Toby Baker, Leroy Chapman, and Joyce Connely. Standing: Sue Cookerly, Elizabeth Kemm, Alicia Hagar, Joan Myer, Carla Hoskins, Larry Habermehl, Kathryn Walker, Karen Williams, Elese Frazier, Jane Barlow, Maureen Vincent, and Betty Board.

Maureen Vincent was 1957 Crossroads Queen. Elese Frazier was one of the first blacks to graduate from JJC, and a Homecoming Queen candidate in 1955.

Edwin B. Strong, Jr., recipient of the Alumni Association's Outstanding Alumnus Award for 1980, graduated from JJC in 1956. Completing his doctor of philosophy degree at the University of Kansas, Strong became a professor of Political Science at the University of Tulsa and then advanced into administrative responsibilities. In 1992 he assumed the presidency of Culver-Stockton College in Canton, Missouri.

Strong is the brother of Annetta St. Clair, associate professor of Political Science at MSSC. Photo courtesy of Annetta St. Clair

(Top) Members of the 1957–1958 Assembly Committee confer on future plans in this gathering. Pictured are, from left, seated: Lela A. Smith, English; May Pool, Mathematics; Loretta Frazier, librarian; Connie Herron, student; and unidentified student. Standing: Duane Hunt, student; Hubert Bird, student; Milton Brietzke, Speech and Drama; and Merrill Ellis, Music.

Hubert Bird, a Music major, graduated from JJC in 1959. An award-winning composer, and a professor at Keene State College in New Hampshire, Dr. Bird created "A Celebration of Promises" in honor of Missouri Southern's fiftieth anniversary. Lela A. Smith served from 1947 to 1966 as an English teacher. Loretta Frazier was a longtime chairman of the Assembly Committee and Southern's librarian from 1948 to 1969. Merrill Ellis taught music at JJC from 1951 to 1962.

(Bottom) Alumni Association officers and faculty sponsors for the 1951–1952 school year gathered for this photograph. From left: Orie A. Cheatham, sponsor; Dorothy Stone, sponsor; Buford Zumwalt, vice president; James C. Willey, sponsor; Jack Parker, president; and Franklin Edwards, board member.

Parker, a war veteran and a 1947 graduate, was president of the Student Senate in 1946–1947. Later, he became a prominent Joplin businessman.

Stone, was the principal sponsor of the Alumni Association for many years. Cheatham taught accounting from 1950 to 1958. Willey was a Chemistry instructor from 1946 to 1958.

Language Club continued to function. Among the new honorary societies, Phi Theta Kappa, a national arts and science scholastic fraternity, was most important with Pi Alpha Pi and Theta Mu Gamma being set up in the business and music fields, respectively.

New service clubs also sprang up at this time. The Circle K Club gave students an opportunity to become involved in community service, and the Young Democrats and Young Republicans gave students a chance to be active in politics.

Assemblies, made convenient by the weekly universal free period, had been a part of student life since the college's founding. The programs, presented by student groups or by outside speakers, helped hold student organizations together and were an important factor in offsetting the growing centrifugal effect of commuting. Many of these programs were quite entertaining and some were memorable. In an October 1949 assembly, held to introduce candidates for the student body presidency, a motorcycle was brought into the auditorium to dramatize the campaign of a candidate. Much to the discomfiture of the college dean, the candidate made his entrance riding down the aisle in a "little crate car" pulled by the motorcycle. A band followed and shots rang out in the balcony. After delivering his campaign speech, the budding politician left the same way he had entered; in spite of all his efforts, he did not win the election.

Alumni gatherings and homecoming festivities had become a firmly established part of the college's traditions by the 1950s. The formally established Alumni Association helped hold the swelling ranks of graduates together and an alumni-student banquet was held each spring in which a distinguished alumnus addressed the audience. The Homecoming activities held each October or November provided a second yearly opportunity for the alumni to visit their alma mater.

The Joplin Junior College of 1947–1962 still offered students a rich extracurricular program. Aside from the limited number of organized clubs,

This 1954 Crossroads *Queen coronation ceremony suggests the elegance of these annual balls, the principal formal dances of the junior college era. Pictured, from left: Mike Roth; Diana Martin, 1953 Homecoming Queen; Bob Capps; Mary Brookshire; Walt James; Patty Gray, 1953* Crossroads *Queen; Patty Deatherage (with crown), 1954* Crossroads *Queen; Richard Humphrey; Charlene Dale; Bob Jackson; Suzanne Ranum, and Wayne Carter. In the foreground: Steve Humphrey, crown bearer; and Linda Kelley, flower girl.*

This fall of 1963 Student Mixer, held in the college gymnasium, was typical of these events. Dating from the early years of the college, they were the first college-sanctioned social events of the new school year and an opportunity for freshmen students to become acquainted with one another.

In this 1966 photograph, Cleetis Headlee appears in a characteristic pose, editing copy for The Chart. With a master's degree from the University of Missouri, she came to JJC in 1946 at the time of a heavy influx of veterans.

Though an excellent teacher in English, Headlee is best remembered for her twenty years, 1948–1967, as adviser to The Chart, during which she took over a rather amateurish publication and built it into a college news organ of professional competence.

With the advent of the four-year college, Headlee served as acting chairman of the new Division of Humanities and Fine Arts, 1967–1970. She retired in 1976, after thirty years of service, with the title of professor emeritus.

Chart *staff officers for the 1956–1957 school year are pictured here. From left: Marian Scott, feature editor; Jerry Cooper, associate editor; Ron Martin, editor; Carolyn Peterson, copy editor; and H. B. Campbell, business.*

Martin is a leading example of the outstanding journalism students who served on The Chart *staff in this era. After completing his degree in journalism at the University of Missouri, he worked on several prominent newspapers connected with the Gannet chain. Later Martin had charge of establishing* USA Today *and served as its executive editor until, in 1989, he became editor of the* Atlanta Journal and Constitution.

An enthusiastic Chart *staff posed on the main staircase of the college's new quarters at Eighth and Wall during the 1958–1959 school year. From left, front row, are: Charles Krokroskia, Dale Allen, Donna Engle, and Marion H. Ellis, editor. Second row: Jerry Bunting, Jo Ann Rutherford, Nelly Ann Trewyn, Jewell Frownfelter, and Marilyn West. Third row: Jim Robson, Rose Marie Wood, Donna Fullerton, and Betty Lee. Back row: George Hatzfeld, George Snow, Gary Trim, Pat Van Hooser, Don Hubatka, Donna Stewart, and Roberta Rodgers.*

Later, Ellis was a member of a team of five reporters for the Charlotte Observer *who won a Pulitzer Prize for a series of articles on the brown lung disease. Ellis, Mary Jane Lang Grundler, and Robert M. Headlee were selected as MSSC's Outstanding Alumni for 1988.*

(Top) Officers of the 1960–1961 staff of The Chart are shown at work on an upcoming edition. From left: Clair Goodwin, Jr., sports editor; Carolyn McCurry, copy editor; Bob Bishop, business manager; and Sue Winchester (on phone), editor.

Clair Goodwin, Jr., is now editorial page editor for the Joplin Globe where he has worked for more than thirty years. Sue Winchester participated in major plays and was 1961 Crossroads Queen.

(Bottom) The Stage Band is shown rehearsing with Russell Benzamin, instructor, during the 1964–1965 school year. Band members are, from left, front row: Claire Howard, Tom Higdon, Richard Hobbs, Terry Basom, Lon Vineyard, and Mike Smith. Second row: Bill Snodgrass, Bill Roberts, Ron Bortles, James Lewis, Mike Graves, Bill Vance, and Larry Rose. Back row: Randy Graue, David Hughes, Gary Roney, John Gardner, Greg Simmons, Sam Davis, and Keith Garber.

Russell Benjamin, who taught at Southern from 1962 to 1966, revived the band program, which had been neglected for several years, by establishing both Stage and Concert bands.

there were orientation mixers each fall, Christmas parties, caroling in the halls at Christmas time, cheering sections at games, and numerous other activities that gave students a sense of involvement beyond the classroom.

JJC's two leading publications, *The Chart* and the *Crossroads* were also well established by the 1947 to 1962 era. *The Chart*, though winning some awards, had been issued erratically in the 1942 to 1951 period and the makeup and quality of writing varied. Credit for building *The Chart* into a publication worthy of the college's growing academic reputation belongs largely to Cleetis Headlee, chief adviser in the years 1948 to 1967. Headlee, an English instructor, had a love for quality writing and a desire to develop the skills of students interested in journalism. In the 1950–1951 school year, she introduced *Survey of Journalism*, the college's first course in journalism. It provided a pool of trained workers for *The Chart* staff.

Under Ms. Headlee's sponsorship, *The Chart* blossomed into a publication of merit. She perceived its role as one of serving the student body, parents, and community, as well as being a laboratory of learning. *The Chart* focused on news pertaining to the college almost exclusively. Ten issues were published each year and an end-of-the-year *Review* issue was added in the mid-1950s.

The Chart emerged as one of the important college news organs of the state. Each year the staff journeyed to Columbia for the Missouri College Newspaper Association Workshop and Awards Ceremony. Almost every year they won something and usually garnered some of the top awards. A number of the staff members went on to attain distinguished careers in journalism.

The *Crossroads*, like its sister publication, *The Chart*, upheld JJC's growing reputation for excellence. Consistency and quality were hallmarks of the *Crossroads* in the 1947 to 1966 era. Year-by-year it presented a clear cross section of college life in an attractive package and never missed a yearly issue in the entire junior college era. Prior to 1949, publication was supported by selling advertisements, but in that year the college began subsidizing the costs and the advertisements were eliminated.

As in other academic areas, the junior college maintained and strengthened its programs in Drama, Speech, and Music. Merrill Ellis was in charge of the General Music program through the 1950s and early 1960s, but this was supplemented with T. Frank Coulter's Joplin Civic Symphony and Oliver Sovereign's Choir.

The use of one instructor for both drama and speech limited these programs until the late 1950s when they were expanded by the addition of a combination

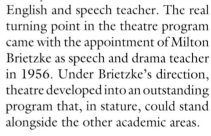

English and speech teacher. The real turning point in the theatre program came with the appointment of Milton Brietzke as speech and drama teacher in 1956. Under Brietzke's direction, theatre developed into an outstanding program that, in stature, could stand alongside the other academic areas.

Athletics, an area in which JJC had never been outstanding, emerged in the period 1947 through 1966 as a worthy adjunct to the college's strong academic program. Football and basketball continued as the major competitive sports with limited efforts in track and golf.

The football team, which had always been the weak link in JJC's competitive sports, improved remarkably in the late 1950s. Prior to that it started up inauspiciously after World War II, gaining only two winning seasons in the seven-year period 1946 through 1952; with the team sliding into a particularly deep slump in 1951 and 1952.

Dudley F. Stegge, who replaced Edward R. Hodges as head football coach for the 1952 season, proved to be the coach who pulled the football Lions out of their mediocrity. Taking over a weak team, Stegge endured a 1–6 losing season, but his team's 31–6 victory over Fort Scott was the only game the Lions won in two years of play. Stegge's deepest embarrassment came when he had to forfeit a game and $250 to the El Dorado, Kansas team because he could not field a full squad of players. The faculty, disgusted over the Lion's poor performance, voted in favor of doing away with football, but College President Roi Wood rejected the recommendation. Wood, always a strong supporter of the junior college, felt that maintaining a football team—the only public junior college in Missouri that did so—added to JJC's distinctiveness.

Stegge's worst handicap had been his inability to recruit good players. Wood moved to resolve this problem by revamping the scholarship program. The Athletic Department's thirty scholarships, worth only $33 per semester—not enough to attract quality players—were raised to near $100 and Stegge found his recruitment problem greatly alleviated.

The 1953 season ushered in a new era in JJC football as Stegge moved to improve the program. He recruited players locally, within a thirty-mile radius of Joplin, where he knew the coaches and the schools. Both he and the assistant coach scouted for promising players. In these years, the basketball coach served as assistant football coach while Stegge, in turn, served as an assistant in basketball and as athletic director.

At this time, Stegge also led the football team into the Interstate Junior College Conference, a consortium of Missouri, Kansas, and Oklahoma junior colleges. Though the teams who played in the conference varied, the Lions

Members at the College Players, one of JJC's most popular academic clubs, posed for this photograph during the 1957–1958 academic year. From left, front row: Jim Hunt; Bill Easley; Fred Tullis; Dale Richards; Mike Robbins; and Frank Sadler. Second row: Sondra Gumm; Gwen Theis; Carol Campbell; Shirley Byrd; and Nancy Chadwell. Third row: Marilyn Harrison; Janice Roper; Suzanne Waggener; Sue Burris; and Jane Lohr. Back row: Donna Engle; Carolyn Updegraff; Donna Finley; Bob Townsend; Ralph Jacobs; Milton Brietzke, sponsor; Duane Hunt, president; Larry Catron; Murray Lorenzen; and Jerry Seger.

Duane Hunt and Gwen Theis, who later married, completed their bachelor's degrees at Southwest Missouri State College and their master's at the University of Arkansas. Duane has taught Speech and Theatre at Southern since 1963 and Gwen has been director of Public Information since 1976.

Milton Brietzke, with a master's degree from Western Reserve University, came to JJC in 1956 as a Speech and Drama instructor. He took over a neglected theatre curriculum and built it into a strong program that added to the college's growing reputation for academic excellence. Later he became director of the new Theatre Department. Brietzke, who retired in 1987 after thirty-one years, received the Outstanding Teacher Award for 1987.

The Diary of Anne Frank, *directed by Milton W. Brietzke, was a major theatre production in the spring of 1959. The players in this scene are, from left: Sondra Gumm (Mrs. Van Daan); Glen Meadows (Mr. Van Daan); Bonnie Cogbill (Mrs. Frank); Jim Lobbey, standing (Mr. Frank); Judy Conboy (Margot Frank); Gary Hunter (Mr. Dussel); and Gwen Theis (Anne Frank).*

Jim Lobbey was then president of the College Players. Later he became a prominent television personality in Joplin. Conboy and Theis (Hunt) both returned to Southern as employees; the former as a professor and the latter in administration.

Conrad Gubera played the role of John Procter and Bonnie Cogbill that of Elizabeth Proctor in this scene from The Crucible *by Arthur Miller. It was a major play of the spring of 1960. Gubera returned to his alma mater in 1967 and has been a member of Southern's Sociology faculty since that time.*

Coach Dudley Stegge's championship winning 1957 football team appears in this photograph. From left, seated: Manager Jerry Chew, D. Fortner, D. Clapper, M. Vowels, G. Harper, T. Dixon, B. Brown, J. Buterbaugh, B. Slinker, L. Wilmoth, H. Cantrell, and J. Atteberry. Kneeling: Bill Kelley, C. Younger, B. Lawson, L. Kellenberger, B. Smith, L. McNellis, T. Wolfe, F. Stangl, D. Staggs, and G. Wallace. Standing: D. Weil, E. Sprenkle, R. Watts, J. C. Kuhn, Jerry Kelley, D. Harris, T. Owens, M. Gunn, S. Ardito, C. Mooney, W. Gibson, W. Bishop, R. Giles, and Jack Golden.

With a record of 4–0 in conference play, this became the first football team in JJC history to win an Interstate Junior College Conference title. Their success was so overpowering that they held their opponents scoreless in six of the eight games played, and two of those games were won by scores of 68–0.

The team's most outstanding players were Myrl Gunn, Buster Brown, and Bill Kelley. Gunn, a fullback from Joplin, became the first JJC football player to receive the NJCAA All-American First Team Award. He later became a Joplin policeman.

Football Coach Dudley F. Stegge appears here during the 1958 season at a time when his "Steggemen" dominated the Interstate Conference. He had an identical twin brother and they played football side by side through high school and at Kansas State College, Pittsburg; both later became football coaches.

Stegge deserves much credit for taking over a discredited football program in 1952 and turning it into a worthy complement of JJC's superior academic curriculum. In 1964, after twelve seasons as head football coach and athletic director, Stegge stepped down to become director of Student Activities.

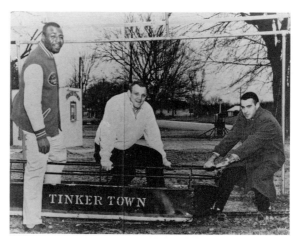

J. D. "Stormy" Love (left), a star tackle on the Lions football team, appears in this 1960–1961 amusement park scene with two unidentified players. A bulwark of the Lion's strong defensive line, the 220-pound Love became one of the few JJC players to ever receive NJCAA All-American honors.

A professional boxer, the Joplin native gave it up to attend college because, he said, "I don't want my brains scrambled like an egg." A graduate of Southern, he has followed a career as a Joplin policeman.

The cheerleaders are shown decorating goal posts at Junge Stadium in preparation for the 1962 Homecoming game with traditional rival Fort Scott. The Lions lost to the Greyhounds 0–27. Cheryl Martin was crowned Homecoming Queen at halftime.

This huge bonfire attracted a large crowd of students to the 1962 Homecoming rally. Bonfire and wiener roast rallies were a long-established Homecoming tradition, but in the early 1960s the bonfires, usually held near Junge Stadium, began to assume spectacular proportions as an urban renewal project downtown made truckloads of scrap lumber available at little or no cost.

The cheerleaders are shown in action supporting the football team at Junge Stadium during the fall of 1958. The seven cheerleaders are: Judy Conboy, Donna Finley, Jewell Frownfelter, Jan Hillhouse, Judy Kingsland, Dixie Moffett, and Shirley Trim, captain. Their mascot is little Kathy Stegge, daughter of Football Coach Dudley Stegge.

Judy Conboy (directly behind Kathy Stegge) returned to Southern in 1969 to become a long-term member of the Sociology faculty.

Myrna Goode, 1954–1955 captain of the cheerleaders, appears in a typical pose. After following a career as a public school teacher, Goode returned to Southern as dean of women in 1973; in 1984 she assumed the new post of coordinator of the Learning Center. Goode married Glenn D. Dolence who is now the college's vice president for Student Services. Her brother, Larry W. Goode, also graduated from JJC and is now an associate professor of Accounting at MSSC.

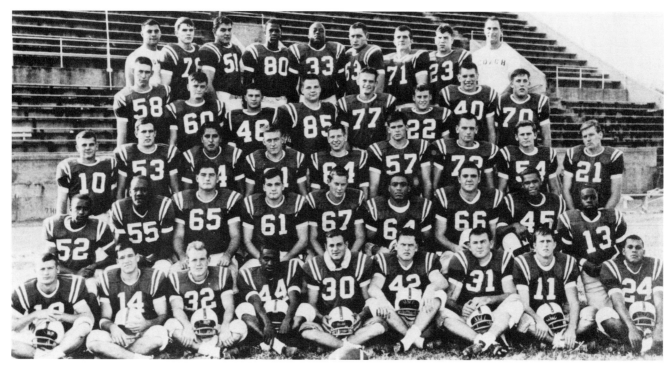

Rated No. 3 in the nation among junior colleges, Coach Ronald Toman's 1965 championship team pose here for their group photograph. From left, front row: Dye, Fretwell, Keys, Witherspoon, Mack, Barnhart, Alexander, Hutchison, and Simmons. Second row: Bean, Sanders, Drouin, Moehling, Cumbia, Jones, Urbanowicz, Turner, and Fountain. Third row: Wade, McKnight, Peak, Clenn, Gilbert, Winslow, Williamson, Trawick, and Sutton. Fourth row: Drake, Wood, Fronterhouse, Walker, Lamb, Harris, and Ledl. Back row: Assistant Coach Jennings, Fritchey, Ryder, Frazier, Mitchell, Gerke, McKillip, Wilkerson, and Assistant Coach Gold.

most commonly played teams from the Kansas junior colleges at Fort Scott, Independence, Parsons, and Highland, as well as the Pittsburg State College "B" team. Other opponents were the Oklahoma Military Academy at Claremore and the Missouri military academies of Wentworth at Lexington and Kemper at Booneville. These three academies, because they did not actively recruit players, ordinarily fielded weak teams and often did not even score against the Lions. On the other hand, the Lions, badly outclassed, discontinued playing the powerful Coffeyville, Kansas and Miami, Oklahoma junior college teams.

Stegge's new program began to show results when the Lions placed second in the three Interstate Conference seasons of 1954 through 1956. The latter was an especially noteworthy year, with an overall performance of 6–1–1. Most memorable was the devastation wreaked on the military academies. Kemper fell to the Lions by a score of 54–0, Wentworth by 55–0, and Oklahoma by a spectacular 84–0, a margin of victory never equalled again in the junior or senior college eras. The Lions tie game resulted from an unusual deadlock with the Pittsburg State College "B" team in which neither side scored.

The second place conference showings for three consecutive years had gained much prestige for Stegge's football Lions, but they reached new heights by winning Interstate Conference championships for the next four years, 1957 through 1960. By 1959, the Lions were at the height of their prestige with the press fondly referring to them as the "Steggemen." They won all three of the conference games and a then record nine players were named to the Interstate Conference's 1959 all-star football team. Six of Stegge's outstanding players in these years were named to junior college All-American teams: Bob Speedy, 1956; Myrl Gunn and Bill Kelley, 1957; H. B. Davis, 1958; J. D. "Stormy" Love, 1960; and William "Bull" Hayes, 1961.

After four years of fielding championship teams, Stegge was unable to dominate the Interstate Conference in his final three years as a coach. Weakened by the loss of several strong players, the 1961 team, though establishing a creditable 5–3 record overall, suffered the Lions' first loss in a conference game since 1956. The next year was even worse as Stegge experienced his first losing season since 1952. In 1963, he returned with a strong team but it failed to gain another conference title.

Stegge had been head football coach and athletic director for twelve seasons. Taking over a discredited program in 1952, he had brought the Lions into the Interstate Junior College Conference and established them as a powerhouse there. Though JJC primarily basked in the excellence of its academics, his championship gridders complemented this and reinforced the institution's stature as one of the state's leading junior colleges. Stegge enjoyed great respect among both the faculty and students, but after so many years as a coach, he wanted a less demanding job and assumed the newly created post of director of student activities in the fall of 1964.

Ronald Toman replaced Dudley Stegge as head football coach in the summer of 1964 and he proceeded to restructure the football team. Enjoying close connections with the University of Missouri's popular football coach, Dan Devine, Toman was able to acquire some promising freshmen players. His recruiting efforts were also aided by local business and professional people who raised funds to house the athletes in the Connor Hotel. The next year, this group formally organized their fund-raising efforts into a Booster Club that eventually became known as the Lionbackers. Toman's success soon gave rise to comments that he was coaching a farm team for the University of Missouri, but there was no such formal arrangement. Though Toman retained the best of the local players, the team was soon dominated by recruits from Kansas City and St. Louis as well as from states like Illinois, Pennsylvania, and Florida. The traditional practice of recruiting local boys exclusively for the team had been broken and would never return.

Toman experienced three successful years at the junior college. In his first year, he led the team to an Interstate Conference title, winning all four of the conference games and establishing an overall 6–3 record. With seven regulars returning, Toman entered the 1965 season coaching a powerful team. He had an offensive line whose players averaged over two hundred pounds, but the defensive line was even more formidable. This strong team went on to complete the most successful season in the annals of the junior college. Sweeping the Interstate Conference championship and all nonconference games, they finished the season with a perfect 10–0 record, the only year in which a junior college football team won all its outings.

Toman's Lions gave fans a spectacular display of their potency when they pulverized the Haskell Institute team, 73–6. The rout began when Lion halfback Donald Bean returned the opening kick-off with an 88 yard touchdown run. Toman sent the first-line team to the showers at halftime, but the reserves still pounded out an additional 32 points in the second half. Overall, the Lions gained 632 yards rushing while limiting the demoralized Haskell Tigers to 38 yards.

The nationally ranked Lions anticipated a bowl bid after their successful 10–0 season. They especially hoped to play in the Junior Rose Bowl game at Pasadena, California, but the bid never came, at least in part because the college did not have a marching band.

With a number of Toman's first-string players graduating, and in some

Head Football Coach Ronald Toman (left) and Assistant Football Coach Douglas Landrith find their spirits undampened after being run through the shower by exuberant players celebrating completion of their unbroken 10–0 winning season in 1965.

Toman, Southern's football coach from 1964 to 1966, was once a student assistant to the University of Missouri's Coach Dan Devine. Though never operating a "farm team" as sometimes claimed, Toman did have sufficient connections to tap a pool of talented players who had been spotted by the university's recruiters. Toman resigned, after three years, to accept an assistant coachship at Wichita State University.

Guard Curtis Jones demonstrates the form that helped make him a formidable figure for the 1965 Lions' defensive line. Jones, Skip Drouin, Dick Kruse, and Hank Urbanowicz formed Coach Toman's principal defensive line. It was said of them that they were "big, fast, and sometimes mean"—and they often made the difference between winning and losing. Statistics for the year showed that the Lions averaged 302.5 yards rushing per game while their opponents were held to only 69.5 yards.

Urbanowicz was later a prominent player at the University of Miami and Jones at the University of Missouri.

The 1954–1955 basketball team pose in this photograph. With a new coach and a number of inexperienced players, the squad experienced a losing 9–11 season, but bounced back the next year to win the IJCC Championship. From left, front row: Drexel Harris, Don Steele, Jim Allen, Joe McKenzie, Ralph Brock, Laverne "Shorty" Stewart, and Frank Anderson. Back row: Richard Humphrey, George K. Jackson, Ed Nealy, Dick Hammond, Ron Richardson, and Coach Buddy Ball.

Richard Humphrey is the son of E. O. Humphrey, JJC's first football coach. He later became director of admissions at Southern. Stewart was one of the first blacks to enter JJC's athletic program in the fall of 1954.

Buddy Ball came to JJC in the fall of 1954 as basketball coach. During his five years at JJC, he won three IJCC championships.

instances moving on to gain the national spotlight on big university teams, he was left with a 1966 team top heavy with freshmen. The Lions gained overall success with a 6–3 season, but the losses were sufficient to deny them another conference title.

Early in February 1967, Toman resigned to accept another position. In his three seasons at MSC, he had steered the Lions away from their local orientation by recruiting players nationally, and had established himself as one of the college's most successful coaches.

Though JJC's basketball program had always enjoyed more overall success than football, due primarily to the greater local reservoir of players the college could draw on, in the 1948–1962 period basketball followed a pattern similar to football by achieving an unprecedented success that further reinforced the college's prestige.

After the basketball Lions won a championship in the 1947 Missouri Public Junior College Conference (MPJCC)—the only undisputed first place they ever won in this conference—the team went into a five-year slump in which they performed poorly. Their principal conference opponents were the junior colleges at Bolivar, Flat River, Hannibal–La Grange, Jefferson City, Moberly, Monett, St. Joseph, and Trenton. The football Lions never participated in this conference because none of the other members had football teams.

The Lion's fortunes began to improve under a new coach, Don Testerman. Up to this time, one individual had served as head coach of both basketball and football, helped by an assistant. Starting with Testerman, each area gained its own mentor while both coaches served alternately as each others assistants. Also, increased athletic scholarships boosted the recruitment of talented players, as they did with the football program. With a strengthened team and a talented new coach, the basketball Lions, in 1952–1953, won a MPJCC co-championship with Hannibal–La Grange. The next year, Testerman's last season, the team lacked the in-depth talent necessary for a conference win, but managed to gain a tie for second place.

In 1954–1955, Buddy Ball began a five-year tenure as coach, a period that saw the basketball Lions win three conference championships. Ball's first year seemed unpropitious as the team lost over half their games, accented by a humiliating 55–102 loss to Moberly, but this dismal performance was assuaged by a 107–43 rampage over the hopelessly weak Kemper Military Academy.

The following year, Ball's team joined the Interstate Junior College Conference (IJCC). There they found a degree of success that had always eluded them on the tortuous Missouri public junior college circuit. In the IJCC, they faced a slate of opponents already familiar to the football Lions.

Success came quickly to the basketball team on the new circuit. For two consecutive seasons, 1955–1956 and 1956–1957, the Lions won the IJCC championship. The next year, weakened by a loss of seasoned players, they slipped to third place in conference play, but sprang back in 1958–1959 to win their third IJCC championship in four years.

A new coach helped usher in the new decade as Douglas "Doug" Landrith began a mentorship of the basketball Lions that would extend to the end of the junior college era. Inheriting a weak team, Landrith rebuilt it and, in 1960–1961, gained a tie for the IJCC championship. After another off-year, Landrith's team came back, in 1962–1963, to win the last basketball IJCC championship in the junior college era.

The next four years were marked by heavy losses for the basketball Lions. At a time of increasing competition for tall players, Landrith's teams lacked the necessary numbers of talented big men. Limited in the scholarships he could offer and overburdened with other responsibilities, Landrith could only recruit locally unlike football which, under Coach Toman, was beginning to cast a national net for players.

The 1965–1966 season marked MSC's final year in the IJCC. The next year, the basketball Lions played as an independent team while officials searched for a suitable four-year college affiliation. Caught in this awkward transitional phase, the Lions still played some of their traditional rivals, but added to these were a new group of contestants whom they had never played before. Handicapped by mediocre players, this 1966–1967 season ended disastrously for the Lions with a 1–20 record; their worst performance in the junior college era. Seemingly the team should have done better and in their one victory of the season, the Lions won decisively, 119–84, over Oral Roberts University's "B" team.

Coach Landrith built a close rapport with his team that season and, in spite of mounting losses, the Lions maintained their competitive spirit. This became evident in a game against Missouri Western College late in the season. The Lions journeyed to St. Joseph with ten players for the game. It turned into a hard-fought contest with Alan Toler, MSC's leading scorer, sinking 30 points. But fouls began to mount against the struggling Lions and, with four minutes left in regular play, six of them had fouled out leaving only four on the floor. In spite of this handicap, the Lions deadlocked the game 96 to 96, forcing it into a five-minute overtime period. Plagued with more fouls, the Lions were reduced to two players on the floor for the final 2:41 minutes of the game, finally losing by a score of 97–105. Some 43 fouls had been called against the aggressive Lions who were probably playing beyond their own natural abilities.

This disappointing season marked Coach Landrith's eighth year as head basketball coach. His responsibilities had been building over the years and, at this time,

A snowball fight rages at the front steps of the junior college during the winter of 1958–1959. This was JJC's first year at the Eighth and Wall location. Students found their new quarters roomier and more comfortable than their old domicile. However, like the old building, this new edifice was a former high school located in a congested downtown district where expansion to accommodate a growing college would be impractical.

The junior college's 1962–1963 basketball team appears here in an eye-catching V-formation. From left: Gary Keeling, David Hammett, Don Karnes, Kenney Bowman, Sam Knight, Gary Crawford, Don Kellholfer, Larry Berner, Gary Hambright, Art Cortez, and Bruce Hammett, with Coach Douglas Landrith in the center. The team won the IJCC championship with a 13–1 record, the last conference championship the basketball Lions would win as a junior college.

Kenneth Bowman, an outstanding player in basketball and football, received the MSSC Outstanding Alumnus Award for 1976.

Coach Douglas Landrith graduated from JJC in 1948. He returned to Southern in the fall of 1959 as basketball, golf, and tennis coach and retired in 1983.

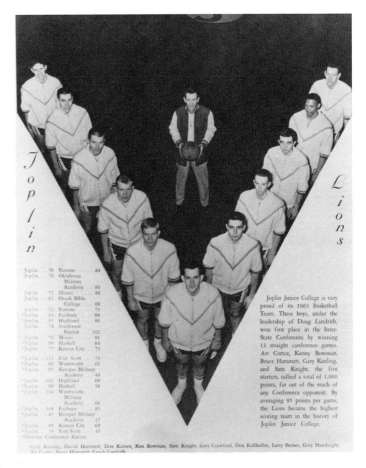

Joplin	78	Parsons	84
Joplin	76	Oklahoma Military Academy	80
Joplin	72	Miami	80
Joplin	82	Ozark Bible College	69
Joplin	51	Parsons	73
Joplin	84	Fairbury	88
Joplin	95	Highland	86
Joplin	74	Southwest Baptist	102
Joplin	76	Miami	81
Joplin	99	Haskell	84
Joplin	77	Kansas City	75
Joplin	112	Fort Scott	75
Joplin	89	Wentworth	62
Joplin	95	Kemper Military Academy	44
Joplin	106	Highland	69
Joplin	99	Haskell	58
Joplin	104	Wentworth Military Academy	69
Joplin	108	Fairbury	83
Joplin	85	Kemper Military Academy	57
Joplin	83	Kansas City	69
Joplin	95	Fort Scott	45

*Denotes Conference Games

Joplin Junior College is very proud of its 1963 Basketball Team. These boys, under the leadership of Doug Landrith, won first place in the Inter-State Conference by winning 13 straight conference games. Art Cortez, Kenny Bowman, Bruce Hammett, Gary Keeling, and Sam Knight, the five starters, tallied a total of 1,000 points, far out of the reach of any Conference opponent. By averaging 95 points per game, the Lions became the highest scoring team in the history of Joplin Junior College.

Gary Keeling, David Hammett, Don Karnes, Ken Bowman, Sam Knight, Gary Crawford, Don Kellholfer, Larry Berner, Gary Hambright, Art Cortez, Bruce Hammett, Coach Landrith.

Leon C. Billingsly, the fifth dean of Joplin Junior College, is shown here in his first year, 1961–1962.

Born in 1925 and reared on a Christian County, Missouri farm, Billingsly served in the Navy during World War II. Having completed a bachelor's degree at Southwest Missouri State College in 1950, he coached and taught at the Golden City and Lamar high schools for the next four years. Billingsly spent the next five years as superintendent of schools at Golden City and at Pleasant Hill before becoming director of the Laboratory Teacher Training School at Kansas State College, Pittsburg, where he had earlier finished his master's. The next year, 1960–1961, he completed his doctor of education degree at the University of Arkansas and came to JJC that fall for two years. Billingsly spent the next year, 1963–1964, as director of Kellogg Community College, Battle Creek, Michigan, then returned to Joplin to assume the presidency of the new Jasper County Junior College and later Missouri Southern State College, where he remained until he died in 1978.

JJC's old home at Fourth and Byers was torn down after sitting empty for three years. Restoration work in the 1930s never solved the building's basic problems, arising from its unstable foundations. Jacks supported the lower floor and cables in the attic tied the weakening walls together. Cracks opened in the walls from time to time and in 1947 part of the west wall fell out. After the junior college moved, attempts to sell the building proved unsuccessful and the city condemned it as a public hazard. In 1961 the school district sold it for $250 to be razed.

he was also athletic director, assistant football coach, golf mentor, and tennis coach, as well as being a physical education instructor. Overburdened, he asked to be relieved of some of these duties. In a reorganization of the Athletic Department, G. W. "Mike" Bogard was brought in as acting athletic director and assistant football coach, and Frank Davis replaced Landrith as head basketball coach.

In addition to basketball and football, the junior college, in its closing years, participated in intercollegiate golf, tennis, and track events for men. Women's sports continued to be limited to intramural activities except that ad hoc teams were sometimes organized to play similar teams from other colleges.

Coaches Douglas Landrith and Dudley Stegge could devote little time to these minor sports, but each spring the teams did compete in the Interstate Conference Tournament, held in various locations, and in the Missouri State Junior College Tournament held at Lexington each year. In these tournaments, Landrith's golf teams enjoyed the most success, winning the Interstate Golf championship for six years straight, 1960–1965, and gaining the Missouri Junior College crown in five of those six years. Track teams gained a more modest success, usually placing second or third in the tournaments. Tennis received the least attention from the busy coaches and the players largely coached themselves. In 1967, the coaches were astonished when they learned that the tennis team had tied for the state championship.

In its closing years, the junior college maintained an impressive program in athletics that complemented its strong standing in academics. The Lions reached new heights of excellence with their 1962–1963 basketball and 1965 football squads, but the teams began to weaken as they grappled with the uncertainties of changing to a four-year college. By 1966, the process of transition was in full swing.

As the decade of the 1950s wore on, the inadequacy of the college's quarters at Fourth and Byers became more and more evident. Top enrollment in the 1957–1958 season, JJC's last year at this location, was 626, almost exactly double its first season some twenty years before. In spite of the expansions after World War II, overcrowding had become oppressive. Classrooms were so full in the last two years that the administration ceased to actively recruit students. An equally pressing problem was the physical deterioration of the aging building.

Fortunately a solution was at hand. Early in 1958, the school district completed a new high school at Twentieth and Indiana. That fall the junior college moved into the vacated high school building at Eighth and Wall, thus returning to its original home of 1937–1938. Renovations were necessary to accommodate the college in its new, more expansive quarters. Walls were knocked out to build a little theatre and to enlarge the library, as well as other changes and a general redecorating. But the administration allotted little new furniture or equipment to the junior college; this was reserved for the new high school.

In 1962, JJC celebrated its twenty-fifth anniversary with a number of activities. Both *The Chart* and the *Crossroads* featured special sections highlighting events of the past twenty-five years. The principal ceremony was a

silver-anniversary program presented in March. In attendance were members of the Board of Education, alumni, former deans and teachers, as well as friends of the college. Ada Coffey and Martha McCormick were honored as the sole remaining teachers from the original staff.

At the ceremony, veteran faculty members presented what they termed as the most important "landmarks" of the previous twenty-five years. Most significant was the gaining of North Central Association accreditation. Also mentioned was the success of JJC graduates who moved on to senior college and universities. Most impressive, in this respect, were studies which showed that graduates attending Kansas State College, Pittsburg, the University of Arkansas; and the Universities of Missouri at Columbia and Rolla—institutions where many JJC graduates completed their college educations—did as well or better in their junior year than the regular students of these respective institutions. A third landmark was JJC's success in establishing itself as a respected college-level institution and not, as Ms. McCormick so succinctly put it, "just a post-graduate high school." Doubtless their pride, in this respect, was reinforced by a study, four years previously, in which the Federal Office of Education selected JJC as one of the top twelve junior colleges of the nation for a five-week study of its service to the community.

Though Ms. Coffey and McCormick's 25-year tenures captured the spotlight, the faculty as a whole was dominated by veterans. Fifteen of the twenty-eight regular instructors then on the teaching staff had served eleven or more years, but nine of the fifteen had taught for twenty or more years. Perhaps a third of the faculty were extraordinarily effective teachers, not for their years of service or the advanced degrees they held, but because of their ability to inspire students on the level at which they taught. Years later, many former students retained vivid memories of the teaching staff in those golden years of the junior college. They remembered the strong student-teacher rapport, the skill of these master teachers in opening minds to new information, their depth of perception, and the genuine care they evidenced for student problems.

Mathematics Club members ponder an equation in this 1963 photograph. From left, front row: Martha McCormick, sponsor; David Owen; Sheila Gilbert; Gary R. Mulkey, president; Gayleen McKenzie; Jim Crabtree; and Paul E. Jensen, sponsor. Back row: Tom Holt; Carl Gilmore; and Frank Woodbury.

The Mathematics Club was organized in 1958. Jensen retired in 1976 after a tenure of sixteen years. Mulkey returned to MSSC as a teacher in 1977.

(Top)Only eight members appeared in 1959 for this last photograph of the YMCA Club published in the Crossroads. *Once highly popular with students, the "Y's" appeal had declined over the years, but the college's move to new quarters in 1958 hastened its demise. From left, front row: George Payne; Gene Christenson; Robert Brown; and Larry Meacham. Back row: Harold Manker, sponsor; Fred Erdman; Jim Owen; Terry Dixon; Billie Schlupp; and Arnold Irwin, sponsor. Irwin, a highly respected and innovative teacher of political science, died the next year after thirteen years at JJC.*

(Bottom) Only ten members of the Beta Beta Beta sorority appeared for this group photograph in 1964, the last to appear in a Crossroads. *Pictured are, from left, front row; Mary Davis; Janice Lofton; Ruth Sayers; Peggy Weinacht; and Elizabeth McKenney. Back row: Ellen Graber; Celia Hasse; Judy Rainwater, president; Marcia McCullough; and Jane Blake.*

Founded in 1938, Tri-Beta lingered on long after all other JJC social clubs had disappeared, but with the dawn of the senior college era it faded away.

On its twenty-fifth anniversary JJC was, by all accounts, an excellent liberal arts junior college. It also had a small Vocational Education program of commendable quality for which college credit was still available, but enrollment remained light. In the spring of 1961 only seventeen boys were enrolled for the courses in Auto Mechanics, Cabinet Shop, Welding, Machine Shop, and Sheet Metal.

However, significant changes loomed on the horizon. The tightly knit, cozy relationship that had characterized the faculty and the student body was beginning to fracture. Clearly the college was being swept forward into a new era. Few in 1962 could visualize how sweeping those changes would be or in what directions they would lead.

The 1963–1964 academic year proved to be Joplin Junior College's last; the next year it became a district junior college. Missouri's third largest junior college—only those at Kansas City and St. Louis were larger—JJC had existed for a generation and seemed such a solid institution that significant changes were difficult to comprehend.

For all of JJC's prestige, its public school connections were evident in many ways. It occupied, not a campus, but an old high school building and each morning at 9:00 the daily bulletin was read over the public address system. Assemblies were still an established part of student life. Instructors toiled under a fifteen semester hour teaching load, were expected to remain at school until 4:00 or 5:00 p.m., and to sign out. There was no academic rank and no formal departments; teachers answered individually to the college dean.

In the spring of 1964, JJC underwent a North Central Association accrediting examination for the first time since the college gained initial accreditation fifteen years before. The staff's self-study and the examining team's report give an interesting profile of the college at this time.

The examining team commented favorably on President Roi Wood's strong leadership and the excellent liberal arts and university transfer programs which produced transferees who did so well in senior college programs. They noted that a positive attitude and pride in the school prevailed among students and faculty; faculty morale was good even though the salary scale was low. On the other hand, the examiners felt there needed to be more clarity as to what the purposes of the college were. Though they found the Franklin Technical School program to be impressive, they saw a need to promote the technical and vocational offerings more vigorously and to relocate them on campus. Their parting advice was to forget about becoming a four-year college for the present and to concentrate on doing a good job as a junior college.

The self-study delved deeply into the composition of the student body at this time. Some 527 questionnaires that had been sent out showed a continuation of the traditional student body. The ratio of men to women students was three to two, 92 percent were single, 84.3 percent lived at home, 65.5 percent lived in Joplin at least as resident students, and 51.7 percent were employed either full or part time. The district-wide origins of the student body were evident; yet a distinct localism still prevailed. A screening of 1,053 students enrolled in the 1963–1964 school year revealed that 984 came from homes within twenty-five miles of the junior college. A few came from out-of-state with Kansas providing 42 and the other nearby states of Arkansas and Oklahoma furnishing only 4 and 3 respectively.

The self-study also cited the factors that tended to attract students to JJC such as the easy, open-door entrance policy that required only a high school diploma for admission; the convenient location; the good selection of programs, particularly for transfer students; the high academic reputation of JJC; its excellent faculty; and the moderate cost. Fees for resident students—not subject to tuition charges—amounted to only $105 and $100 for the first and second years respectively. Out-of-district costs ran to $265 and $260 for the corresponding years.

Enrollment at the junior college increased markedly as the institution moved into the decade of the 1960s and actions to create a four-year college accelerated. The student count, full and part-time, passed the 1,000 mark for the first time in the fall of 1963 with an enrollment of 1,144; in the fall of 1966, the last year of an exclusively junior college enrollment, the count reached 1,837.

Several reasons for the rapid increase in enrollment are evident. In one sense, it merely reflected a national trend as young people increasingly saw the need for higher education and as their numbers increased due to the post–World War II "baby boom." The expanded Night School program, introduced in the late 1950s, noticeably increased enrollment. The so-called Sputnik scare of the late 1950s alarmed the American public and stimulated a move toward putting more resources into higher education. By the mid-1960s, the Vietnam War also began to stimulate college enrollment. Though more young men were being drafted, deferments were freely granted to those who entered college full time and who maintained a good grade standing. Other federal government aid, in the form of work-study programs and guaranteed student loans, also stimulated enrollment. Creation of the Jasper County Junior College served to further boost the student count by expanding tuition-free enrollment to the whole district. This became evident in the fall of 1964 when enrollment increased by 26 percent over the previous year in spite of the loss of an estimated 100 students to the newly opened Crowder Junior College. Undoubtedly enrollment was stimulated from the fall of 1965 on by students expecting that they would be able to complete a baccalaureate degree without transferring.

The number of graduates rose in the mid-to-late 1960s along with the increased enrollment. In 1966, some 182 graduated and the next year's total reached 252, the largest class the junior college would ever graduate.

The 1967 year also marked the last in which baccalaureate services were held for the graduates. A fixture in college tradition dating back to the first graduating class in 1939, these services were discontinued because of the mounting controversy over mixing formal religion with publicly financed education.

As the school year of 1965 wore on, it became evident the junior college era was coming to an end. The district junior college was but a temporary arrangement. Already legislation providing for a senior college was in place and the transitional phase, which would last another year, was underway.

The junior college had served Joplin and its environs well for a generation. It had been an excellent educational institution and could have continued to serve the area splendidly; but, interestingly, many of the same arguments that had been used to justify a junior college in the 1930s were used to propel it into a four-year institution in the 1960s. Again, a college was seen as a primary instrument for providing expanded educational opportunities and for stimulating economic development in a depressed area.

But the junior college was not a victim of the change, it was merely enveloped into the expanded four-year institution. Its veteran faculty played a key role in the transition, preserving the basic junior college curriculum and helping shape that for the new senior college, as well as preserving old traditions and providing a nucleus around which the new four-year college staff could be built.

(Top) Mr. and Mrs. Harry C. Gockel are shown leaving a plane in Santiago, Chile, during their six-week tour of South America in the summer of 1957. Foreign excursions like this became a tradition with the Gockels. In a 58-day world tour during the summer of 1964 they traveled 28,397 miles. These travels added much depth to Gockel's teaching of Geography.

(Bottom) C. Otis Robinson became the sixth dean of JJC in the fall of 1963, replacing Leon Billingsly. In his two and one-half years of service, Robinson was the last dean of Joplin Junior College, the first and only dean of Jasper County Junior College, and the first dean of Missouri Southern College.

Robinson resigned in January 1966 to accept the presidency of the newly formed Great Bend, Kansas Community College.

CHAPTER III
A TWO-PLUS-TWO COLLEGE

The 1963–1975 period ushered in the most fundamental changes in the college's history as JJC moved from being an appendage of the Joplin public schools to being an independent junior college district capped with a two-year, state-supported senior college. The changes were sweeping as administrators and faculty worked to build an all-new campus, install a four-year curriculum, and deal with an enrollment that ballooned to heights undreamed of a few years before. Yet much remained the same. The student population continued to be drawn primarily from southwest Missouri and, after the initial transition, a core of veteran faculty, joined by a staff of talented newcomers, upheld the tradition of high academic standards so diligently that what had once been the widely respected Joplin Junior College became the equally respected Missouri Southern State College.

As Joplin and the nation at large moved into the decade of the 1960s, an accelerating trend toward higher education was evident, and a September 1966 study by the Missouri Commission on Higher Education pointed out that full-time college enrollment in Missouri grew from 44,537 in 1955 to 95,557 in 1965, an increase of nearly 115 percent; population increases alone could only partially explain this growth, the study noted, because Missouri had experienced slow growth in the 1955–1965 period. The population group of primary college age, eighteen to twenty-one, grew by only 22 percent. In balance, the percentage increase of young people seeking higher education was a more significant factor than the overall growth in college-age population. Counting full-time students alone, the number in college for every one hundred of the eighteen to twenty-one age group increased from twenty in 1955 to over thirty-three in 1965. The commission concluded that these two factors alone: growth in the college-age population and the percentage increase in those attending college, could easily bring about a doubling of college enrollment by 1975.

As the decade of the 1960s dawned, Roi Wood, longtime superintendent of the Joplin public schools and president of JJC, faced a growing dilemma. He came to realize that the Joplin School District, with its limited tax base, could no longer support an expanding junior college and that the college needed to be formed into a district-wide entity of its own. However, existing state law prohibited this; only individual school districts could establish junior colleges. Superintendent Wood, as president of the Missouri Association of School Administrators for the year 1961, used his position to help bring about passage of a new state statute allowing special junior college districts to be set up that would be supervised by elected boards of trustees who would have the authority to levy property taxes. Direct state funding would also be provided at the rate of $200 for each full-time student per year. This statute put Wood in a position to resolve his dilemma.

Local business leaders were sympathetic to Wood's problem, but in informal discussions they came up with a bolder idea than merely setting up a district-wide junior college; namely, why not seek state support for establishing a four-year college in Joplin? The idea of a four-year college for Joplin had been little discussed since the founding of the junior college, but suddenly with the growing public support for expanded higher educational opportunities and a state legislature receptive to the idea, a baccalaureate-degree grant-

(Opposite) This 1964 view of the Mission Hills mansion, with its beautifully landscaped grounds, suggests the elegance of this local estate. Located on the most prominent point of the ridge overlooking Turkey Creek valley, the grounds drop away steeply on three sides. The original vista of this east side of the mansion, where there is a broader expanse of level ground, has been marred by the addition of an annex to the garage area.

JOPLIN JUNIOR COLLEGE

Members of the first Board of Trustees of the Jasper County Junior College District gathered for this photograph shortly after their election on April 7, 1964. From left: Lauren R. Reynolds, Thomas E. Taylor, Elvin Ummel, Gene Taylor, Norval M. Matthews, and Fred G. Hughes.

As the governing body of the new district, these men were responsible for supervising operations of the junior college. All except Gene Taylor served on both the Board of Trustees and the later Board of Regents and all except Ummel were businessmen.

Lauren R. Reynolds, Joplin, died in 1968. The L. R. Reynolds Science and Mathematics Building perpetuates his memory.

Thomas E. Taylor, Carthage, served until his death in 1975. The Thomas E. Taylor Auditorium honors his memory.

Elvin Ummel, a dairy farmer from Jasper, continues to serve on the Board of Regents. The Ummel Technology Building honors his long service to the college.

Gene Taylor, Sarcoxie, served eight years on the Board of Trustees. The Gene Taylor Education and Psychology Building serves as a memorial to his service.

Norval M. Matthews, Webb City, died in 1977 at the age of eight-two, the oldest person ever to serve on either board. Norval M. Matthews Hall honors his memory.

Known as "Mr. Missouri Southern," Fred Hughes, Joplin, was a prime mover in bringing a four-year college to Joplin. His long service to Southern is unparalleled by any other board member. The Fred G. Hughes Stadium honors his dedication to the college.

ing institution seemed both realistic and possible. As business and civic leaders discussed the proposition, they became more enthused with the prospects.

Superintendent Wood felt the four-year college idea had merit and in the closing days of 1962, between Christmas and New Year's Day, he met informally with six local leaders: Mills Anderson, president of the Bank of Carthage; W. T. Morrow, head of the Morrow Lumber Company in Carthage; Fred Hughes, general manager of the *Joplin Globe;* Lauren Reynolds, president of the First National Bank of Joplin; and two members of the state legislature, Senator Richard Webster and Representative Robert Ellis Young, both of Carthage, to further consider the proposal. The group gathered in Wood's office located in an old house behind JJC. With the outside temperature hovering at six degrees above zero, Wood lighted a fire in an old potbellied stove. The warmth was never sufficient for the men to remove their overcoats, but the discussion was portentous for the future of the college. As the men shivered around the stove, a definite plan of action began to emerge. Senator Webster and Representative Young felt that, with adroit political maneuvering, legislation might be pushed through the legislature providing at least for a state-supported senior college division.

In their discussions, the men perceived two basic reasons for seeking a four-year college: primarily, it would reduce the loss of area young people who went away to college and many of whom never returned. Studies showed that about one thousand district youths were attending other colleges and that a large number of these students were attending the nearby institutions of Southwest Missouri State College at Springfield, Kansas State College at Pittsburg, or the University of Arkansas at Fayetteville. Secondly, they felt it would stimulate the economy by providing additional jobs, expanded consumer spending, and attracting new industry.

The men left the meeting determined to feel out sentiment in their own communities and to undertake further action. In February 1963, the Jasper County Development Association (JCDA), a countywide organization of business and civic leaders, created a subcommittee, known as the Committee to Establish a Four-year College in Southwest Missouri, to promote the plan. Fred Hughes of Joplin and Harry M. Spradling, a Carthage businessman, were appointed as co-chairmen. In the meantime, the *Joplin Globe* and the *Carthage Press,* joined by other district newspapers, launched an editorial campaign to promote the four-year plan, while area legislators began drafting a bill to present in the state legislative session that met in January 1963. For the first time in local history a concerted drive was underway to create a four-year college.

By early spring of 1963, plans to promote the four-year college began to take concrete shape. The immediate challenge for action rested with the local legislators. Representative Robert P. Warden of Joplin had served two terms in the House, but Senator Richard Webster of Carthage was a freshmen; only Representative Robert Ellis Young of Carthage, with eight years of service, had extensive seniority.

The legislators agreed that the bill should be introduced in the House; this would give Webster more time to prepare for the struggle in the Senate. Warden and Young introduced a loosely worded bill providing for a branch of the University of Missouri in Joplin. In the meantime, representatives from St. Joseph which, like Joplin, had a well-established junior college, introduced a similar bill. It provided that the university would assume operational costs and bear the responsibility for conducting the third and fourth years of instruction while St. Joseph would operate the junior college and provide all necessary physical facilities. The more specific St. Joseph bill was amended to include Joplin. Political necessity had joined the two cities together and, from that point forward, all planning treated the two proposed colleges as sister institutions.

In the hearings that followed local advocates made a strong case for the senior college in Joplin. They pointed to a nine-county "service area" that would provide the population base for the new college. This service area included the five southwestern counties of Missouri along the Kansas and Oklahoma state lines: Vernon, Barton, Jasper, Newton, and McDonald, and the western portions of the four counties forming the next tier to the east: Cedar, Dade, Lawrence, and Barry. This area contained a total population of 211,350 in 1960 and studies indicated it would be producing nearly 1,600 potential college students yearly by 1970. Proponents also maintained that this area had the largest population concentration in the state without four-year college facilities and that the area's young people deserved fairer access to educational opportunities.

A recurring question in the deliberations revolved around the feasibility of capping a two-year state college on top of an existing junior college. Though an unusual arrangement, promoters learned of one such operation in which Flint College, a two-year branch of the University of Michigan operated in conjunction with Flint Junior College. A delegation, including Fred Hughes and Roi Wood from Joplin, journeyed to Michigan to study the system. They learned that it had functioned smoothly since its inception in 1956, but officials alerted the delegation to one potential problem; namely, the dual policymaking boards, and urged the Missourians to create only one board. The novel two-plus-two concept was accepted by the state legislature without serious opposition.

The Joplin delegation's proposal was weakest on its plans for a campus to house the new university branch. The bill specified that the junior college district would provide and maintain all physical facilities. The promoters proposed a temporary downtown campus utilizing the existing junior college, as well as the nearby Memorial Hall and public library buildings, both city facilities. In addition they would buy two adjacent old houses. The problem of parking in this already congested area was not addressed nor did they realistically consider the availability of these facilities. Though the proponents recognized the necessity of building a new campus, the implication was that this could be postponed indefinitely.

The struggle for passage of the bill in the state legislature did not prove insurmountable. As anticipated the proposal moved through the House of Representatives, dominated by its strong rural membership, without serious contention; but it met formidable opposition in the Senate. Senator Webster, joined by Senator John E. Downs of St. Joseph, struggled to overcome this antagonism. They faced a solid phalanx of opposition from the senators representing areas where existing state colleges and universities were located. These legislators saw the proposed new colleges as rivals which would be competing with their institutions for state funding. Also, the entire Democratic leadership structure of the Senate joined in opposition. "Otherwise," as Senator Webster wryly commented, "it did not look too bad." Fortunately for the bill, twelve of the Senate's thirty-four members were freshmen and they tended to side with Webster, who was one of them. Also, Webster and Downs

Joplin Junior College's transformation into the Jasper County Junior College required a redesign of the college's seal. The new logo is shown here. A committee, chaired by Dorothy Rutherford, coined the new motto, "In Pursuit of Excellence," which summed up JJC's legacy to the new institution. Sophomore Terry Setser designed the artwork. The torch represents knowledge; the atoms, progress; the rays of light, understanding; and the open book signifies scholarship, past, present, and future.

Three years later, Missouri Southern State College, the new state-supported two-year senior college, came into operation and it required an additional seal. A simple design, this MSSC seal featured Missouri's state logo, with its two bears, encircled with the name of the college.

won the support of St. Louis area senators who wanted help in gaining a university branch for their city. In the final vote, the bill cleared the legislative hurdles by comfortable margins.

Though passed by the legislature, the bill met its doom when Governor John Dalton struck it down with a veto. Later, in talking with Fred Hughes, Dalton explained that he did not oppose the idea, but rather the timing. The legislature had also committed the state to establishing University of Missouri branches in Kansas City and St. Louis and three new junior colleges were being formed. He feared the state was taking on too much of a financial burden at one time. Dalton had worked to get the state sales tax raised to 3 percent and he assured Hughes that this new source of revenue would provide additional money for future educational projects like the Joplin proposal. Dalton indicated he felt the proposed Joplin college had more merit than St. Joseph's because of the latter's proximity to existing four-year colleges.

The Four-Year College Committee and other proponents of the expanded college were disappointed by Governor Dalton's veto, but not discouraged. They could see their action had been somewhat hasty and not fully thought out, particularly in regard to providing physical facilities for an expanded school, but there was time in which to solidify their plans and redirect their strategy. The legislature would not meet in regular session until January 1965 and in the meantime there would be an election for a new governor.

Supporters saw clearly that they would have to move immediately to create an enlarged junior college district that could then proceed to build a new campus.

The JCDA took the initiative in organizing the enlarged district, which assumed the name of the Jasper County Junior College District. Boundaries of the new district were not drawn strictly on county lines, but rather encompassed thirty-nine public-school districts consisting largely of rural and small-town schools, but also including the more populous entities of Joplin, Carthage, Webb City, Sarcoxie, Carl Junction, and Jasper. Though located primarily in Jasper County, some of these districts extended marginally into the neighboring counties of Barton, Lawrence, and Newton.

After petitioning the State Board of Education for certification, the 1961 statute required that the issue be submitted to the voters of the new district at the annual school board election held in April. The voters would vote yes or no on creating the new district and would elect a Board of Trustees, consisting of six members, who would be empowered to levy a property tax of up to thirty cents on each one hundred dollars of assessed valuation.

The Four-Year College Committee took the initiative in selecting candidates for the new Board of Trustees. Under the guiding statute, Joplin was entitled to two of the trustees because of its greater population while the remaining four would be elected at large from the other thirty-eight school districts. The committee recommended a slate of six candidates who had been active in the campaign and who would provide a geographical cross-section of the new district. These candidates were: Fred Hughes, Joplin; L. R. Reynolds, Joplin; Thomas E. Taylor, Carthage; Elvin Ummel, Jasper; Gene Taylor, Sarcoxie; and Norval Matthews, Webb City. A fifth "at large" candidate, Wesley Bivens of Carterville,

This wintertime scene, circa 1941, provides a front view of the Mission Hills mansion that has changed little over the years. Facing south, it provides an inspiring panorama of the beautiful Turkey Creek valley below.

The mansion was built in approximately 1920 by Lucius P. "Buck" Buchanan, a wealthy mining developer who was also instrumental in founding the Joplin Stockyards. Built in a Spanish motif at a time when this architectural style was in vogue, Buchanan's inspiration was reportedly a house he saw in Puerto Rico. The house, with a stucco facade and red-tile roof, has eleven rooms and many novel features, including a 62-foot tunnel that connects the basement with the well room.

gained a place on the ballot but was defeated in the voting, while the other six were elected.

In the April 7, 1964 election, the issue carried by a vote of 8,393 for and 2,627 against, an impressive margin of more than three-to-one. In Joplin the margin was an astounding eight-to-one.

The outcome reflected a mounting public support for the new enterprise, but it had a precedent in the five-to-one margin by which voters in 1938 had approved setting up the Joplin Junior College. The campaign had wisely stressed approval of the new junior college district as a perquisite to bringing a four-year college to the area. The publicity that pictured a four-year college as being potentially the greatest boost to the district's economy since the mining boom days, appealed powerfully to a populace who were painfully aware that they were living in an economically depressed area. The surge of support was further buttressed by the fact that all high-school graduates from the expanded district could now enter the junior college without paying the $80 per semester tution, a benefit previously limited to residents of the Joplin Public School District. On the other hand, Joplinites saw the new district as a way of shifting some of the junior college tax burden to other shoulders. Overall, the benefits made the additional property tax more palatable to everyone.

Implementation of the new Jasper County Junior College (JCJC) was officially set for July 1, 1964, the beginning of the new fiscal year. The June 1 commencement exercises for the 1964 graduating class marked the last ceremonial function of the old Joplin Junior College. JJC's 27-year history was honored and Superintendent Roi S. Wood, the outgoing president, received a plaque commemorating his distinguished 20-year service to the junior college.

Figuratively, on July 1, JCJC would be a college without a home since the old JJC quarters they occupied belonged to the public school district, but the Joplin Board of Education generously allowed them to continue to use the building at a nominal rent of one dollar per year plus the operational and maintenance costs. No time limit was initially set, but the next spring the Board of Trustees were officially notified to vacate the building by June 1967, preparatory to opening a second high school there.

The Board of Trustees realized that the new Jasper County Junior College could carry on for the coming 1964–1965 school year without any fundamental changes in operations, but planning for a new campus which had been

under tentative consideration for several months, required immediate action. The trustees moved to assess the full thirty-cent tax levy authorized in the April election, with twenty cents earmarked for operational expenses and the other ten cents reserved for a building fund. In reality, the board realized that much more revenue than this would be needed to establish a new campus, but first they had to seek a site.

In general, the trustees agreed that the new campus should be located to the east side of Joplin, yet close enough to have access to urban facilities. They were sensitive to criticism from rural and small-town elements that the new tax revenues might be used to promote the interests of Joplin businessmen. They wanted a site with easy transportation access to all the junior college district and in which all the residents could take pride. Tentatively, the trustees considered sites near the Carthage Airport, on North Range Line, near the Joplin Airport, and two downtown Joplin locations adjacent to Landreth Park. None of these proposals received serious consideration.

In the meantime, the trustees interest had become focused on the Mission Hills estate located east of Range Line at the intersection of Newman and Duquesne Roads. This property, owned by Mr. and Mrs. Frank C. and Juanita H. Wallower, was a showcase farm devoted to raising purebred Hereford cattle. Visually, the property was dominated by a Spanish-style mansion surrounded by elaborately landscaped grounds. The Wallowers, growing older and finding maintaining the estate to be an increasing financial burden, desired to sell. They were receptive to the idea of turning the farm into a college campus.

Rolla E. Stephens, a Joplin realtor, represented the Wallowers. Earlier he had attempted to develop a subdivision, Mission Hills Estate, on the land, but this effort had failed with only one house built. Preliminary negotiations continued for more than a year. On April 6, 1964, the day before voters approved organization of the new Jasper County Junior College District, Stephens presented the trustees with a specific offer of the main Mission Hills properties. The price quoted for the tracts the board wanted totaled $254,000, later adjusted to $255,000.

Prospects for the new campus at this point were favorable but clouded. Evidently a majority of district residents favored the location. On the other hand, there existed a minority of downtown Joplin interests who vociferously opposed the Mission Hills location, and who continued to promote a site adjacent to Landreth Park. They termed Mission Hills the "stockyards" location and noted its nearness to an asphalt plant. They also pointed to its remoteness, some six and one-half miles from the heart of downtown Joplin. The location, they maintained, would hinder future growth of the college. Furthermore, the urban location would be cheaper because utilities were already in place and federal urban renewal monies would likely be available. Finally, the urban site would help revitalize the downtown district, an area already in decline.

The trustees, convinced the Mission Hills location would best serve the

The ornate Spanish gates at the east entrance to the Mission Hills estate grounds are shown in this photograph. In the immediate foreground is a cattle guard. The Wallowers purchased the gates from the William Randolph Hearst estate, but they were removed before the property was sold to the college and for some years were located at Mrs. Wallower's Table Rock estate. The gates were later donated to the museum at the College of the Ozarks. Courtesy Jacqueline R. Potter collection

larger interests of the district, were not swayed by the opposition; instead they turned to the immediate task of raising the large sum of money that would be needed to purchase the new site and to start construction of the necessary buildings. A gift of approximately $100,000 by George A. Spiva provided the catalyst for a successful fund raising drive to buy the new campus site. The JCDA determined that $300,000 would be needed in addition to the property tax revenues, to buy Mission Hills and start construction on the new campus. The JCDA set up a subcommittee known as "Friends of the College" to solicit donations for the project. Spiva's generosity sparked an outpouring of contributions by individuals and businesses. By October 1964, after only ninety days of solicitations, subscriptions topped the $300,000 goal. The leading business contributions came from Eagle Picher Industries and the Empire District Electric Company, each of which donated $15,000, while the First National Bank gave $10,000.

With the influx of these funds, the trustees were in a position to proceed with the purchase of Mission Hills. On July 15, 1964, contracts were signed giving the junior college district an option to buy the four tracts involved, totaling 230 acres with the buildings located on them, at the agreed upon price of $255,000.

The college gained possession of its new properties in the months to come. With money flowing in from the successful subscription drive, the final transaction, involv-

Mr. and Mrs. Wallower appear in the Mansion's sunroom in this photograph, circa early 1940s. Mrs. Wallower, a lover of animals, maintained a pet cemetery in the northeast corner of the mansion grounds for her favorite dogs. Brass plaques perpetuate the memory of each dog buried there. Mr. Wallower also maintained his office in this mahogany-paneled room. The Wallowers purchased Mission Hills in 1940, shortly after "Buck" Buchanan's death.

Juanita Hammons Wallower was born in 1904 at Fairview, Missouri, and was a relative of John Q. Hammons, a wealthy Springfield real estate developer. Ms. Hammons was manager of the Keystone Hotel at the time she married Mr. Wallower. She died in 1980.

Frank C. Wallower was the son of E. Z. Wallower, a wealthy Harrisburg, Pennsylvania businessman who built Joplin's Keystone Hotel in the 1890s. F. C., with engineering degrees from both Princeton and Columbia University, assisted in managing his father's enterprises and later owned the Golden Rod, one of the richest mines in the Tri-State field. Wallower set up a generating plant to produce electricity for Mission Hills and the mansion was one of the first homes in the Joplin area to be air conditioned. Wallower died in 1970 at the age of eighty-seven. Courtesy Sue Billingsly collection

Frank C. Wallower is shown sitting near the swimming pool at the Mission Hills Estate, circa early 1940s. This Olympic-sized pool was a favorite gathering place on hot summer days, but the water, from a natural spring, was somewhat cold.

At first it was thought the pool would be a valuable asset for the college, but health authorities condemned it because of its deteriorated condition and impure water. It was torn out in 1972 and the site was turned into a Biology pond. *Courtesy Jacqueline R. Potter collection*

Though most people associate Mission Hills with its herds of prize Hereford beef cattle, this scene, near the still existing silo, portrays a time in the early 1940s when the estate was primarily a dairy farm, specializing in Jersey cattle. Mr. Wallower moved the dairy operation from near Tipton Ford when he acquired Mission Hills in 1940. *Courtesy Sue Billingsly collection*

In this photograph, circa 1942, Juanita Wallower converses with the noted actress Constance Bennett near the swimming pool. Ms. Bennett was married to the actor Gilbert Roland who was inducted into the Army in the spring of 1942 and underwent his basic training at nearby Camp Crowder. It was not unusual for the Wallowers to entertain distinguished guests at Mission Hills. Courtesy Jacqueline R. Potter collection

(Photo above) The uniformed chauffeur, Reuben Brazil, appearing in this photograph with Mr. Wallower's 1941 Cadillac, suggests the family's elegant lifestyle. Brazil also served as a butler and performed other household duties. In addition, the Wallowers employed a cook, maid, gardener, secretary, and overseer as well as other seasonal employees in yardwork or the cattle operations.

Mr. Wallower had special need for a chauffeur. He had lost his left forearm and hand in a mining accident and his artificial hand was always covered with a black kid-leather glove. Courtesy Jacqueline R. Potter collection

(Top photo) Juanita Wallower is shown here with one of her prize Hereford show animals. In the mid-1940s, Mission Hills was converted from a dairy to a beef cattle operation and the estate became noted for its line of full-blooded Herefords. These animals often won prizes at cattle exhibitions and occasionally auctions were held at the farm that attracted buyers from a large area.

The Herefords were always Mrs. Wallower's special interest. Once rustlers stole some of her cattle and, though the animals had been mutilated to erase their brand markings, she was able to identify them and they came to her when she called them by name. Courtesy Jacqueline R. Potter collection

George A. Spiva (right) converses with Governor Warren E. Hearnes in front of the newly completed library that bears Spiva's name in this March 1967 photograph. Spiva died about two months later.

Spiva, a wealthy Joplin businessman and civic benefactor, donated four hundred shares of DuPont stock, with a market value of $104,970.72, to be used in purchasing the Mission Hills campus site. He specified that the gift was to remain anonymous, a request which the trustees honored. Spiva's generosity so stimulated donations to the "Friends of the College" fund that by October the fund approximated $300,000.00, including Spiva's gift, and enabled the Board of Trustees to go ahead with purchase of the land. They honored Spiva's beneficence by naming the new library after him.

Spiva made a further contribution to the new college by working to move the Spiva Art Center from downtown to a new building on campus which it shared with the Art Department.

ing the eighty acres north of Newman Road, was completed in early 1966. Ten acres of this land was given to the state of Missouri for a new Mental Health Clinic. Right immediately, the trustees found themselves in the farming business. Some $985 was realized from the sale of soybeans in 1965 and the next year a contract was let to raise corn on the land south of Newman Road.

District leaders had realized from the beginning that a bond issue would be necessary to raise money for a multimillion dollar construction program on the new campus, but this need had wisely been postponed as they worked to create a new junior college district and raise money to buy Mission Hills. With these preliminaries out of the way, the trustees scheduled a special election for May 7, 1965, asking the voters to authorize issuance of $2.5 million in bonds for construction and equipment.

Though the outlook seemed favorable, the Jasper County Development Association and other district leaders mounted a carefully orchestrated promotional campaign including a ceremony dedicating the new campus at which Governor Warren E. Hearnes and President Elmer Ellis of the University of Missouri spoke. Under state law, the bond issue required a two-thirds margin of approval, but support went far beyond this. The final count showed 8,018 votes for and 1,016 against, a margin of nearly 8 to 1. The issue failed to receive even a simple majority of the votes in only three of the forty-one precincts. These were located in the far eastern and northern fringes of the district. As anticipated, Joplinites voted overwhelmingly for the issue with a total of 4,889 votes for and 235 against, a margin of nearly 21 to 1. Several of the voting places tabulated near unanimous votes; the Stapleton School Precinct lead with only two no votes recorded out of a total of 295 cast.

The results of this election were truly impressive. Few local issues gain such strong margins of victory and where a tax increase is involved such an overwhelmingly positive vote is seldom known. But support had been building. A strong groundswell had been evident in the April 1964 election to create the JCJC district, but as residents began to see concrete results with the purchase of Mission Hills, enthusiasm mounted, people began to speak of "our college." Sensing a brighter future for themselves and their children, the electorate had in fact voted for an additional 15 cents tax levy to retire the $2,500,000 bonded debt, raising the total property tax levy for the junior college to 45 cents on each $100 of assessed valuation—a not insignificant increase for the many district homeowners living on limited incomes. The bond issue was paid off in twenty yearly installments of $125,000 plus interest, starting in 1967.

With the Jasper County Junior College District as established fact, the Board of Trustees faced the immediate task of finding a new president. After some deliberations, the board contacted Leon C. Billingsly who had served as dean of JJC for two years, 1961–1963, and was well liked. He had left Joplin to become director of the Kellogg Community College in Battle Creek, Michigan. When Fred Hughes, president of the Trustees, contacted Billingsly he proved receptive to returning and after some negotiations was hired at a salary of $15,000 per year. Billingsly left Kellogg with some reluctance. A larger school than JCJC and endowed with considerable wealth, it faced few immediate problems. On the other hand, Billingsly came from a rural and smalltown background in Southwest Missouri and he saw a golden opportunity to help the economically depressed area youths, whom he knew so well, obtain the benefits of higher education. Coupled to this was the still bright prospect of expanding JCJC into a four-year college. In this, Billingsly sensed an opportunity to play a rare constructive role in creating a significant new state college.

The 1964–1965 school year marked Jasper County Junior College's first under its new name, but 1964 was an election year and its attendant political campaigning portended a bright new future for the college. Missourians would be choosing a new governor since the state constitution limited the incumbent Governor John Dalton to one term. It was against this background, that, in the fall of 1963, Secretary of State Warren E. Hearnes came to Senator Richard Webster's office. Hearnes confided in Webster that he planned to run for governor and that he would launch his primary campaign with stops in Joplin and St. Joseph where he would endorse the proposed four-year college legislation that Governor Dalton had vetoed. Hearnes, a native of rural Southeast Missouri, did not have the support of the Democratic party leadership and he knew he would have to build his support in outstate Missouri. Thus Joplin, though normally Republican, became important to him.

Hearnes was the only one of the three Democratic candidates in the primary who supported the college bill. In the general election, the Republican candidate, Ethan A. Shapley, also supported it; but he provided only token opposition. In a Democratic era, when a Republican stood little chance of winning statewide in Missouri, the Democratic primary, in effect, elected the next governor.

Hearnes' election strategy worked and, true to his word, he called on Webster and Senator John E. Downs of St. Joseph to help write the education section of his inaugural address. In the speech, Hearnes strongly endorsed the proposed four-year colleges for both Joplin and St. Joseph.

Joplin area leaders were elated when they learned of Hearnes' support and it galvanized them into action. One lesson they had learned from Dalton's veto was that more local action was needed; that they, like St. Louis, needed to provide a campus site. It was at this time that area leaders began the concerted drive that culminated in the purchase of Mission Hills.

In January 1965, Jasper and Buchanan County legislators introduced a new four-year college bill. Like the one vetoed in 1963, it provided for senior college branches of the University of Missouri at Joplin and St. Joseph that would operate in conjunction with the existing junior colleges. The same legislative team still represented Jasper County: Richard Webster of Carthage in the

President Leon Billingsly is shown handing a $65,000 check to Mrs. Juanita Wallower in this circa January 1965 photograph. Standing are (left) Herbert Van Fleet, college attorney and Rolla E. Stephens the realtor who negotiated the sale. The college purchased the 230-acre Mission Hills site in four separate transactions, taking possession as money became available from the successful fund-raising drive. Mr. and Mrs. Wallower contributed $15,000 to the new college; the Mission Hills Estate, $5,000; and Rolla E. Stephens, $2,500.

This solemn group of dignitaries are watching Governor Hearnes sign House Bill No. 210 on July 22, 1965. The legislation enabled Missouri Southern and Missouri Western colleges to set up state senior colleges at their respective institutions. Standing behind the governor (fully visible) are from left: Senators John E. Downs, St. Joseph, and Richard Webster, Carthage; and Representatives Jim Williams, St. Joseph; Robert Ellis Young, Carthage; Ronald F. Reed, Jr., St. Joseph; and Robert Warden, Joplin. Visible are the many pens Hearnes used in affixing his signature. The ceremony was held on a stretch of south Main Street that the City Council renamed Hearnes Boulevard as a token of appreciation. As a further mark of esteem, the Board of Trustees announced that the new administration-classroom building on campus would be named Hearnes Hall. Missouri Western College officials also named a building in honor of the governor.

With this signing, Hearnes fulfilled his promise to Joplin and St. Joseph residents that if he gained the governorship he would help the two cities gain state senior colleges.

Of the local legislators, Senator Webster and Representative Young were key figures in their respective chambers. Representative Warden, a House member, 1960–1966, also played a creative role, but lacked Young's seniority. Young, who eventually served thirty-two years, had been in the House since 1954. Webster was a powerful promoter of Southern's interests and served in the Senate for twenty-eight years. He died in 1990.

Senate and Robert Warden of Joplin and Robert Ellis Young of Carthage in the House of Representatives. All three worked diligently for the measure.

In the meantime, the Missouri Commission on Higher Education (MCHE) had authorized Dr. George L. Hall of the University of Michigan to make a survey of the higher educational needs of Joplin, St. Joseph, and the delta areas. Hall's study, which was released just one month before the legislature met, used much of the Four-Year College Committees' earlier study to conclude that there were sufficient students in the nine-county service area to justify the addition of junior and senior years to JCJC. But the Hall report differed significantly from the earlier bill vetoed by Governor Dalton in that Hall called for the new senior colleges at Joplin and St. Joseph to be operated as independent state colleges under their own boards while the existing junior colleges would continue to operate under their separate boards. Hall cited an example of a similar operation in the Miami, Florida area, but Joplin and St. Joseph leaders had already studied the successful example in Flint, Michigan. The MCHE gave cautious endorsement to Hall's proposals, but also called for a greatly strengthened junior college program.

The bill, after moving through the House of Representatives with comparative ease, passed on to the Senate. There the opposition was formidable, but Webster had a strong ally in Senator John E. Downs of St. Joseph. Furthermore, Webster, now with three years seniority in the Senate, was himself emerging as a powerful figure in the legislature. Serious doubts, reinforced by the Hall report, were being raised about the wisdom of extending the University of Missouri system to encompass the two new schools. After some political negotiations, the bill that finally emerged specified that the new state senior colleges at Joplin and St. Joseph would be under their own boards, but start-up of the new schools would be supervised by the University of Missouri.

However, powerful opposition still remained. Veteran senators from areas with established state colleges, saw the Joplin and St. Joseph schools as upstarts who would cut into their money pie. At this point, Webster and Warden coauthored a compromise that made the bill more palatable. This new legislation provided simply that university status could be extended to the major existing state colleges. Senator Webster, a master of political logrolling, once remarked to his colleagues, "you've got to know what other people want and how bad they want it." The leaders of these colleges wanted university status very badly and they pressured their legislators to ease up on the opposition and let the bill pass. Thus the legislation, known as House Bill No. 210, finally passed both houses by comfortable margins.

With the passage of House bill No. 210 imminent, the issue of naming the new college had to be resolved. Many Joplinites disliked the designation Jasper County Junior College, feeling it lacked distinctiveness, but looked on the name as temporary pending passage of legislation to set up a state-supported senior college. The names Missouri Southern and Missouri Western were discussed by the board, but no decision was made and the bill moved through the legislative committees with the name blank. Webster preferred the name Missouri Western, but St. Joseph pre-empted that designation with the bill going to conference committee for final resolution. Webster and Warden had to provide a name immediately, but the telephone lines to Joplin were not functioning so they wrote in the name Missouri Southern State College and it proved acceptable.

In May 1965, the board resolved to change the name of the junior college to Missouri Southern College and this became the name the institution usually went by for several years, though officially the senior college was Missouri Southern State College. In 1972, the Board of Regents/Trustees changed the

Paul R. Shipman, with a doctorate in education from the University of Arkansas, came to MSC in 1965 as an assistant to President Billingsly and presided over business affairs of the college for the next twenty-one years, a period when the college quadrupled in size. Maintaining oversight over the extensive campus construction projects of that era fell under his jurisdiction as did the organization and supervision of the building maintenance and groundskeeping staffs. His title was elevated to that of vice president for Business Affairs in 1973. Shipman retired in 1986.

name of the whole college to the latter designation and this first appeared in the 1972–1973 catalog.

House Bill No. 210 now needed only Governor Hearnes' signature to make it official and this became the occasion for a special ceremony in Joplin on July 22, 1965. Present were legislators from Buchanan and Jasper counties, civic officials, and administrators from both Missouri Southern and Missouri Western colleges. After a luncheon at the Hollywood Inn, the dignitaries traveled to south Joplin for the signing ceremony. Hearnes affixed his signature to the new statute before the attentive audience and praised the people of the district for their, "We can do it ourselves" philosophy.

Before the new senior college could function, the statute required the governor to appoint a five-member Board of Regents whose members would serve five-year terms with the initial appointments staggered from one to five years. The Regents were vested with power to administer all four years of instruction, though the levying of taxes and the earmarking of junior college funds was left in the hands of the Board of Trustees.

The Jasper County legislators, Webster, Warden, and Young, wrote Hearnes urging him to appoint the five regents from the present six- member Board of Trustees in "the interests of continuity." When Governor Hearnes announced his appointments, effective October 13, 1965, he honored the legislators' request except that in one instance he appointed an outsider, Mills Anderson. The appointments were: Fred G. Hughes, Joplin; Thomas E. Taylor, Carthage; Lauren R. Reynolds, Joplin; Norval M. Matthews, Webb City; and Mills Anderson, Carthage, serving five-to-one-year terms in that order.

In their organizational meeting the Regents moved to coordinate the two boards as much as possible. Gene Taylor and Elvin Ummel, the trustees left off the new board, were appointed treasurer and secretary respectively of the Board of Regents. In turn, Mills Anderson was appointed treasurer of the Board of Trustees. Fred Hughes, president of the Trustees, also became president of the new Board of Regents. Though the two boards could not have identical membership, and became more diverse with the passage of time, they worked with little friction. The fact that both had Fred Hughes as president for many years helped to bring about this harmony.

Local leaders could be proud of their role in gaining a state- supported senior college for the region. They had worked hard and effectively as had the very able group of legislators that represented Jasper County. Governor Hearnes' timely support provided a welcome windfall, but the community's strong commitment proved most crucial. Legislators in Jefferson City were tremendously impressed with the eight-to-one majority by which the bond issue passed and by the rapidity with which the community raised the funds to buy Mission Hills. Finally, the prestige of Joplin Junior College cemented the support. Legislators felt they would be placing the new senior college on a firm foundation.

Once Governor Hearnes signed the enabling legislation in July 1965, officials of the junior college turned vigorously to the process of implementing a four-year college. Aside from the routine of regular classwork, the school was a beehive of activity as administrators and faculty labored with the myriad problems of setting up a senior college curriculum and expanding the administrative and teaching staffs.

Changes were made in the administration in the next few months. In August 1965, Paul R. Shipman became an assistant to the president in charge

Missouri Southern's first division chairmen are shown conferring with one another in this photograph. From left, Dr. James Altendorf, Science and Mathematics; Dr. Charles Niess, Education, Psychology, and Physical Education; Dr. Ervin Dunham, Humanities and Fine Arts; James K. Maupin, dean of Semi-Professional Technical Education; Keith Larimore (partially concealed), Business and Economics; and Harry Gockel, Social Science.

Prior to this time, the junior college had never maintained a structure of administrators below the level of the college dean, but North Central advisers made it clear that such an organization of division heads would need to be in place before the college could gain accreditation for its senior college program.

Altendorf and Dunham remained at MSC for only three and two years, respectively. The other four stayed on at the college for many years. Maupin and Gockel were the only division chairman to come from the old junior college staff.

of business affairs. Fred Cinotto, was hired as curriculum coordinator in November. The following January, C. Otis Robinson, dean of the junior college since 1963, resigned to take a new position in Kansas. Fred Cinotto replaced him as acting dean and a few months later as full dean.

As the fall semester opened in September 1965, excitement permeated the staff and student body. Everyone realized that fundamental changes were at hand for the 38-year-old junior college. The state legislature had appropriated $40,000 for planning the new senior college offerings. As this money became available, serious work began on developing a curriculum and structure of degrees for the new baccalaureate program.

President Leon C. Billingsly (left), Dean Fred Cinotto (right), and Faculty Association President David C. Bingman with their wives are shown at a recognition dinner held by the MSC faculty on April 10, 1967, to honor Billingsly and Cinotto for their work in obtaining preliminary North Central accreditation for Southern. Some 102 faculty members and guests attended the dinner and President Billingsly received a prolonged, standing ovation.

Fred Cinotto, as curriculum coordinator, had played a key role in gaining the accreditation. He became acting dean in February 1966 and full dean a few months later. Though effective, Cinotto lacked senior college administrative experience and a doctorate, limitations which the North Central examiners found unacceptable. Edward Sterl Phinney replaced him as dean in August 1967 and Cinotto held miscellaneous posts until he retired in 1973. Later honored with the title of emeritus professor, Cinotto died in 1991 at the age of eighty-three.

The successful implementation of the new senior college program depended heavily on the cooperation and enthusiasm of MSC's staff of veteran instructors. Many had held their positions long enough to see several administrators come and go. They formed a tightly knit faculty family, somewhat ingrown, but very professional in outlook and possessed of a great pride in the venerable junior college. Martha McCormick, by this time the sole survivor of the original staff of 1937, epitomized this group. Though she realized an expanded college was needed to better educational opportunities for the area's young people, she regarded the change with misgivings. McCormick feared a rapid expansion that with its attendant new course offerings and influx of inexperienced teachers, would dilute the strong academic standards that had made JJC one of the top twelve junior colleges of the nation. Most of the veteran teachers shared her view. They would rather MSC remained a strong junior college than become a mediocre four-year institution but, like Ms. McCormick, they were not obstructionist in their outlook. They saw the need for a four- year college, and sensed that it, too, could become an outstanding center of learning. With that in mind, they entered vigorously into the planning process, but with a determination to make the junior college's excellent liberal arts program a core on which the senior program would be built.

House Bill No. 210, stipulated that the establishment of senior-level colleges at Joplin and St. Joseph, must meet requirements established by the University of Missouri Board of Curators before they could go into operation. Accordingly, an Advisory Board was set up at Columbia to coordinate and review work on the curriculums for the new colleges. Also, president Elmer Ellis of MU appointed a special consultant to observe progress at Joplin and St. Joseph, particularly as to the addition of physical facilities and the enrollment trends. Drawing on reports of the Advisory Board and the consultant, Ellis would then make his recommendations to the Board of Curators.

By October 1965, Fred Cinotto, MSC's new curriculum coordinator, was on the job conferring with faculty groups. His expertise and connections proved of great help in gaining North Central accreditation for the new program. Initially Cinotto worked with a faculty committee in drawing up general education requirements for the new baccalaureate program. Veteran teachers on the committee insisted that it preserve key elements of the junior college's widely respected liberal arts programs. Some forty-eight to fifty-three credit hours in five different areas of general education were specified for a baccalaureate degree.

The college was fortunate in that the North Central Association sent Dr. Edward B. Blackman, an assistant dean of Michigan State University, as a consultant on preparing for the preliminary accreditation examination. Blackman especially urged the staff to aim for a four-year curriculum that would equal the quality of the two-year program that had been reviewed so favorably in 1964. He saw the college as possibly being vulnerable for lack of an adequate library. Though concerned at first about the tight timetable, he came to praise the staff for their industry and became a strong supporter of MSC.

To expedite the curriculum planning process, President Billingsly cancelled all classes on March 2–3–4, 1966, so that the faculty could participate in planning workshops. Consultants brought in from other colleges and universities for these workshops and at other times, were very helpful in rounding out a basic four-year curriculum.

By the spring of 1966, President Billingsly faced a crucial decision; should he push ahead and try to gain North Central Association approval to start the senior college program in the fall of 1967 or should he wait another year. Billingsly realized that pressing for accreditation at the earlier date was a gamble, but he saw certain positive factors that convinced him to push ahead. For one thing, he felt it was necessary to keep up the momentum, otherwise enthusiasm would falter. Also, a survey had just indicated a probable enrollment of five hundred for the junior year and the MU Board of Curators had approved adding the third year on an experimental basis to test the enrollment potential, but this would be contingent on North Central granting preliminary accreditation. Other factors that weighed heavily in Billingsly's decision was the great prestige of the junior college, the strong community support, and the ambitious campus construction program with four buildings either under way or in advanced stages of planning. On the other hand, the hurdles to be surmounted were formidable. The library needed to be expanded, new division chairmen hired, and a self-study drawn up. With these steps successfully completed, a team of examiners would make an on-campus survey, and the North Central Association Executive Board would hand down a final decision in the early spring of 1967.

Governor Hearnes is shown addressing a crowd at the formal dedication of Missouri Southern College and its new campus on Sunday, October 29, 1967. Behind Hearnes is the new administration-classroom building that bears his name. In his remarks, Hearnes termed the college, "a catalyst for progress." The dedication ceremony culminated three days of festivities and was followed by an open house which gave visitors an opportunity to tour the new campus.

This unidentified student is shown receiving a ticket for illegal parking near the junior college at Eighth and Wall during the 1965–1966 school year. A serious parking problem developed in the closing years of the junior college at its downtown location. Off-street parking had never been provided except for a few administrators. On class days several hundred cars lined the five-block area surrounding the college. Residents complained and police issued tickets, but no attempt was made to resolve the problem because of the impending move to the new campus.

President Leon C. Billingsly is shown here in his office at the Mission Hills mansion during the 1966–1967 school year. He occupied the sunroom where Frank C. Wallower had once had his office. The overcrowding problem at MSC's downtown location had become so severe that Billingsly decided to move to the unfinished Mission Hills campus; his old office was turned into a classroom.

Before the self-study could be completed the new administrative structure and degree program had to be set up. As a part of curriculum development, the State Advisory Board had approved the creation of six academic divisions and a structure of degrees. The degrees initially offered consisted of three baccalaureate degrees: bachelor of arts, bachelor of science, and bachelor of science in education, while the junior college offerings of associate of arts and associate of science degrees were continued.

Creation of the new divisions required immediate action. North Central officials insisted that new chairpersons be in place by July 1, 1966, to help in finalizing the curriculum and in drafting the self-study. Accordingly, Dr. Billingsly proceeded to make the necessary appointments.

With the acceptance of the self-study, submitted in the late summer of 1966, arrangements were made for the four-member North Central examining team to appear on campus January 12–13, 1967. The team consisted of the chairman, Dr. Alan O. Pfnister, dean of Wittenberg University; Dr. Leslie W. Dunlap, director of libraries, University of Iowa; Dr. F. E. Oliver, director of Office of Financial Analysis, University of Michigan; and Dr. Sidney Titelbaum, City College, Chicago. After conferring with selected administrators, faculty, and students, the team held a luncheon meeting with the Board of Trustees at Mickey Mantle's Holiday Inn. The examiners were complimentary of Billingsly and the faculty, but expressed serious reservations about the adequacy of the library's holdings.

Dr. Dunlap was especially critical. He charged that MSC administrators were overly anxious to gain accreditation and insisted that the library have twenty-five thousand volumes on hand and catalogued within six months, which he said was impossible. Gene Taylor, a trustee from Sarcoxie, later recounted that he told Dunlap, "Let me tell you something fellow. We will get the ——— books!" and indeed the books were in place for the beginning of the fall semester. Though the library was being rapidly expanded at this time, fueled in part with liberal federal grant monies, the problem was serious because the junior college library of over eleven thousand volumes belonged to the Joplin School District and the college was able to purchase only about five thousand volumes that were not needed for the new high school. By the time of the North Central visitation, the library had been built up to approximately twelve thousand volumes.

Evidently the North Central team left MSC with a favorable overall impression. Perhaps most of all, they were so impressed by the spirit with which college officials, the staff, and the community had overcome seemingly insurmountable odds that inadequacies like the library seemed likely to be soon resolved. In their report, they recommended accreditation to the forty-member North Central Association Executive Board. Billingsly and Cinotto were called to Chicago to appear before the board. On April 5, the board handed down a decision granting MSC preliminary accreditation for a period of three to four years. The school was authorized to add a third year in the fall of 1967 and a fourth year the following fall and to grant baccalaureate degrees.

The granting of preliminary accreditation touched off a period of celebration at the college. On the morning of April 5, tension mounted among the faculty and students as they anxiously awaited word of the North Central decision. About noon Billingsly called to report that approval had been

In another move to deal with the overcrowding problem at Eighth and Wall, this old house, located on Ninth Street adjacent to the then public library, was one of two rented to provide additional office space for the 1966–1967 school year. Offices for the new division chairmen were set up in this building. Somewhat reminiscent of a haunted house, jokesters referred to the old structure as "Munster Hall," a name derived from "The Munsters," a popular television program at the time.

This master plan for development of the new MSC campus was drawn up in the summer of 1965 by Hare and Hare, a Kansas City site planning and landscape architectural firm. The plan projected development over a fifteen-year period that would accommodate a student population of 6,473 by 1980, an overly optimistic estimate. Though the plans were soon revised, the grouping of the initial four buildings to form an oval was followed, as was the main parking lot facing Newman Road. The grouping of the dormitories north of Newman Road has been followed as to location, but the idea of a married students housing complex was never implemented. Most significantly, Hare and Hare's plan to locate the football stadium, in the Turkey Creek valley flood plain has been abandoned in favor of a location on higher ground east of Duquesne Road, but in 1965 the college owned no land there.

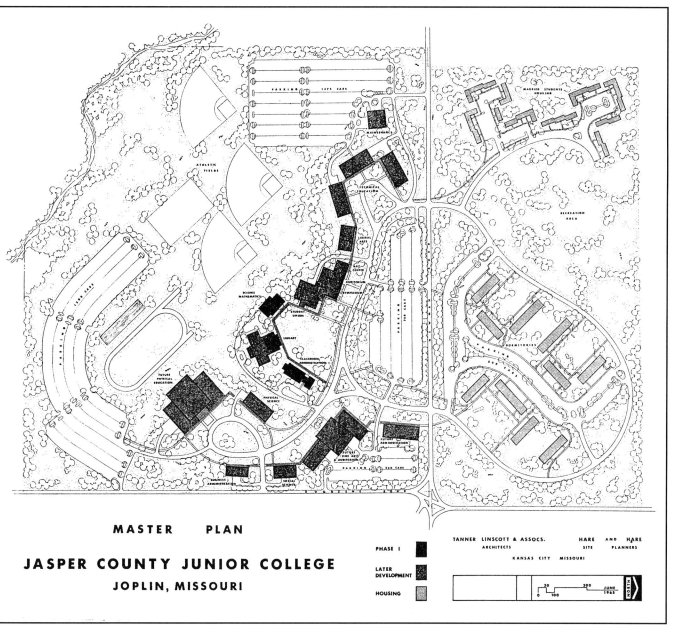

MASTER PLAN

JASPER COUNTY JUNIOR COLLEGE
JOPLIN, MISSOURI

granted and it was immediately announced to the classrooms over the public address system. A delegation from the college greeted Cinotto at the airport when he returned that afternoon. Later the faculty held a recognition dinner at which Billingsly and Cinotto were honored with gifts of appreciation. Perhaps Fred Hughes, president of the Board of Regents/Trustees, best summarized the importance of gaining accreditation when he commented, "I don't think any of us fully appreciate the significance of the accreditation. I'm sure that if we could put the clock ahead ten years, we would be pleasantly surprised at the changes which will have taken place."

Another occasion for celebration came in the fall of 1967 with the formal dedication of the four-year college and its new campus. The festive mood was reinforced when, on the day before ceremonies began, the MU Board of Curators unanimously approved MSC's fourth year of instruction. This date, October 26, 1967, marked the surmounting of the last legal hurdle and made MSC officially a full four-year college. The three days of festivities culminated with a formal dedication ceremony and open house on Sunday afternoon, October 29, at which Governor Warren Hearnes delivered the principal address. As the excited crowd toured the new campus that afternoon they too saw, as in Hearnes' remarks, the college as a "symbol of progress" and "culmination of a dream."

Clearing the academic hurdles presented the vital first step in establishing a four-year college, but the construction of a campus furnished another necessary component. The Mission Hills estate provided a beautiful setting, but its mansion and cluster of farm buildings was far from being a college campus. This would change in the next ten years as fifteen major new buildings were constructed along with the attendant building of streets, parking lots, athletic grounds, and the remodeling of older structures. A new campus would have been built even if the institution had remained a junior college, but the implementation of a four-year curriculum accelerated the process so that by 1975 Missouri Southern State College had a campus of striking proportions and architectural integrity for a college of its size.

While planning and construction of the new campus proceeded, the mushrooming student enrollment imposed a serious strain on the junior college's limited physical facilities. The move to the Eighth and Wall location in 1958 had provided seemingly commodious quarters, but once enrollment passed the one thousand mark pressure began to mount and when the student count reached fifteen hundred in the fall of 1965 additional emergency quarters became mandatory.

Starting that fall, the administration took several steps to deal with the problem. The gymnasium was turned into a student center and the Physical Education classes were moved to the YMCA where the college paid $1,000 a year for the use of their facilities. Art classes were moved to the Spiva Art Center. The next fall, space was rented in the Episcopal Church Annex. President Billingsly moved his office to the Mission Hills mansion and two old houses were rented from the Joplin R-8 School District for office space. Some of the new technical courses in Automotive Technology and Nursing were held at Mission Hills.

The Board of Trustees and President Billingsly approached the task of planning for the new campus with caution and a high degree of professionalism. They wanted attractive buildings that would accent the natural beauty of the landscape and spacing of the buildings that would preserve the openness of the

On a cold, snowy February 3, 1966, this crowd gathered to witness a groundbreaking ceremony for the new Missouri Southern campus. The site is that of the Spiva Library, the first major building to be constructed. Participating in the ceremony are, from left: Elvin Ummel, Fred Hughes, Gene Taylor, Robert Ellis Young, and Mills Anderson. All except Young, a state legislator, were Regents/Trustees.

In this photograph, excavation is underway for the new George H. Spiva Library in the early spring of 1966. In the background stands the ranch-style house that MSC purchased from Max and Peggy Whitehead for $35,000. Later it was moved to the location where it now serves as the Alumni House. In the far background may be seen the tops of the large trees that had to be removed for construction of the main parking lot facing Newman Road. Completed in February 1967, the library was the first new building on campus to be ready for occupancy. Too small in size almost from the beginning, it was more than doubled in area in 1973.

campus; but they also wanted practical buildings, solidly constructed, easy to maintain, and that could be expanded. Convenient access streets and adequate parking for the large student population who would commute by automobile was also seen as a necessity.

The Trustees interviewed several architects in the late summer of 1964 before hiring Frank McArthur of Tanner-Linscott and Associates, a Kansas City architectural firm. They were impressed with McArthur's practicality and his quick facility for rendering their ideas into attractive designs.

Under McArthur's guidance, an image of the campus began to take shape. In styling the new buildings,

This November 10, 1966 photograph, looking north, shows the exterior of Hearnes Hall nearing completion. Hearnes Hall and the L. R. Reynolds Science and Mathematics Hall were built together under a joint contract. With 40,390 square feet of floor space, Hearnes was the largest building on campus until the Taylor Performing Arts Center was finished in 1975. A fire during construction delayed completion and it was not finally finished until early June 1967.

some consideration was given to a Spanish motif in keeping with the existing mansion, but this was rejected in favor of a southern colonial theme as suggested by the college's name and its regional location. The design would feature a blend of bricks and Carthage stone accented by white, squared columns and white trim.

McArthur also advised that a long-range master plan for campus development be drawn up before "a single spade of earth was turned." The board employed Hare and Hare, planners and landscape architects, to accomplish this. The plan called for a main campus to be located on the high ridge overlooking Turkey Creek to the south, anchored on the west end by the mansion complex and extending eastward to Duquesne Road.

Funding a construction project of this magnitude was a sizeable undertaking for an institution with Southern's limited tax base and did present some problems, but none that produced more than temporary delays.

Many of the first buildings constructed, plus auxiliary projects like the parking lots, streets, and remodeling of older structures, relied heavily on funds from the $2,500,000 bond issue approved by the voters in May 1965, but there were other sources such as revenue from the property tax, state aid, and student fees. Interestingly, construction of the library, the first new building on campus, did not rely on the bond money. With $700,000 on

(Top) President Billingsly is shown inspecting construction on the L. R. Reynolds Science and Mathematics Hall. Like Hearnes Hall, with which it was built concurrently, Reynolds Hall had two floors above ground in front and three in the back. Construction proceeded smoothly and the Reynolds Building was ready for occupancy in mid-May 1967, the second building to be completed on campus. An expansion in 1988 nearly doubled its size.

(Bottom) This view of the Mansion Annex under construction shows how it was built as an extension onto the three-car garage section of the mansion. A hurriedly conceived plan drawn up when it became clear funds could not be raised immediately to build a college union, it amounted to a temporary cafeteria and student lounge that could be converted into classroom space when the cafeteria moved. Built at a cost of only $125,990, after the cafeteria moved it housed in succession the School of Business Administration, the Social Science Department and part of Communications, and finally the Learning Center.

hand, augmented by anticipated federal aid, the Trustees proceeded with the library project three months before voters approved the bond issue.

Federal grants proved to be an unexpected bonanza. The Higher Education Facilities Act of 1963 extended federal matching monies to eligible colleges for construction. In Missouri the Commission of Higher Education distributed these funds. Though the Commission tried to distribute them equitably, some colleges were unable to proceed immediately with planned construction and left over funds were reallocated to institutions, like MSC, with an active construction program. Up to 1975, approximately $1,400,000 in federal funds were received for use in constructing buildings. The sum could have been larger, but the need to expedite construction caused the board to bypass this source of funds for several buildings. Another federal source, the National Defense Education Act, extended generous grants for library books and educational equipment that enabled the college to meet the heavy expenses of expanding in these areas.

The Board of Trustees initially planned to construct four buildings: the library, a science and mathematics building, a classroom-administration building, and a community center. These were perceived as the minimum accommodations for a functioning college and they needed to be completed by the fall of 1967 when the college had to vacate the downtown location. Plans for the community center were altered when the Spiva Art Center offered to help build a fine arts complex that would house their collection. This and higher than estimated costs caused elimination of a planned theatre and gymnasium for the community center. Revamped plans called for a larger gymnasium in another location and the conversion of a barn into a theatre. The latter was ready for use on time, but it was the spring of 1968 before the gymnasium could be completed.

Though President Billingsly realized that academic facilities were the heart of the emerging campus, he also felt that service facilities for the students were vital. A college union was needed and residence halls were a necessity if the institution was to continue to grow. With this in mind, he had worked with area legislators to get a new state law passed allowing small colleges to issue revenue bonds for building service facilities with student fees to be used to pay off the bonds. The president hoped to use this statute to issue revenue bonds immediately and possibly have residence halls and a college union completed by the time the new campus opened, but the bonds could not be sold on acceptable terms; MSC was too new to have an established credit rating. Mobile housing units were then brought in for athletes and construction was started on a low-cost annex to the mansion that would provide a temporary cafeteria and student center. It was not until 1969 that a small college union could be opened and the following year before two residence halls were ready.

In many ways the major phase of constructing the campus came at an ideal time. The federal government was promoting an expansion of higher education facilities with generous grants, the public was receptive to paying higher taxes, and construction costs were low compared to what they would be in a few years with the onset of heavy inflation. Southern was fortunate too in that it benefitted from a keen competitive situation among contractors. Minford Potter, an executive of the M-P (Mayes-Potter) Construction Company, expressed an intention for his concern to build the new college. Eventually M-P built ten of the major projects by submitting the low bids and in fact constructed all the major buildings in the first three years. The first five of these were constructed at a cost of approximately $18 per square foot, not including architectural engineering fees or original site development, a figure that would seem remarkably low only a few years later.

As the new campus began to develop, another problem began to surface. In choosing the Mission Hills location, the college had taken itself into a rural area devoid of most city services. Though the administration was able to obtain the needed utility connections by paying for them, this still left the college without adequate police and fire protection and no zoning laws to control development in the surrounding area. When President Billingsly and the Trustees heard rumors that a group planned to open a "beer joint" adjacent to the south edge of the campus, they prevailed on the City Council to annex the campus and in August 1967 Joplin voters approved annexing 1,080 acres encompassing the campus and the surrounding area.

By the end of 1975, MSSC had a well-developed campus. Adequate facilities were in place to serve the immediate needs of the various departments. With the gymnasium and the new stadium completed, most athletic events could be accommodated on campus. The recently finished performing arts center provided more space for speech and theatre classes and plays as well as a place for school assemblies and community cultural offerings. The planting of trees and shrubbery, much of which was donated by individuals and service clubs, helped to soften the spartan landscape. In 1969–1970 the college began an ongoing program of acquiring additional land on the east side of Duquesne Road and by 1970 the campus encompassed 310 acres. That same year, the college acquired a home for President Billingsly in keeping with an old, but dying, college tradition. The house was sold in 1989.

At the end of the spring 1967 semester, construction of the new campus had progressed sufficiently for the college to vacate the downtown location as required by agreement with the Joplin R-8 School District. The move was a small-scale operation because virtually all the equipment belonged to the school district. A crew of school employees and fifteen students completed the move on June 7, l967, using one van and three pickup trucks.

The summer session began on the day following the move. Accommodations were minimal, but sufficient for the low enrollment of about 225. The library was functional, but most of the classes had to be held in the Science and Mathematics Building because of the unfinished state of the other structures. Students and faculty were excited to be on the expansive new campus and relieved to be away from the overcrowded downtown building.

The real test for the adequacy of the new quarters came with the opening of the fall 1967 semester when the full complement of over two thousand students descended on the new campus. On Monday morning, September 11, the first day of fall classes, President Billingsly and Administrative Assistant Paul Shipman stood on the portico of Hearnes Hall observing the bumper-to-bumper traffic on Newman and Duquesne roads with growing dismay. The two parking lots, built to accommodate twelve hundred cars, overflowed and late arrivals among the fifteen hundred vehicles, parked along the roadways and on the campus grass. A massive traffic jam developed at Range Line and Newman Road with a lesser tie-up occurring at Seventh and Duquesne. The situation relieved itself somewhat in the days to come as students staggered their hours of arrival and departure, and formed car pools. Also, temporary dirt parking lots were opened up and the Inter-City Transit Company offered bus service, though it never proved very popular.

The spacious new campus was sorely needed to deal with the increasing student population. In the five-year period 1962–1967, enrollment had almost doubled. With the advent of the fall 1967 semester, enrollment jumped to another historic high of 2,411 students, a 31 percent increase. Most of this gain came from the addition of the new, surprisingly large, junior class of 531. Larger than anticipated numbers of juniors had transferred in from the seven

(Top) A rather abbreviated College Union appears here as it originally looked. A delay in selling revenue bonds, to be paid off with student fees, held up the project for more than a year. The union opened in late May 1969 with the first event being a twirp dance followed a few days later by a breakfast for the graduating Class of 1969. An addition, completed in 1979, nearly doubled the size of the union and the name was changed to the Leon C. Billingsly Student Center.

(Bottom) This photograph shows the Robert Ellis Young Gymnasium in it's original state. Completed in April 1968, delays in starting the project caused Athletics to depend on off-campus and makeshift facilities for their first year on the new campus. Additions to the gymnasium included an extension of the front lobby area in 1976 and a major addition to the north, completed in 1982, that added a swimming pool, racquetball courts, and offices.

area junior colleges while many earlier graduates of JJC returned to continue their college education; also a surprising number transferred in from larger senior colleges and universities.

The new four-year college did offer an attractive opportunity to average students of modest financial means. The Board of Regents/Trustees continued to operate under their original philosophy of a quality college open to all at very reasonable cost. The "open door" admission policy admitted any graduate of a fully accredited Missouri high school without further certification, but out-of-state residents were required to rank in the upper two-thirds of their high school graduating classes. Fees for full-time junior college division district residents, enrolled for fifteen semester hours, totaled $100; out-of-district students paid $145; and out-of-state enrollees were charged $205. The senior college division levied fees of $145 for Missouri residents and out-of-state students paid $205. All fees included a $30 textbook rental fee, $15 of which was refundable when the books were returned. Estimated costs for room and board per semester were $375. Few institutions at that time could offer students an opportunity to obtain a baccalaureate degree from a fully accredited college at such low cost.

A strong impetus to increasing enrollment in the 1967–1975 period came from benefits available to students in the form of scholarships and student-aid programs. The four-year college stimulated an interest in setting up scholarships and fifty-five new ones were created in 1968 alone. In addition to the scholarships, a number of student-aid programs were available, some of which were supported by federal grants. The largest at this time was the student loan program, federally guaranteed and partially forgiven under some conditions. Federal veterans benefits also became significant as Vietnam War veterans returned. MSSC actively recruited them and by the spring semester of 1975 some 814 veterans and their dependents were receiving benefits.

The Hare and Hare Master Plan enrollment projections badly underestimated the rapid growth up to 1970, but grossly overestimated growth in the 1970s. In reality, enrollment growth slowed in the early 1970s and actually declined from the previous high for the three school years 1971–1973. The decline had several causes. Many young people sought technical training that would quickly qualify them for a job rather than seek a college degree. With American involvement in the Vietnam War declining, fewer young men were entering college as a way of gaining draft deferments. But, most importantly the demographics of the area's nearly static population base tended to hold down college enrollment. But in the fall of 1974 enrollment again reached a new historic high and continued a slow upward advance through the rest of the decade. Over the long run, the growing realization among

This 1967 aerial view, looking southwest across the intersection of Newman and Duquense roads, shows the campus as it looked when Southern completed its move to this new location. Evident is a campus of few buildings, vast expanses of empty land, no shrubbery, and few trees except for a cluster around the mansion premises. Clearly visible are the new parking lot facing Newman Road; the cluster of three buildings, Hearnes Hall, Spiva Library, and Reynolds Hall on the oval; and the new Art and Music complex immediately to the east. The only other new building was the Mansion Annex, partially concealed by the trees. In the immediate foreground, at the southeast corner of Newman and Duquesne roads, is the Messick Truck Company. Shortly after this photograph was taken, the Ecumenical Campus Ministery purchased this location and turned the main building into a student center. The college now owns this property and it is the planned site of a multimillion dollar arena.

This circa 1972 aerial view of the MSC campus shows the extensive growth that had taken place in the five years since the college moved to its new home. The view looks southward with the intersections of Newman and Duquesne roads to the extreme left. At the extreme right center may be seen the Matthews (now Ummel) Technology Building, completed in 1970. Just to the south is the silo and adjoining Barn Theatre. Behind them are the two modular dormitory units that housed athletes until 1970. Farther east is Kuhn Hall, and across from it is a parking lot where Matthews Hall now stands. On the oval, the new College Union is visible to the right. Southeast of the oval is the new gymnasium. North of Newman Road, in foreground is the new Anderson Police Academy, completed in 1971, and to the east are the two new residence halls that opened in 1970.

The school year 1968–1969 marked completion of MSC's first four-year cycle of classes and was followed by the first commencement exercises in which baccalaureate degrees were issued. Some 198 baccalaureate degrees plus 88 associate degrees were conferred in this landmark ceremony held on Sunday, June 1, 1969, in the gymnasium. Dr. George A. Spiva, Jr., son of the late George A. Spiva, Sr., one of the college's principal benefactors, delivered the keynote address. The first recipient of a four-year degree, by virtue of heading the alphabetical list, was Barbara Blackford, who received a bachelor of arts degree in Sociology.

In this fall of 1965 photograph, Horace Shapley, an evening student, is shown cutting a cake on the occasion of his eightieth birthday. Looking on from the left are: Dr. Lloyd L. Dryer, two unidentified students, Dean James K. Maupin, and Harry C. Gockel. Shapley, a farmer from near Lamar, entered JJC in 1961, after his wife died, because, he said, "I made up my mind that I was not going to spend the winter alone . . . with the cats, dogs, and mice, watching television." He graduated in 1969, at the at the age of eighty-three, with an associate of arts degree in Sociology, the oldest person ever to graduate from Southern. His twin brother, Harlow, was a world-famous Harvard astronomer. Both men are now dead.

young people, especially females, that college training was necessary for their future careers, and the returning of older people to college for the same reason, kept MSSC growing.

The move to a senior college status in the 1967–1968 school year did not immediately result in a class of graduating seniors. The 1968 commencement was actually the last such ceremony as a junior college. Though Southern had been offering upper-division classes for one year, no student yet qualified for a baccalaureate degree. Only eighty-two received their degrees, the smallest graduating class since 1954. The drop was due to many students deciding to bypass the associate and stay on for a four-year bachelor's degree. Held on Sunday, June 2, in the just completed Physical Education Building, this last graduating ceremony of the junior college was also the first to be held on the new campus.

May 1969 marked completion of MSC's first fourth-year class and the occasion for the first commencement in which baccalaureate degrees were issued. Though four-year commencement exercises were a regular yearly event from 1969 on, there were changes. Initially, exercises were also held at the end of the summer sessions and fall semesters, but these were soon dropped in favor of a once-a-year ceremony. In 1973 the Board of Regents/Trustees approved a proposal to establish a new senior tradition of engraving the names of the graduates on the campus sidewalks, starting with the 1969 class, but this resolution was never carried out.

The addition of third and fourth year classes sparked sweeping changes in the administration. In August 1967, Edward Sterl Phinney became dean of the college, replacing Fred Cinotto. With a background as an academic dean, he had the experience necessary to implement and coordinate the new four-year curriculum starting that fall. Upon Phinney's death in August 1973, Floyd E. Belk replaced him as acting dean. Belk, who had advanced through the ranks as a teacher and administrator in the Joplin public schools and Missouri Southern College, continued Phinney's program, working to assure that high academic standards were maintained and that a strong general education curriculum was preserved at a time when such basic education programs were tending to fragment into uncoordinated "cafeteria" type choices, often lacking in intellectual enrichment. New teachers, being hired, were carefully screened to make sure that their academic credentials were strong and that they were effective classroom teachers.

Administrative titles were also changed in a move to provide more clarity. In April 1974, Floyd Belk assumed the new title of vice president of Academic Affairs and Paul R. Shipman became vice president for Business Affairs. At the same time, division heads had their titles elevated from that of chairman or associate dean to that of dean. These changes more clearly identified the levels of administration and eliminated confusion in the use of the title of dean.

Changes in the academic divisions of the college in the early 1970s, ran deeper than the adoption of new titles. The initial structure, dating from 1966, provided for six divisions. Though minor changes were made in the next few years, those divisions remained essentially intact until the 1970–1971 school year when Humanities and Fine Arts, Science and Mathematics, and Social Science were combined into a new Division of Arts and Sciences under the initial chairmanship of Dr. Harold Cooper. This move reduced the excess of divisions to four while many of the duties in the merged divisions were shifted to department heads.

New programs were continually being developed to better serve student

New programs were continually being developed to better serve student needs. In 1974 a new Division of Continuing Education was established with David C. Bingman, a biology teacher, becoming its director. This program aimed to serve a broader spectrum of educational needs than could be met by the regular on-campus academic courses. A series of noncredit courses and workshops were set up to serve an adult population and regular credit courses were offered off-campus in neighboring towns to give the college a broader geographical reach. Also, an "over 60s" program was set up under which senior citizens could attend regular classes, tuition free, if room was available.

As JCJC neared the transition to a four-year college, the size of the faculty grew along with the increased student population. The full-time teaching staff had grown slowly over the prior decade and stood at thirty-one for the 1963–1964 school year. Two years later the figure had increased to forty-one.

The teaching staff was also in a state of transition at this time. With the passing years, the junior college teaching staff had become more locally oriented in background. The earlier faculty had been quite cosmopolitan, with widespread geographical backgrounds and many with master's degrees from large universities. This slowly changed in the 1950s. Many new teachers came from the Joplin High School. Often they had been reared within a fifty-mile radius of Joplin and an increasing number had gained their master's degrees at Kansas State College in nearby Pittsburg. In the 1965–1966 school year, nine of the faculty had master's from the Pittsburg institution and five of these had also received their baccalaureate degrees from there. This did not reflect a decline in the quality of the teaching staff. Many of these Pittsburg graduates were fine teachers, but it did give a more local flavor to instruction. Also, a seemingly inevitable part of this growing local orientation was that former JJC students began to come back as faculty. By the 1965–1966 school year, there were eight of these.

Another step in preparing for the four-year college involved the establishment of professional rank for the faculty effective with the 1966–1967 school year. Prior to this time, all the teaching staff had been ranked as instructors and were paid on a scale dependent on seniority and education. The new system, which aimed at encouraging faculty to get their doctorates, established the ranks of instructor, assistant professor, associate professor, and professor. Advancement from one rank to another was dependent on several factors. The initial salary schedule ranged from $6,000 for an entry-level instructor with a master's degree to $12,500 for a full professor at the top of the scale. Compulsory retirement was set at age sixty-five, but individual teacher contracts could be extended on a year-to-year basis at the discretion of the president.

The implementation of the four-year program and the burgeoning student population brought about the hiring of new faculty on a scale never before experienced by the college. The addition of the junior and senior years in 1967 and 1968 touched off the most spectacular growth. The full-time teaching

Edward Sterl Phinney became dean of the college in August 1967. Phinney's chief responsibility was to implement the new senior college academic program getting underway that fall. In his six-year tenure, he worked to build a well-rounded academic program, and with the support of a strong faculty, he succeeded in preserving the college's reputation for excellent academics.

Dr. Phinney came to MSC from Taylor University where he had held administrative posts for twelve years; he died in August 1973 at the age of sixty-one. The Phinney Recital Hall, a part of the Fine Arts complex, honors his memory.

Floyd E. Belk, appears in this photograph as vice president of Academic Affairs, a position he held from 1974 to 1990. Belk worked to maintain the college's tradition of having a strong academic program and was particularly active in retaining and improving MSSC's core curriculum. In 1990 he was one of three honored nationally by the American Association of State Colleges and Universities for lifetime contributions to academic programs. In that same year, Belk, a JJC graduate, received the Outstanding Alumnus Award.

After serving on the staff of the Joplin public schools for 14 years, he completed his doctorate in education at Oklahoma State University in 1966, and began his 24-year career at MSSC. He retired in 1990.

staff rose to 96 in the fall of 1967 and to 124 the following fall. Vigorous growth continued until the total reached 145 in the fall of 1971. After that the rate of increase slowed as the student population stabilized and the new programs were fully implemented.

A fear that MSC might not be able to fill all of these new positions with qualified personnel proved unfounded as the tight supply of teachers, caused by the expansion of colleges nationally, began to ease. The North Central Association accrediting team had been insistent that MSC hire faculty with doctor's degrees wherever possible. By the 1971–1972 school year, some 30 percent of the staff had doctorates and another 12 percent were nearing completion of their degrees.

Though the influx of new teachers gave a more cosmopolitan cast to the faculty, it also became more formal in organization, and less close-knit as a social group. But in many ways it remained the same. There were still a sizeable number of veteran teachers from the junior college who acted as a stabilizing element and who tended to import on the newer teachers their concern for quality teaching and close personal contact with the students. In the fall of 1967, five teachers remained on the staff who dated back to the 1930s: Martha McCormick, 1937; Lillian Baker Spangler, 1938; Arthur Boles, 1938; Harry C. Gockel, 1939; and Dorothy Stone, 1939. In a few more years they would all be retired. The Board of Regents/Trustees, in 1973, dropped the prohibition against spouses of faculty being employed by the college, but they were required to remain in different departments. In the fall of 1969, the old junior college Faculty Organization was replaced with a formal Faculty Senate consisting of twenty-five members and an Academic Policies Committee was set up to give the faculty a voice in the merit of proposed new academic programs.

The implementation of an upper-division program in the years 1967–1968 and 1968–1969 entailed the addition of a large number of new courses and a whole structure of baccalaureate degrees that had not been offered before. Bachelor of arts degrees were initially catalogued in the major areas of English, History, Music, Political Science, and Speech and Drama. Bachelor of science degrees were available in Biology, Chemistry, Business Administration, and Mathematics. Bachelor of science in education degrees were available with certification in most of the major academic areas, plus Elementary Education. A stream of additions and changes followed after this with baccalaureate degrees being added in Psychology, Sociology, Environmental Health, and General Studies. In 1975 the Speech and Drama Department was split, with the former becoming a part of the Language and Literature Department while the latter (under its new name of theatre) moved to the Fine Arts Department.

A survey of the first five years of the baccalaureate program, 1969–1973 inclusive, show that 1,524 students graduated with majors in the following percentages: Education, 51; Humanities, 18; Business Administration, 17; and Natural Sciences, 14. Not surprisingly, Southern was regarded as primarily a teacher training institution for the public schools in its early years. When young people thought of seeking higher education many looked to a major that would prepare them for a specific occupational field. Teaching seemed to

fill this need. Jobs were local and, as the post–World War II "baby boom" generation flowed through the public schools, such positions were usually available. In the early 1970s the teacher market began to tighten and students tended to turn to another job-oriented academic area that offered more immediate opportunity; namely, Business. By the 1973–1974 school year some 29.5 percent of the student body were majoring in the Business Administration areas, and in a few more years it emerged as the college's principal division in terms of majors and credit hours generated.

Clearly Education was the most dynamic of the college's new divisions as well as being the largest. Charles F. Niess, chairman of the division, knit together an able faculty team and organized an advanced program. The North Central Association accrediting team in 1971 found the program to be "vigorous and innovative." Accreditation by the National Council for Accreditation of Teacher Education (NCATE) posed the most formidable challenge, but Southern's program, in 1974, gained acceptance for a full ten years. The examiners lauded the program for the way in which it had been shaped to meet the needs of area public schools. But even before this, reports filtering back from public schools administrators commented on how well trained the beginning MSC teachers were.

The addition of a senior college program tended to overshadow other curriculum changes because of its sheer massiveness, but there were important changes, particularly in the Vocational-Technical area, that were both extensive and significant. The Hall Report that sanctioned the addition of a senior college had also called for a strengthened junior college program. The Hall Report conclusions were further reinforced by a 1965 survey of the employment needs in the Jasper County Junior College service area by Harlan L. Haglar, a Michigan State University graduate student. Haglar spent three months in the area surveying seven hundred local firms. His study indicated a definite need for more people with college-level training in the technical fields of Business Administration, Automotive Repair, Industry, and Medicine. The need for a stronger junior college program was further accented when studies showed that approximately 25 percent of the student body was placed on academic probation or suspension at the end of the fall 1966–1967 semester as a result of their poor grades. Though near the national average, it convinced Dean Fred Cinotto, who always had a deep sympathy for underprivileged students, that the college needed a broader range of terminal, vocational-type programs to accommodate these students.

Even if the senior college had never materialized, Southern was faced with a complete restructuring of its Vocational-Technical program as a result of the college's severance from the Joplin R-8 Public School System in 1964. The Franklin Technical School programs belonged to the school district and only a few on-campus vocational courses, mostly in business and drafting, were left. To cope with the problem, President Billingsly set up a

New teachers for the 1965–1966 school year are shown grouped on the front steps of the newly renamed Missouri Southern College following their first faculty meeting. Front row, from left: John Eli, Larry Martin, Edra Cox, Bobbie Short, Barbara Frizzell, and Glen Smith. Back row: Wayne Habermehl, G. K. Renner, John Gilmore, Dale Bates, Ervin Dunham, Alfred H. Rogers, and Paul Shipman.

Of these thirteen, Larry Martin, Bobbie Short, G. K. Renner, and Paul Shipman continued at the college for many years as teachers or administrators. Only Larry Martin, a professor and head of the Mathematics Department, is still at MSSC; the other three are retired.

Edra Cox, a Business teacher, died tragically at her home, only six weeks into the fall semester, a victim of carbon monoxide poisoning resulting from a clogged flue. She was a sister of Missouri State Senator Noel Cox from Ozark.

(Top) Harrison M. Kash is shown in this 1967 photograph with veteran Chemistry instructor Eula Ratekin at the time of her retirement. Kash, a longtime Chemistry teacher, joined the JJC staff in 1958. As of 1992, he had the longest tenure of any of the current teaching faculty.

Ratekin came to JJC in 1942. One of the few new teachers hired during the war, she was laid off the next year and spent a year doing research for Eagle-Picher before returning to JJC. An impressive teacher and an enthusiastic and cultured person, Ratekin belonged to the National Audubon Society and was an avid bird watcher. She died in 1991 at the age of ninety-two.

(Bottom) Charles F. Niess, chairman (later dean) of the Division of Education, Psychology, and Physical Education was one of MSC's original division deans appointed in July 1966. Dr. Niess, who remained with Southern until 1978, is remembered for his vigorous role in setting up MSC's program for the training of public school teachers.

new Division of Semi-professional and Technical Education, later renamed the Division of Technology. James K. Maupin headed the new division. Dean Maupin pushed the new programs vigorously and advisory committees, consisting of area leaders in the various fields, were set up to determine the need and later to act in an oversight capacity to keep the programs up to date.

With the institution of the first senior college courses in 1967, MSC still offered a full range of associate of arts degree transfer programs, but these declined in popularity with bachelor's degrees being offered. The associate of science degrees became largely the province of the new Vocational-Technical programs and they grew rapidly in popularity, being offered largely in the Technology and Business fields.

Between 1966 and 1975 the new Division of Technology developed rapidly. Drafting and Design had been carried over from the junior college era, but new technical programs were added in Machine Work, Environmental Health and Radiology. A planned program in Cosmetology never succeeded and one in aviation never progressed beyond offering a five-credit hour basic course at a local flying school. The most noteworthy new programs were in Automotive Technology; Nursing; Data Processing and Computer Programming; Law Enforcement and Criminal Justice; Dental Hygiene and Dental Assistant; and Military Science.

The Mission Hills campus, while resplendent in its natural setting and its newness, initially had a centrifugal effect on the cohesion of both students and the faculty. Gone was the sense of community that once prevailed in the junior college where most activities were confined within four walls. The faculty, with common ties already loosened by their growing numbers, and now finding themselves isolated geographically in separate buildings on the roomy campus, tended to splinter into new groupings based on their academic areas. Students, too, rapidly lost much of their personal contact as they no longer daily rubbed elbows in the crowded hallways of the old building. Southern, always something of a commuter college, became even more so; with classes over, students tended to drive away in their cars. To the extent they did socialize, students related more to their majors than in the junior college where the curriculum was more generalized.

The Chart took cognizance of the growing apathy on the new campus and called for more activities and a change of attitude on the part of students. The sense of isolation was especially strong in the first two years. Student life was "dead after 4:00 P.M." There were no residence halls except for the temporary units for athletes. No adequate union existed; the cafeteria served this purpose. Examples of student apathy and lack of activities abounded. The traditional beginning of the school year mixer for the fall of 1967 was held on the college parking lot where students could dance free to the tunes of the "Pink Peach Mob." The Crossroads Ball of 1970 further accented student indifference. When *The Crossroads* could no longer afford to finance it, the Student Senate allocated $1,000 so this traditional formal dance could be continued. Though free, only about two hundred people showed up to dance and see the queen crowned.

The dreary emptiness of after-hours life on the campus slowly began to change. The College Union opened in May 1969 and the newly established College Union Board began to bring in more activities from 1970 on. The first residence halls opened in the fall of 1970 with 252 students living there. Other than a few athletes, this was the campus' first resident population. But the problem of apathy continued to plague the college and in 1973 the Student Senate formed an apathy committee to plan activities that would generate more campus social and cultural life.

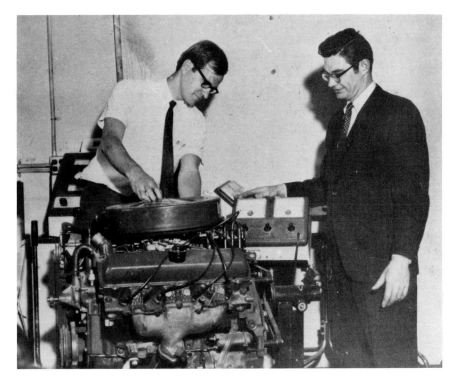

James K. Maupin appears in this 1967 photograph as dean of Semi-Professional Technical Education (later School of Technology). With a master's degree from Kansas State College, Pittsburg, Maupin came to JJC in 1955. He retired in 1992, rounding out thirty-seven years of service, a then unequaled tenure.

The only Biology instructor up to 1963, Maupin, though an excellent teacher, turned more to administrative work. He has left his most lasting mark in building the new School of Technology, virtually from the ground up, into a worthy complement of the other academic divisions.

(Top) Roger E. Adams (left) and Dwight E. Mason, Automotive Technology instructors, are shown in this 1970 photograph. Mason started the Automotive Technology program in the fall of 1966 and Adams joined him the next year. Mason left MSSC in 1975 for another position.

Auto Tech remained strong for several years, but began to decline in the 1980s as automobile manufacturers set up their own specialized training programs. MSSC's program was cancelled in 1987 after twenty-one years of operation and Adams, who has a doctorate in education, left to establish his own business.

(Bottom) The first teaching staff for the new Nursing program confer in this fall of 1966 photograph. From left are, Jenean Sears, Betty "Bessie" Vediz, and Juanita Hulen. Ms. Vediz set up the program, which began in the fall of 1966, and headed it until 1969. Ms. Hulen and Sears left the program after short tenures. Ms. Sears later completed her doctorate and became a professor of Nursing at the University of Kansas Medical Center.

The Nursing program grew out of a shortage of nurses that had been aggravated by the closure of St. John's Hospital School of Nursing a few years before. It, along with Automotive Technology, were the first technical programs set up by MSC and Nursing was a huge success from the beginning.

(Top) The newly constructed Kuhn Hall is shown here as it appeared in July 1969. Built primarily to house the Nursing program and the Health Clinic, it was named for Dr. J. R. Kuhn, Jr., a veteran Joplin medical doctor who promoted establishment of the nursing program. Dr. Kuhn long attended the pinning ceremonies, presenting each graduating nurse with a long-stemmed red rose.

(Bottom) This photograph shows the new Mills Anderson Police Academy after its completion in 1971. In 1977 it was more than doubled in size and housed not only law enforcement, but also the ROTC Program and the Campus Security Office.

The Law Enforcement Program, beginning in the fall of 1969, rapidly grew into one of the strongest of the college's technical areas. MSSC was the first college in southern Missouri to have such a program located on its campus.

Geographic isolation and spartan facilities were not the only factors generating a sense of apathy on campus. The Vietnam War provided another. That long war had begun to undermine academic achievement in the last year of the junior college as MSC experienced an influx of students who enrolled primarily to escape the draft and who were lacking in motivation. A more significant turning point came in 1968 when the Tet offensive in Vietnam and the assassination of Martin Luther King and Robert Kennedy alarmed many Americans and filled them with a sense of disillusionment. These events left many MSC students with a deep feeling of alienation. This sense of malaise led to demonstrations and violence on many college campuses, but in Southern students, who came largely from a conservative social background, it tended to generate apathy rather than militancy.

The years 1969 and 1970 were the time of greatest concern. College administrators remained anxious and feared the organization of demonstrations that might degenerate into violence, but nothing serious ever developed. Comments on the students' mood in that era tend to emphasize their apathy rather than their hostility. Only a few small discussion groups gathered from time to time, usually on the campus oval. The most serious disturbance came in October 1969 when a Vietnam moratorium rally, sponsored by a Committee to End the War in Vietnam, was held beneath a large oak tree on the campus oval. Several speakers delivered brief addresses. The crowd, consisting of an estimated 350 to 400 students, became more divisive with a group of Vietnam veterans congregating in front of the College Union to heckle the speakers, but there was no violence. A mathematics professor, newly hired that fall, spoke most forcefully against American involvement in Vietnam. Shortly after this, coming under heavy administrative disfavor, the math teacher resigned and took another teaching position in New Zealand.

Personnel and students at Missouri Southern were reminded of the vagaries of the weather when tornados hit the campus in 1971 and again in 1973. The 1971 storm struck on Wednesday, May 5, at approximately 7:00 P.M. while night classes were in session. The tornado narrowly missed the main campus buildings, but wrecked some nearby private property. Hardest hit was Anderson's Trailer Park one mile east of the campus on Newman Road. Several MSC students lived there and one, Rick Johnson, was killed by debris when he sought shelter in a nearby ditch. Several people were injured. On campus, damage to the buildings was slight though the glass in several cars was broken by the sudden drop in pressure. It had been a near disaster and steps were taken to install a new warning system on the College Union with double the volume. The old siren could not be heard clearly within the buildings.

The deadly 1973 storm struck at dawn on May 11. Fortunately few people were on the MSC campus at that hour, but three were killed and more than

Students are shown here on May 5, 1967, engaged in "Frontier Day" antics, one of the last student activities at the old downtown junior college. Followed by a day of "shooting up" the campus, participants retreated to McClelland Park for a picnic followed by a dance that evening on the First National Bank parking lot. Annual "Spring Fling" activities such as this were a tradition that carried over to the new Mission Hills campus.

one hundred injured elsewhere. On campus no buildings suffered heavy damage, but many trees were uprooted and debris strewn across the campus.

The establishment of a four-year college touched off an intense period of restructuring student organizations and the formation of new ones. Most interesting was the reappearance of Greek social fraternities and sororities. None had survived the junior college era, but such organizations seemed a traditional part of four-year college culture. When a survey of the student body indicated an interest in such clubs, new administrative rules, aimed at discouraging the formation of ill-considered student organizations, were drawn up that placed a two-year moratorium on the formation of nationally affiliated Greek societies, but allowed local units to form immediately.

Much activity was also evident in other areas of student interest. Among the academic clubs only the College Players, Mathematics Club, Modern Language Club, and Student National Education Association maintained their long-established identities. Few honorary scholastic societies had ever existed in the junior college era and only the strongest of these, Phi Theta Kappa, a national arts and science affiliate, continued to function. With the establishment of a four-year curriculum, new honorary societies began to form in the various academic areas. Among the miscellaneous general and service organizations that had existed from time to time, only the Cheerleaders, Circle "K," Young Democrats, and Young Republicans moved intact into the four-year college era, but they were soon joined by a number of new clubs, some of which were of a transitory nature. Few religious societies had ever formed among junior college students, and none existed at the time of the transition, but church affiliates moved quickly to form new clubs to serve the four-year student population.

Student government and service organizations were modified to better meet the needs of a four-year college. Student government was changed to accommodate the new junior and senior classes without any fundamental restructuring. The old Assembly Committee and the Student Cabinet, which had played separate roles in arranging extracurricular cultural and social activities, were replaced with a new College Union Board. The new CUB, consisting of ten student and faculty members, under the chairmanship, initially, of the College Union director, used a portion of student fees to bring in films, lectures, and entertainment and to plan and direct social activities such as the Crossroads Ball. The CUB, with its more professional direction and expanded funding, helped enrich the cultural and social life of the student body.

The advent of the four-year college brought about greatly expanded programs of departmentally sponsored activities for public school students. These programs aimed to stimulate the interest of youngsters in academics and to acquaint them with the facilities of the college through activities consisting of contests, entertainment, and games. Among these were forensic tournaments, Children's Theatre, Math League competitions, mock United Nations Security Council sessions,

Julia Hudson is shown here being crowned 1974 Crossroads *Queen by Bruce Lais, chairman of the College Union Board. A candidate of Kappa Alpha and elected by a student body vote, Hudson was the last queen to be recognized in the pages of the* Crossroads. *The Crossroads Ball, a venerable institution of the junior college, dating from 1939, quickly lost its appeal in the more diverse social setting of the four-year college. It was dropped after 1978.*

History Conference contests, Foreign Language Field Days, music festivals, and business seminars.

The Alumni Association strengthened its organization as MSC turned into a baccalaureate degree granting institution. Starting in 1968 annual dues were established as a requirement for active membership. The fees were used to fund two annual scholarships, publish a quarterly newsletter, and to contribute funds for the betterment of the college. Starting in 1971, the association began giving Outstanding Alumnus Awards to alumni who gained recognition in their professions. The first award went to Dennis Weaver. The traditional Homecoming social activities were continued.

The Chart and *Crossroads* continued to be the school's principal publications as it moved into the senior college era, but both publications went through a transitional period between 1967 and 1975 in which serious problems had to be resolved.

In 1967, Cleetis Headlee ended her long tenure as adviser to *The Chart* when, on her recommendation, journalism was expanded into a full minor. Eugene J. Murray headed the new program and served as adviser to *The Chart* until 1972.

Under Murray's guidance, *The Chart* underwent significant changes in character. Up to this time, it had been a small institutional-type publication of high quality but with coverage concentrated almost exclusively on school-related events. Starting in the fall of 1970, *The Chart* switched to a newsprint format; also it expanded in size and used many more photographs. Along with this expansion, a deterioration in the quality of *The Chart* soon became evident, though not all issues were bad. The reproduction of photographs was often poor, but, more importantly, the journalistic quality declined. Typographical errors became bothersome. *The Chart* seemed less focused and featured considerable editorializing. Some of the editorials were quite penetrating and mildly reflected the student militancy of the Vietnam era while others dwelt on the apathy of the MSC student body. On the other hand, the staff sometimes failed to give adequate coverage to routine campus events.

In the fall of 1972, Richard Massa became teacher of journalism and adviser to *The Chart*. He found serious problems. The equipment was primitive,

The new Lion Pride Marching Band is shown performing in the Maple Leaf Festival parade at Carthage in the fall of 1968 fresh from its first appearance at the MSC-Arkansas State football game. The seventy-member band is being led by drum major Tom Black assisted by twirlers Diane Doran, Francis Benton, Gloria Bland, Linda Jackson, Jacque Moody, and Anita Hawkins. Music professors Delbert Johnson and William Taylor directed it.

Southern had been without a marching band since the early years of the junior college and its absence was seen as hurting the college's image, but the cost of the program had held up its implementation.

Officers of the Mathematics Club are shown in this photograph taken during the 1975–1976 school year. From left: Robert Dampier, vice president; Sharon McBride, historian; Cynthia Carter, president; and Sam Miller, secretary-treasurer.

After graduating from MSSC in 1976, Cynthia Carter, from Carthage, earned her doctorate at Cornell University and later became an associate professor at the University of Alabama, Birmingham. Along with Floyd E. Belk, Cynthia (Carter) Haddock received MSSC's Outstanding Alumnus Award for 1990.

Conferring in this 1973 photograph are officers of the Student National Education Association. From left: Dr. Lloyd Dryer, adviser; Kent Estes, past vice president of the Missouri SNEA; Patsy Younker, historian; Connie Billingsly, president; Debbie Shanks, secretary; and Marsha Klein, vice president.

Connie Billingsly, daughter of the late MSSC president Leon C. Billingsly, was SNEA Homecoming Queen candidate in 1972. An elementary education major, Connie (Billingsly) Goodwin later became principal of the intermediate school in the Carl Junction public school system.

Members of the new Council on International Relations and United Nations Affairs (CIRUNA), organized during the 1967–1968 school year, appear in this photograph. From left, front row: Leigh White and Susan Kelley. Back row: Jack Newman, Terry Helton, Ramona Christman, Douglas Lawson, and Joe Schoeberl. Sponsored by Annetta St. Clair, CIRUNA grew out of the old Collegiate Council for the United Nations (CCUN). Like the CCUN, CIRUNA was concerned primarily with training a team to participate in the annual Midwest Model United Nations convention in St. Louis.

Schoeberl, who completed a doctor of jurisprudence degree at the University of Missouri, Columbia, later became prosecuting attorney of McDonald County.

Officers of the Society for Advancement of Management (SAM) appear in this 1973 photograph. From left are: Larry Crowder, treasurer; Jerry Black, president; and Kreta Cable, secretary.

Kreta (Cable) Gladden, sponsored by SAM, became the 1972 Homecoming Queen. A 1973 MSSC graduate, she later earned a doctorate in education from the University of Arkansas. Gladden is currently director of Alumni Affairs at Southern.

Members of the Afro-American Society (AAS) gathered for this casual group photograph during the 1975–1976 school year. From left, first row: Aaron Johnson, Bill Hayles, Melvin Wilson, Michel Bauer, and Randy Johnson. Back row: Damon Clines, Robert Burks, Willie Williams, Kenric Conway, Larry Barnes, John Watson, Gordon David, and Dr. Henry Morgan, sponsor. Barnes, Conway, and Williams were outstanding football players.

Organized in 1970, the Afro-American Society remained active through that decade, but ceased to function after 1980.

College Republican officers, from left, Stephen Holt, president; Douglas Endicott, vice president; and David Holz, parliamentarian, seem pleased with "Hiram," their elephant mascot, during the Missouri College Republican meeting which MSSC members hosted in 1973.

Founded in 1958, the College Republicans is one of the college's oldest service clubs. In 1970, the organization changed its name from Young Republicans to that of College Republicans.

During the 1988 and 1992 political campaigns, the College Republicans sponsored visits by presidential candidate George Bush to the MSSC campus and, in the former year, by vice presidential aspirant Daniel Quayle.

This donkey mascot seems pleased to pose with a group of the MSSC Young Democrats in 1970. From left are: Bill Parker, William Murray, Penny Shaw, Joe Leonard, Ellen Roughton, Charlotte Duke, and Herbert Gailey, president.

Dating from 1958, the Young Democrats is one of the oldest service organizations on campus. A memorable event for them came with Democratic presidential candidate John F. Kennedy's visit to the Joplin airport in October 1960. The club presented him with a bouquet of gold mums.

Members of Delta Phi Delta pose on the steps near the Mansion in this 1971 photograph. Present are, front row, from left: Dana Dooley; Penny Patterson; Jo Spille; Dixi Gossett; Donna Bement; and Connie Travis. Back row: Charlotte Duke; Audrey Gray; Jane Dasbach; Pam Perkins; Susan Barnett; Debbie Pottero; Mary Lou Sayers; Christi Nichols, president; Connie Duke; Toni Taylor; Frances Rose; Cathy Martin; Kristen Bailey; and Mrs. Davis, sponsor.

Founded during the 1968–1969 school year, Delta Phi Delta became the first Greek sorority to be organized on the four-year college campus. Beta Sigma Chi followed it a few months later and in 1973 Lambda Beta Phi came into existence. DPD received a national Zeta Tau Alpha charter in 1974 and in 1992 was one of the two sororities still on campus. Greek organizations, while they have had a continuous record on campus since 1968, have never been strong.

So popular was the Mu Sigma Gamma fraternity that some members had to pose in the tree to get in this 1970 group photograph. Shown are from left, in tree: John Sykes; Leonard Waggoner; Leon Royer, president; Bob Wilson; and Tom Jensen. Middle row: Bob Mayberry; Paul Poynor; Tom Laster; Tom Wicks; Ron Mitchell; Lea Kaffenberger; Tom Fenton; David Raper; Danny Burns; Rod St. Clair; and Jim Christiansen. Bottom row: Jim Kingore; Jim Webb; Chuck Gibson; Rick Bennet; Gary Willard; Dennis Ditto; Chris Baker; Mike Booe; Wayne Cox; and Jim Adams.

Founded during the 1968–1969 school year, Mu Sigma Gamma was the first Greek fraternity formed on the four-year college campus and was followed a few months later by Pi Beta Lambda. MSG affiliated nationally with Sigma Nu in 1973 and has continued under that name.

Three of MSC's four first junior class officers, chosen in a September 1967 election, are shown strolling across campus. Pictured are Gary Davis, vice president; Leigh White, secretary; and Ron Richard, president. Senior class officers were added the next year to round out the full complement for a four-year college. Class officers, a part of the college since its founding in 1937, were dropped in 1982 as being superfluous.

Ron Richard later became a prominent Joplin businessman and, more recently, a member of the City Council.

Richard Massa, shown here, joined the MSSC staff in 1972 as an Associate Professor of Journalism and adviser to The Chart. With bachelor's and master's degrees in Journalism from the University of Missouri, Columbia, he came to Southern with a rich background of experience.

Massa rescued The Chart from the doldrums it had slipped into and built it into a leading small-college newspaper that received many awards. Massa then turned to establishing a new Department of Communications and became its head in 1980. It is one of the fastest growing academic areas on campus.

Donna Lonchar, 1974–1975 editor of The Chart is shown laboring to meet a publication deadline. Under Lonchar's editorship, The Chart reached new heights of journalism as it moved into investigative reporting. In 1985, as wire editor of the Santa Ana, California Register, Lonchar was a member of the staff that won a Pulitzer Prize for its spot news photography of the Olympics.

In a memorable example of investigative reporting two Chart reporters' 1979 exposé of a local massage parlor's operations attracted widespread attention and resulted in one of the reporters having the brake lines on her car cut in retaliation.

This two-room guesthouse, immediately west of the Mission Hills mansion, became The Chart's home from 1967 to 1975 when it moved to Hearnes Hall. Atop the post in the foreground is one of the lanterns which came to symbolize the college.

The two drama instructors, Duane Hunt (left) and Milton Brietzke stand outside the newly converted Barn Theatre in October 1967. A change of plans that eliminated a proposed theatre for the new campus, caused Brietzke to undertake converting the old barn, adjacent to the silo, into a temporary theatre. Limited to a budget of $30,000, most of the work had to be done by a few college employees, including Hunt and Brietzke. The ground floor was used for auxiliary services while the stage and auditorium were located in the hayloft. With a stage only twenty feet wide by eighteen feet deep and a seating capacity of 144, the new Barn Theatre provided a large measure of intimacy, but its limitations taxed the ingenuity of those putting on the plays. Though considered temporary, the Barn Theatre was "home" to the Drama Department for the next nine years.

consisting mostly of typewriters and miscellaneous secretarial items. It would take a few years to resolve the equipment problem. A more immediate concern was the staff, as two or three dedicated staff members were doing most of the work and deadlines were being missed. Professor Massa spent most of his first year correcting the staff problems. In his second year *The Chart* showed much improvement, running a twelve-page format with increased national coverage and more human-interest stories. An aggressive staff of reporters also picked up significant campus developments. By 1975, *The Chart* was a markedly improved newspaper over what it had been at the beginning of the decade and it won the Missouri Newspaper Association's "Best in Class" award, the highest such award *The Chart* had ever received.

In the transition period 1967–1975, the *Crossroads* suffered from many of the same problems that plagued *The Chart*. Trouble started with the 1967 issue. Prior to that, all students paid for the yearbook as part of their activities fee, but at this time the compulsory charge was dropped and students had the option of ordering the publication for five dollars. Sales dropped, compounded not only by the cost, but also by the growing apathy on campus and the poor quality of the yearbooks. When only six hundred students purchased the 1971 *Crossroads* the Board of Trustees voted, "with regret," to drop the yearbook, but stipulated that it could be revived if students showed enough interest. Thus, after thirty years of continuous publication, the *Crossroads* was cancelled, but it proved only temporary. With over eight hundred orders in hand, publication was resumed for the 1973 issue.

Significant departmental publications began to appear with the advent of

The Barn Theatre opened on October 20, 1967, with a two-day performance of Anna Karenina. *The cast included faculty as well as students. Pictured in this scene from the play are, from left: Trij Brietzke, Milton Brietzke, Tim Elliott, Toni Zbranek, Duane Hunt, Stanley Graham, and Gwen Hunt. Trij Brietzke and Duane Hunt adapted* Anna Karenina, *a Leo Tolstoy novel, for the performance; Milton Brietzke directed it.*

the four-year college. One of the most important of these was the *Winged Lion*, introduced in the spring of 1972. A joint product of the English and Art departments, it aimed to provide an outlet for the creative talents of students in those fields. Initial advisers were Joseph Lambert and Henry C. Morgan in the English field and Nathaniel Cole from the Art Department. Once established, the *Winged Lion* proved to be an enduring publication that has continued through the years.

The Drama Department found itself as a stepchild of MSC's move to the new campus in the fall of 1967. While other academic departments enjoyed quarters in new buildings, drama found itself presenting plays in a converted barn. Though the Barn Theatre fell short of providing the comfortable accommodations the department had enjoyed in the old building, it did lend a certain rustic atmosphere and intimacy to the department's presentations. Milton Brietzke, drama instructor at this time, saw the crowded quarters for the audience and players as a challenge and an opportunity to develop more of an appreciation of theatre as an art form.

In this period, the Drama Department introduced Children's Theatre, which proved to be one of its most popular innovations. At first the performers toured area schools presenting such spectacles as *Reluctant Dragon* to fascinated youngsters. Later, with the completion of a spacious auditorium, children were bussed in for most of the two or three children's plays presented each year.

The Drama Department received due recognition of the excellence of its work when it was selected as one of seven colleges that would tour overseas military bases during August 1968 to entertain service personnel.

Drama was selected for this honor largely on the basis of its outstanding reputation, but immediately because of its brilliant presentation of *Finian's Rainbow* in the spring of 1967. The MSC troupe took this play on a tour of the Northeast Command, which included Newfoundland, Labrador, Greenland, and Iceland.

The move to a four-year college curriculum brought about changes as fundamental in Missouri Southern's athletic program as it did in the academic area. Though the academic areas started offering upper division courses in the fall of 1967, the athletic teams remained in junior college competition. The college retained its membership in the National Junior College Athletic Association (NJCAA), but affiliation with the regional Interstate Conference was terminated.

Actor Dennis Weaver and his wife, Gerry, are shown leaving the Spiva Art Center during their visit to Joplin on October 20–21, 1967.

Weaver, who came to Joplin to participate in the city's first Fall Festival of the Arts, was at the height of his career at this time.

While at MSC, Weaver spoke to the student body at a convocation, participated in dedication ceremonies for the Barn Theatre, and attended a performance of Anna Karenina.

Pictured is a scene from A Doll's House. *Directed by Gwen Hunt, it was one of the major productions presented at the Barn Theatre during the 1967–1968 season. Appearing from the left are: Mike Braeckel, Toni Zbranek, and Paul Shanahan.*

Zbranek played the leading role of Nora in this classic 1879 play by Henrik Ibsen. She graduated from MSSC in 1970, and earned her doctorate in drama at the University of California, Los Angeles. Toni (Zbranek) Smolen later taught drama at California State University, Fullerton.

Tim Elliott and Trinket Plumb are shown in a scene from Finian's Rainbow, *a musical comedy presented in the spring of 1967. This elaborate production, using a cast of forty drawn from the Drama and Music departments, was one of the plays Milton Brietzke was most proud of in his long career of teaching theatre at the junior college and MSSC. The impressive presentation won the Drama Department an invitation to tour military bases the next year, but a simplified version had to be developed for this purpose.*

The next year, MSC moved completely into four-year college sports competition, abandoning its venerable junior college rivals and terminating membership in the NJCAA. Athletics now joined the National Association of Intercollegiate Athletics (NAIA). Finding no enthusiastic welcome into any of the regional conferences, MSC remained an independent in the national organization until 1976.

The expanded athletics program brought about the formation of support organizations. In the spring of 1968, the Lionbackers Booster Club, consisting of local supporters of the college's athletic program, became fully organized and began holding annual banquets in which outstanding athletes of the year were honored. Four years later, Richard Humphrey, an MSC faculty member, sponsored establishment of the E. O. and Virginia Humphrey Award, in honor of his father, who was the first football coach at Joplin Junior College, and his mother.

With the move to the new campus in 1967, it was no longer convenient to house basketball and football players on athletic scholarships in the Connor Hotel and mobile dormitory units were set up near the Barn Theatre. The two units accommodated forty-six athletes.

The fortunes of the football team typified many of the problems faced by MSC's competitive sports in the period 1967–1976. Drawing on Coach Toman's legacy, the new mentor, Jim Johnson fielded a strong team, recruited nationally, and completed the season 8–1. Having climbed to a number four ranking in the NJCAA poll, Coach Johnson's charges hoped for an invitation to play in the Junior College Bowl game at Las Vegas, Nevada, but were turned down for the lack of a marching band and because of the distance involved. In spite of their strong football teams over the years, the junior college Lions never received a bid to play in a bowl game.

The 1968 season marked Southern's move into four-year football competition. A completely new schedule of opponents had to be worked out. Athletic Director Mike Bogard and Coach Johnson experienced a difficult time doing this and had to contact over 150 schools in order to fill out a ten-game schedule. Most colleges had few open dates and, even if they did, they hesitated to play newcomers like the Lions. Coach Johnson's difficulties were compounded by the fact he had a weak team, many of the players from his nationally ranked 1967 team having graduated or transferred to other colleges. The weakness became evident in the Lion's very first game as a four-year college, a contest with Northeast Oklahoma State College which they lost 0–45. Another of MSC's opponents that first year was Pittsburg State University. It marked the beginning of a lasting rivalry between the two neighboring schools. The Lions also lost this game 3–14.

The next two seasons 1969 and 1970, under a new coach, Reuben Berry, saw little change in the Lion's fortunes. James L. Frazier replaced Berry as coach in 1971 and began to build a strong team. Though the 1971

August in Missouri is never this cold. Members of the Finian's Rainbow *group pose in Greenland during their Northeast Command tour of military bases that also included Iceland, Labrador, and Newfoundland. The troupe only performed their abbreviated version of* Finian's Rainbow *five times because many bases did not have large enough stages, but they presented their auxiliary variety show twenty-eight times.*

Some thirteen students, plus instructors Milton Brietzke and Duane Hunt, took part in the actual tour that covered over sixteen hundred miles. The cast consisted of Lyle Ways, Pat Pickett, Stan Graham, Tim Elliott, and Judy Sage. Chorus members included Ray Basye, Steve Kluthe, Kathy Watkins, Joe Kingore, Judy Ardrey, Paul Shanahan, and Toni Zbranek plus Gloria Brittenham as accompanist. Pictured, from left, wearing coats, are Judy Sage, Ray Basye, Pat Pickett, Judy Ardrey, and Kathy Watkins. Partially obscured behind Ms. Ardrey is an unidentified officer.

season's 4–6 record seemed another disappointment, it marked MSC's best yet performance as a four-year college and heralded a brighter future for the Lions.

Coach Frazier faced the 1972 contests with a seasoned team containing twenty-one returning veterans and five junior college transfers. Well disciplined and trained to a keen competitive edge, the squad eventually finished the season 12–0, a record unmatched by any other team in Southern's football history. However, some of the games were very close. A hard-fought 7–0 victory over the University of Nevada at Las Vegas provided an example. The Las Vegas Rebels regularly played some of the powerhouse teams of the West Coast, but the tough Lion defense held them scoreless, stopping Rebel drives within the ten-yard line on three different occasions.

The Lion's string of victories mounted steadily. On November 11, Culver-Stockton College fell to the Joplin team, 63–12, in the last regularly scheduled game of the season. By this time the NAIA Division II poll rated the undefeated Lions number one nationally and only the playoff contests remained between them and a national championship.

The playoffs were scheduled to be held in Joplin's Junge Stadium. In the semifinals, on November 25, the Lion's defeated Doane College of Crete, Nebraska, on a cold, blustery Saturday afternoon. Southern's stalwarts dominated the game, slopping across the field, long since churned into a sea of mud, to an impressive 24–6 victory. On the following Saturday, the Lions faced Northwestern College of Orange City, Iowa, for the championship. Some four thousand fans packed Junge Stadium for the hard-fought, thrill-packed game. The talented Iowa team dominated most of the play, leading 7–0 at halftime. The Lions finally scored a touchdown in the third quarter but the Red Raiders gained another one early in the fourth, only to be countered by a second Southern trip to the end zone. Unfortunately, the Lions' two-point conversion failed and they were left trailing the Iowans 14–13, with little more than three minutes left to play. The Raiders, in possession of the ball, found themselves blocked by a staunch Southern defense and were forced to kick on the fourth down. The nervous Iowan's snap sailed too high, barely touching the punter's fingertips and bounding aimlessly into the Southern end zone where Lion tailbacker Sam Kealoha quickly covered it, thus giving the MSC team a touchdown. The two-point conversion was good and the Lions, by a score of 21–14, had won the NAIA Division II national football championship, the only time in the college's history that the gridders have gained a national championship.

The victory left Joplinites in a festive mood. Jubilant fans ranged through town honking horns in the aftermath, President Billingsly declared the following Monday a school holiday, and the Joplin City Coun-

The Thomas E. Taylor Performing Arts Center completed in late 1975, appears to the left in this photograph. Built at a cost of $2,935,241, the 53,358 square foot auditorium, seating 2,036, was much the largest and most expensive structure yet erected on the campus. The Theatre Department found the new auditorium a great improvement over the Barn Theatre, but its sheer size caused productions to lose some of their intimacy with the audiences.

cil passed a resolution praising the Lions for the honor they had brought to the area.

Accolades were showered on the deserving Lions in the aftermath of their 12–0 championship season. Coach Frazier commented: "You win the close ones on discipline and that's what made the difference." Later he remarked that luck was a factor. Both were accurate observations, but it was mostly the Lion's tight cohesiveness under stress that enabled them to win last-minute victories in the face of what seemed like certain defeat.

The 1972 championship marked a turning point in the image of Southern's football teams and in fact the college's whole program of varsity sports. Up to this time MSSC's athletic teams had gained little respect from other midwestern four-year colleges of a similar size, but the prestige of a national championship helped change this. From this point on a developing competence in sports complemented by the emerging quality of its new upper-division academic program tended to enhance MSC's reputation as a quality college.

The Lions never regained the brilliance of their 1972 performance. The 1973 squad disappointed Coach Frazier. Though potentially talented, graduation had exacted its usual toll of strong players and the team ended the season with a losing 4–6 record.

The 1974 and 1975 teams were strong, but not of championship caliber, establishing a 6–3 record in the former year and 7–3–1 in the latter. These teams were memorable for their strong individual performances with five receiving NAIA District 16 honors in 1974 and seven the next year, but as teams they were prone to lapses in their play. In a memorable 1975 game against Fort Hays State College, the Lions led 21–0 at halftime yet ended by losing the game 24–32. A dismayed Coach Frazier left the field speechless.

By 1975, the football Lions were a solidly established team in their own circle of competition. Since 1970 they had won thirty-five games, lost twenty-five, and tied in two. Though they still played as an independent, their overall winning record, and especially their championship performance in 1972, marked them as a power to be reckoned with in the NAIA.

In basketball, the other major area of intercollegiate competition, the Lions established a 1967–1968 to 1975–1976 record that compared favorably with that of football. Though they won no national championship, they did compete in the NAIA national basketball tournament twice. Overall, the Lions established a credible record of 140 wins and 114 losses in this nine-year period, but these statistics masked the fact that the basketball team had some

MSC's 1972 NAIA, Division II, national football championship team posed for this photograph. Present were from left, front row: Assistant Coach T. Calwhite, T. Starks, J. LaBlank, R. Barnes, Coach J. Frazier, S. Hamilton, K. Stracke, D. S. Evans, and Assistant Coach E. Wuch. Row two: M. Cole, J. Watson, T. Jackson, R. Harding, J. Varns, R. Fidler, B. Korner, and D. Pendergrass, and K. Howard. Row three: L. Williams, S. Ward, M. Mitchell, L. Hill, K. Anders, P. Sallee, D. Efird, R. Hall, and C. Henricks. Row four: M. Wilson, J. Balentine, M. Galbraith, J. Duda, J. Busalacki, N. Alkire, M. Mourglia, F. Gnerlich, and R. McReynolds. Back row: D. Guler, S. Kealoha, R. Hocker, J. Wolverton, L. Cameron, B. Busken, D. L. Evans, H. Moyer, and D. Dodd.

This was the only football team in the senior college's history to win a national championship, and many honors were bestowed on the Lions individually for their 12–0 winning season. Jim Frazier was named NAIA Coach of the Year nationally and for District 16. An NAIA All-American award went to Terron Jackson (First Team) and Honorable Mention honors were extended to Jack Duda, Barry Korner, Jack Varns, and Terry Starks. A number of players also received District 16 First Team and Second Team awards. Jackson and Ray Harding were later named to the MSSC Hall of Fame.

Posing near the practice field are the coaches who led the 1972 football squad to a national championship. From left: Tony Calwhite, Ed Wuch, Head Coach Jim Frazier, Jim Hoots, and Charles Wade.

Frazier came to MSSC in 1971 as head football coach. He stepped down from that position at the end of the 1985 season, but continued as athletic director, a post he had assumed in 1977. Frazier compiled a 97–52–5 record as head coach, one of the college's longest and most successful. One of only three of the college's coaches to earn national Coach of the Year honors while at Southern, Frazier also received the MSSC Hall of Fame honor.

Fred G. Hughes Stadium is shown as it appeared shortly after its opening. Seating 6,866, the stadium was innovative for its time in that it became the first college or university stadium in Missouri to have an artificial turf playing field. Hughes Stadium opened with a winning, 20–13, game against Emporia State College, September 6, 1975.

From 1937 through 1974, the football Lions relied primarily on Junge Stadium, a sports facility of the Joplin public schools. While Junge was a substantial stadium, it came to be overused and near the end of a rainy season wits jokingly referred to it as the "Joplin hog wallow."

of the strongest players in its history though it often lacked strength in depth. Frank Davis coached the Lions in the first seven of this nine-year period. R. C. Shipley, replaced him for the 1974–1975 and 1975–1976 seasons.

Davis' first year, 1967–1968, corresponded with MSC's last year in junior college competition. No longer in a conference, the Lions' played a few of their traditional rivals but mostly an odd assortment of new comers including the Metropolitan Junior College of Kansas City; Crowder College; and the School of the Ozarks. The Lions ended the year 9–18, but after the 1966–1967 disaster coach Davis had had to build essentially a new team. As in football, he recruited widely, drawing heavily on Kansas City, St. Louis, and Tulsa, but also casting a national net.

The year 1968–1969 marked MSC's entrance into four-year college basketball competition. Other then the University of Missouri, St. Louis, and Washington University, Southern played an assortment of small colleges located in Missouri, Kansas, Oklahoma, and Arkansas. The Lions gained a 16–16 season, a much better showing than the previous year in spite of the stiffer senior college competition.

In the next four years, the Lions, with seasoned teams, emerged as strong contenders in NAIA District 16 competition. The 1969–1970 and 1970–1971 teams won second place in the District 16 playoffs at the end of the seasons and mentor Davis was named Coach of the Year for the former year. In the next two years, the Lions reached new heights. In both seasons, the team won the playoffs thus capturing the NACA Division 16 championships for the first time in the college's history and advancing into the NAIA National Tournament in Kansas City; there they lost in the early rounds of both tournaments.

After experiencing four strong years, the Lions went into a slump and suffered three consecutive losing seasons. Coach Davis resigned at the end of the 1973–1974 year and R. C. Shipley, assistant football coach since 1969, replaced him, but the Lions showed little improvement in the next two years.

Looking back on the 1967–1968 to 1975–1976 period, the basketball Lions had closed out their junior college years with a dismal season in 1967–1968, but in the following seven years, as a four-year college, they had established a respectable record. Few college teams can be consistently good over a period of years, but the Lions had placed first or second in District 16 competition for four of the seven years and played in the national tournament twice.

Soccer was the most original of the sports that Missouri Southern moved into in the early 1970s. Little known at an earlier time in the United States, it was slowly emerging in these years as a competitive sport in the public schools and in colleges and universities with low budgets. Credit for introducing the sport at Southern belongs to Harold W. Bodon, then an assistant professor of French and German. Bodon, a native of Germany, grew up with the game and had coached high school teams in California.

Harvey Derrick, Southern's 1974–1977 place kicker specialist is shown in action. Derrick's records for 1975, his most outstanding year, include the most field goals made in one season, 13; the longest field goal kicked, 57 yards; and the most points scored by kicking in one season, 64. These records have never been broken. Many honors were bestowed on Derrick and in 1992 he was named to MSSC's Silver Anniversary Commemorative Football Team.

A notable example of the nontraditional student, Derrick was known as the "old man" of the football squad. He reached his twenty-ninth birthday during the 1975 season, was married, had two children and had already followed a varied career.

Bodon perceived soccer not only as an intriguing sport but also as a game that would give young men who had been outstanding athletes in high school, but who lacked the physical size to be successful in college basketball or football, a chance to compete. Unfortunately few had played soccer or even seen a game, but with patient coaching and some experience they could become good players.

Bodon's next step was to turn soccer into an organized MSSC sport. In the spring of 1972 he established intramural teams to compete on campus. The response was such—some fifty students volunteered—that he entered a team into intercollegiate competition that fall. Funds were a serious problem. The Student Senate granted $600 to help defray travel costs and other expenses, but the Athletic Department helped very little. Bodon entered competition with nineteen players, almost all of whom were novices. The teams that were played included Rockhurst College, Forest Park College, Lindenwood College, Oral Roberts University, and Northeast Oklahoma A & M. The season ended 1–9–3 for the budding soccer Lions, not a depressing outcome for an amateur team seriously lacking in experience.

In the next three years, the Lions emerged as a mature soccer team. Returning lettermen added stability to the squad and the addition of soccer programs in local high schools made it easier to recruit experienced players. The 1973 team had a 5–8–3 season, but in the next two years the Lions swung from being a losing team to being winners with an overall record of 13–4–3 in 1974 and 14–2 the next year. Coach Bodon organized an MSSC Soccer Tournament in 1974 and the Lions won first place in it both that year and in 1975.

Coach Bodon's soccer Lions had come far in their first four years of play and achieved a measure of distinction in NAIA District 16 play, but the MSSC Athletic Department still relegated the team to the status of a club rather than a full-fledged varsity sport. Coach Bodon conducted his burdensome soccer duties as a service activity in addition to his full load as a foreign language professor. Funding continued to be a problem, and it stemmed partially from the fact that development of the soccer program coincided with that of women's athletics, thus saddling athletics with huge additional costs.

Baseball, along with women's sports and soccer, was another of the new athletic areas that the college moved into as a four-year institution. Under the leadership of Coach Edward W. Wuch, the Lions entered their first year of intercollegiate baseball competition in 1972. The young, inexperienced team ended the season with a credible 11–13 record. The next year, with more experience, the Lions broke even with a 13–13 performance. In 1974, Coach Wuch's careful recruitment program began to bear fruit as the team swept to a 33–19 record. The following year, with seven returning starters, the baseball Lions emerged as top contenders in District 16 competition. Their 33–15 record earned them a berth in the playoffs, but the team fell short of the District 16 championship. Overall Coach Wuch's team had made an impressive start for MSSC baseball.

The minor sports, track, golf, and tennis, made the transition to four-year competition without serious problems. Golf, under Coach Douglas Landrith's guidance remained the most successful of the minor sports as it had been for several years. In the spring of 1968, Landrith's linksmen, competing for the final time in the state junior college tournament at Lexington, won the state championship for the eighth time in a ten-year span. At the same meet, the much neglected tennis squad won the doubles championship. Coach Landrith, in 1970, established an MSC Invitational Golf Tournament, later known as the Crossroads of America Golf Classic. Played each spring, these tourna-

Fred Hatfield, a transfer student from Crowder College, is shown making one of his spectacular jump shots during the 1969–1970 season. A strong rebounder, Hatfield is best remembered as a field-goal artist. His percentage of successful field goal attempts, .615 for the 1969–1970 season and .588 for his two-year career, have never been exceeded. Many honors were bestowed on Hatfield and in 1993, he was named to MSSC's Silver Anniversary Commemorative Basketball Team.

ments attracted participation by as many as thirty important midwestern colleges and universities.

The track team in 1973, after several lean years, experienced one of its most successful seasons under coach Mike Bogard. Twelve new school records were established with Ken Jones setting three and Kerry Anders two.

The upgrading of selected women's teams to a status of formal intercollegiate varsity sports alongside the men's teams provided the most significant new development in athletics during the 1967–1975 time period. Women's athletics teams had competed in sports throughout the college's history. Mostly these were intramural teams that grew out of Physical Education classes, but they sometimes competed against squads from other colleges or with local independent teams. In the late 1960s, an MSC women's softball team played each summer in the Joplin Softball Associations' Women's Softball League. Their opponents were local independent teams such as the Neosho Gidgets, the Eagle-Picher Cuties, and the Cajun Queens.

The real turning point in women's athletics came with the Education Act of 1972. Its Title IX provided that colleges or high schools denying equal athletic opportunities to women would lose their federal funding. Nationally colleges and universities formed an Association of Intercollegiate Athletics for Women (AIAW) to set up guidelines for the new programs and a Missouri state branch, the MAIAW, formed the unit within which Southern's teams played. The AIAW-MAIAW became defunct in 1982 as the governance of women's athletics merged more fully with that of men.

Members of the 1969–1970 basketball team pose on the bleachers in the MSSC gymnasium during the season. In front is P. Young, trainer. From left, front row: T. Vogel B. Adams, F. Hatfield, R. Krogh, G. Wofford, J. Oestreich, and J. Carter. Row two: D. Denny, D. Arnold, B. Wagner, J. D. Thomas, T. Agnello, C. Johnson, and G. Fulton. Back row: G. Warden, G. Boyd, M. Eastmen, C. Hoynson, S. Dixon, and H. Cox.

This team proved to be MSSC's first strong contender in four-year competition. Possessed of a number of able players of whom Fred Hatfield, John Thomas, and Bill Wagner were most outstanding, the team compiled a 21–8 record.

Wagner, a native of Republic, was a mainstay of the MSSC team for three years. The highlight of his career came in a 1971 game against Ozark Christian College in which, though suffering from a bruised ankle, he shot a spectacular 100 percent, bucketing all 10 of his attempted field goals and all four of his charity shots. In 1993, Wagner was named to MSSC's Silver Anniversary Commemorative Team.

Charles "Mouse" Ward (left) is shown blocking a soccer opponent in this dramatic 1972 action shot taken during the team's first year. The squad selected Ward as their outstanding defensive player in the first three years of competition.

Missouri Southern moved in step with other colleges to implement the new requirements. Though specific guidelines did not apply until 1976, a program of women's athletics was well underway by that time. An attempt to form a girl's basketball team in 1972 failed for a lack of commitment. Two years later, a group of girls appealed to physical education instructor Sallie (Roper) Beard for help in forming another team. Athletic Director Max Oldham granted Beard $3,000 to finance three women's teams for intercollegiate competition: Basketball would start that fall of 1974 with softball and tennis to be added the following spring. Volleyball and track were added to this list in 1975 and 1976 respectively. The initial 1974–1975 budget provided only for equipment, a limited travel allowance, and jerseys for the girl's uniforms. No athletic scholarships were made available.

The new women's athletic program began in the late fall of 1974 with basketball practice. The girls trained under a difficult schedule, beginning practice at 6:00 A.M., the only time gymnasium facilities were available to them. Play began with a loss to Evangel College at Springfield on December 4, but the season turned out propitiously for the budding "Lady Lions" with a 9–2 overall record. The tennis program began in the spring of 1975. Coached, as was basketball, by Sallie Beard, the team established an impressive 8–2 record. The softball team also started that spring. The overburdened Beard also coached this, but with the assistance of Roscoe Evans. The inexperienced softball girls met with many reverses ending the season 3–9, but overall the Lady Lions had achieved a respectable first year in a competitive field where all the teams were still in the formative stages and lacking in resources.

At the end of the 1974–1975 season, the tiny women's sports program had received little publicity, and Coach Beard sought to gain some recognition for them by holding a sports banquet. The Lionbackers refused to invite the Lady Lions to their annual awards dinner because of a lack of funds. At this point, the Association of Women Students, the Compass Club, and the Student Senate came to Beard's rescue by sponsoring a women's sports banquet.

In the 1975–1976 school year a stronger women's athletic program materialized. A new physical education instructor, Geraldine Albins, was added to assist Sallie Beard. Albins formed the first girl's volleyball team during the fall semester. It established a credible 12–9–3 record and placed fourth in the new state MAIAW tournament. Beard's basketball team provided the highlight of the 1975–1976 season with a 15–6 overall record, placing first in District 16 competition and taking fourth in the MAIAW state meet.

At the conclusion of two years, the women's sports program was still in its formative stages. It did not have the depth of talent or the sophistication of the long-established men's sports, nor did it have the recognition and attendance-drawing power. A lack of funds for scholarships, recruitment, and general operating expenses kept the program on a modest scale. Without a large pool of recruits to choose from, the individual sports tended to be dominated by a few talented athletes who, starting with volleyball in the fall, moved through the school year playing in as many of the seasonal sports as they could fit into their schedules. But once established, the program grew, matured, and attracted more talented players until the time came when some of the girls' teams achieved championship stature.

By 1975 MSSC had established a successful four-year athletic program that paralleled developments in the academic sector. This was evident not only in senior college competition, but also in the addition of baseball, soccer, and women's sports which added depth to the program. Initially accepted into the four-year college community with some misgivings, the Lions were forced to travel long distances to find teams who would play them, but this changed as the MSSC squads proved their merit in competition. The 1972 national championship in football marked a turning point. The MSSC team, in only their fourth year of senior college competition, had gained an honor that many small colleges never achieve. Though they had their ups and downs, as in all college athletics, by mid-1970 the Lions were solidly established in NAIA, District 16 competition as teams of considerable prestige.

After some eight years, 1967–1975, of offering upper division classes Missouri Southern was a firmly established four-year college. Its future received official sanction in March 1971 when the North Central Association of Colleges and Secondary Schools approved full accreditation for the maximum period of ten years. This meant that after four years of probation the college was now fully accepted into the family of four-year colleges.

The North Central report reflected a generally positive tone. The examiners praised the dynamic leadership of President Billingsly and the effectiveness of the Boards of Regents and Trustees. Though still somewhat dubious about the complex two-plus-two organization, they noted that it had worked smoothly, a fact they attributed largely to the caliber of the persons serving on the boards. Like so many other outsiders, they were intrigued by the mutual understanding and strong support between the school and community. The examiners found the academic programs to be generally strong though there were weaknesses in certain areas. The examiners also praised the professional qualities of the faculty and the emphasis on quality teaching. The team commented favorably on steps being taken in recruiting to reduce the provincialism of the faculty, but noted that most of the teachers had

Soccer team members pose on the bleachers at their playing field in this fall of 1975 photograph. Pictured from the left are, front row: G. Conlee, A. Johnson, P. Knight, J. Zieger, D. Price, G. Ullo, and M. Edwards. Row two: A. Miller, D. Sims, C. Maloney, C. Valentine, J. Callahan, R. Johnson, and W. White. Back row: W. Tichacek, D. Travers, T. Wood, B. Mueth, D. Johnson, C. Harper, and Coach Harold W. Bodon.

This was the soccer Lions last year as a club sport and, with a 14–2 winning record, their best season yet. Aaron Johnson was the team's leading scorer.

come from the immediate four-state area of Missouri, Kansas, Oklahoma, and Arkansas and that 33 percent of the current faculty had one or more degrees from Kansas State College at Pittsburg.

As the year 1975 came to a close, Missouri Southern entered a transitional phase. A sound four-year curriculum had been put into operation, a strong athletic program had gained regional recognition, and ten years of almost continuous construction had turned a rural estate into a splendid, widely admired campus. The tempo of student enrollment, after a brief slump in the early 1970s, was beginning to pick up, but the lavish flow of federal funds to expand higher education had begun to slow. The future held a mix of problems, some old, some new, some foreseeable, and some the product of chance.

The MSSC baseball team appears here during the spring of 1975 season, its fourth year in intercollegiate competition. With a 33–15 record, it was the team's best year up to this time. Pictured are, from left, front row: T. Hilton, D. Miller, S. Carlton, B. Blankenship, K. Schroer, unidentified, T. Allen, unidentified, and Coach Ed Wuch. Second row: unidentified, J. Eberhard, C. Chickering, M. Hagedorn, D. Smith, P. Morgan, P. McClarty, unidentified, D. Yocum, M. Coburn, and unidentified. Back row: M. Butler, M. Vaughan, unidentified, S. Ketchum, B. McAfee, B. Baker, and D. Beasley.

Several players received recognition for their strong performances but Mike Hagedorn was most outstanding. Since 1982 the Pierce City native has served as an assistant to baseball coach Warren Turner. In 1992, Hagedorn became the first MSSC baseball player to be named to the Letterman's Alumni Association Hall of Fame.

Coach Edward W. Wuch started the baseball program in 1972 and headed it for five years during which time he established a 118–80–1 record. In the fall of 1976 he joined the Education Department and in 1990 he became director of Educational Media and Services.

Members of the first Lady Lions basketball team gathered for this photograph during the 1974–1975 season. Players shown are from left, front row: Theresa Francisco, Juanita Elbrader, Linda Ummel, Debbie Nelson, Roanna Patterson, and Terri Dresh. Back row: Betsy Taylor, Cheryl Allen, Coach Sallie Roper, Janet Gladwin, and Cindy Hearn. Intercollegiate competition in women's sports began in the fall of 1974 with this squad and was followed in the spring with teams in softball and tennis.

A graduate of Southern, Coach Beard earned her master's degree at Pittsburg State University. She began teaching at MSSC in 1972 and coached or helped organize all the original Lady Lions athletic teams. In 1976, she became women's athletic director. Limiting her coaching to track and field, Beard was named NAIA District 16 Women's Track and Field Coach of the Year for 1981 and again in 1983. After 1983 she devoted full-time to being women's athletic director. In 1992, Beard became the first woman to be named to the Letterman's Alumni Association Hall of Fame.

The Lady Lions volleyball program started in the fall of 1975 with this team. Members pictured are, from left, front row: Teresa Wilcox, Patty Crane, Debbie Downs, Belynda Doby, Sherry Yeager, and Karen Gordon. Row two: Brenda Randolph, Barbara Lawson, Linda Ummel, Cheryl Frazier, Debbie Phillips, and Coach Geraldine Albins. Karen Gordon and Barbara Lawson became the first Lady Lions recruited under a new scholarship program for women athletes.

Geraldine Albins was added to the Physical Education staff in the fall of 1975 to assist Sallie Beard in the newly formed women's athletic programs. Albins left after three years, leaving behind a credible 60–39–5 record in volleyball.

CHAPTER IV
A TIME OF TRANSITION

Missouri Southern State College entered a transitory phase in its development during the late 1970s and early 1980s. After a brief lull in the early 1970s, steady growth set in. The two-plus-two arrangement of a state-supported senior college capped on a locally supported junior college was finally replaced with full state funding. Cracks began to appear in the leadership structure with important changes emerging in the Board of Regents and the administration. The new team of leaders seemed less sure when dealing with severe crises brought on by an ill-conceived faculty merit rating system and with deep budgetary cuts. But at the same time the college reached new heights in the quality of its academic programs.

After nine years of intense activity, construction on the new campus slowed in the 1976–1982 period. Since 1966 some fifteen major edifices had been completed. The new buildings formed an impressive complex, striking in their newness, though the Spanish-style mansion, the silo, and the Barn Theatre remained prominent landmarks that reminded visitors of the campus' rural origins. Much of the construction consisted of additions to existing buildings with only the Gene Taylor Education-Psychology Hall, the Norval M. Matthews Technology Building, and the residential apartment complex, being entirely new structures. The M-P Construction Company of Carthage, which had built most of the original campus, continued to be the dominant contractor, but the Billingsly Student Center expansion was their last major project. A shift in financing also occurred at this time. The Mills H. Anderson Police Academy addition and the construction of Gene Taylor Hall were the last buildings to be built with JCJC capital improvement funds. The Norval M. Matthews Hall was the first major structure to be financed largely by state appropriations.

In the late 1970s and early 1980s a growing need for the college to construct more student residential units became evident. Such facilities had always been regarded as necessary to promote the growth of the college by drawing students from beyond the local, commuting vicinity of the institution, but a sharp rise in the cost of gasoline in this period greatly accelerated the demand. Many students who had been commuting twenty and more miles by automobile began to seek on-campus housing.

Women's on-campus living facilities presented the most pressing need. A wing of Webster Hall, not needed for men, had been converted to women's accommodations in 1974 to house the overflow from the South Hall dormitory. Two years later, the college installed two modular units to provide temporary housing.

By 1976, a shortage of accommodations for men also began to develop and the old speech and theatre classroom trailers, no longer needed, were converted into a men's dormitory for 24 honor students. Addition of the prefabricated units in 1976 had raised the total campus residential capacity to 380, but this proved insufficient and college administrators were soon plagued with another waiting list. An extensive building program, using the college's legal authority to issue revenue bonds, which could be paid off with student fees, seemed the logical solution.

A campus poll showed that students preferred a cluster of small apartment-type units in a landscaped setting over the traditional hotel-like dormitories. In

(Opposite) This composite photograph, from the 1979 Crossroads portrays President Billingsly in his later years. The following remarks give insight into how many perceived him at the time of his death:

Julio S. Leon, president of Missouri Southern: "He was right for Missouri Southern in the early years. It needed a particular person and that person was certainly Billingsly. The college is very fortunate he was available."

Annetta St. Clair, associate professor of Political Science: "He was a very friendly, outgoing person. He welcomed everyone with an idea into his office. As some instructors recollect, he made them feel like family."

Joy Thompson, secretary to Billingsly for eight years: "He was a powerful man. And he did run the college in that sort of way. . . . He had a facility for knowing what was going on around the campus."

Clark Swanson, editor of The Chart: "He had a feel around him that told you he was in charge and things were under control."

Jim Ellison, associate editor of The Chart: " . . . what made him stand taller than other men of his stature, was his caring."

Fred G. Hughes, president of the Board of Regents/Trustees: "He had a good academic background, which is important. But he had a great business head as well. . . . And besides that he had a good strong dose of common sense."

Howard Dugan, director of Physical Plant, appears here in a pose familiar to students over the years as he toured the campus checking on needed maintenance. Always conscious that newcomers often gained their first impression of the college from its physical appearance, Dugan worked to insure that that impression would be a favorable one. North Central examiners remarked on how superbly Southern's buildings and grounds were maintained.

Dugan joined the college staff full time in 1970 and two years later became superintendent of Buildings and Grounds. As the college expanded, Dugan's job grew and by the time he retired in 1990, he supervised a staff of fifty-five who cleaned, secured, and maintained the extensive campus.

A section of two modular housing units is shown moving north on Range Line at dawn during the summer of 1976, just after leaving the Holiday Inn where they were purchased for $45,000. The units, known as the South Hall Annex, were intended as temporary housing to relieve the shortage of accommodations for women students. Providing housing for thirty-two women, the units remained in use for the next sixteen years, but the deteriorating condition of the thirty-year-old structures caused them to be abandoned after the 1991–1992 school year.

the fall of 1980, five of these structures built by the Goetz Construction Company, opened to student occupancy. Each of the five two-story buildings contained eight, two-bedroom apartments housing a total of 160 students. With completion of the new apartment complex, the old honors dormitories were sold and this left the college with nine residential units that provided accommodations for 550 students, sufficient to ease the housing problem for most of the next decade.

As the campus grew, the question of naming the new buildings arose. Traditionally many colleges and universities had named buildings after important benefactors and this practice was informally adopted for the new campus, but no systematic procedure was worked out until the 1970s.

In the history of Joplin Junior College, 1937–1964, only one building was ever named after a college personage, this being the student union, designated Blaine Hall in 1947 to honor the retiring first dean. With the college's removal to Eighth and Wall, this building was abandoned and no other college structure was so named.

Officials renewed the naming process with the start of construction on the new Mission Hills campus. Hearnes Hall came first and this was soon followed by the Spiva Library, the Spiva Art Center, Reynolds Hall, and Kuhn Hall. Other new buildings remained unnamed, most notably the Physical Education Building which was known simply as the "Gymnasium" for eleven years.

In 1975 President Leon Billingsly appointed a committee for the naming of buildings. This committee made several recommendations, most significantly that the new North and South Residence Halls be named after Harry E. Blaine and Edna C. Drummond from the junior college era. Also, the committee suggested naming the new stadium after Billingsly himself. Billingsly specifically rejected naming any building after himself while he still played an active role in college affairs and he expressed reservations about naming any buildings after Joplin Junior College notables on the grounds that if one was honored then it would establish a precedent for naming others. He did accept the committee's recommendation for naming South Hall after Edna C. Drummond, but the Board of Regents did not accept this and South Hall remained unnamed. In the next two years the Regents did name three other buildings following the committee's and Billingsly's recommendations:

Performing Arts Center	Thomas E. Taylor	1976
Music Recital Hall	Edward S. Phinney	1977
Technology Building	Norval M. Matthews	1977

In 1978 another committee submitted its recommendations to Billingsly. Again he rejected some of them, but four that he did accept were approved by the Regents:

Gymnasium	Robert Ellis Young	1978
North Hall	Richard M. Webster	1978
Police Academy	Mills H. Anderson	1978
Stadium	Fred G. Hughes	1978

At this time the Board of Regents established guidelines for the naming of buildings. These rules specified that structures could be named after former staff members, alumni, former Regents or Trustees, or financial donors who had made important contributions to the college; only under exceptional circumstances were buildings to be named after people still active in college affairs. Ironically, this latter rule had previously been violated by the Regents in several instances.

After honoring the four legislators and board members in 1978, the process of naming buildings became more active as new construction or unexpected developments opened up opportunities. When the college union expansion was completed in 1979, it was named in memory of the late president of the college, Leon C. Billingsly. In the spring of 1977, the original technology building, completed in 1970, was named after Regent-Trustee Norval M. Matthews. Matthews died a few months later and when the new technology building was completed in 1980 his name was transferred to it. A few years later, the original technology building was renamed for Elvin Ummel, a longtime member of the Board of Trustees and future member of the Board of Regents, who earlier had had only a small greenhouse named after him. In 1979 the Education-Psychology Building, completed two years earlier, was named after then Congressman Gene Taylor, a former member of the Board of Trustees. With these changes the Board of Regents had completed the process of naming a building after all the original members of the Boards of Trustees and Regents.

Missouri Southern's student population experienced steady, though not spectacular growth, in the 1976–1982 time period. Enrollment, full and part-time, stood at 3,748 in the fall of 1976 and in fact declined slightly in 1979, but rebounded the next fall to 4,013, marking the first time Southern's enrollment surpassed the 4,000 mark. College population growth reflected a national trend, but the early 1980s, in spite of an economic recession, high inflation, and faculty unrest on the local campus, ushered in a period of steady growth at Southern that was above the national average. The full and part-time student count in 1982 reached 4,478, a figure some 11 percent above that of 1980. With low tuition and a growing reputation for quality academics, the college was appealing to a broader population base.

The composition of MSSC's student body did not change appreciably in the six-year period 1976–1982. Minority ethnic groups remained very small, with most students being old-stock Americans of European extraction. Unlike earlier decades in the college's history, the ratio of men to women students had changed with the

General William Westmorland, commander of American forces in the early part of the Vietnam War, is shown addressing a student group during a campus visit on May 2, 1980. Westmorland's appearance was an example of the prestigious personages occasionally brought on campus by the then College Union Board to broaden student's cultural and intellectual horizons. In the afternoon, the retired general joined Kappa Alpha members in their annual mock storming of the Carthage courthouse.

The bland sameness of dormitory rooms can challenge students to use originality in decorating them. This young man has exercised unusual ingenuity to make his room in Webster Hall appear if not "like home," at least as an expression of individuality.

This aerial view shows Southern's residential hall complex as it existed in 1992. In the immediate foreground are South Hall (left) and Webster Hall, now North Hall (right), the original dormitory structures on campus, dating from 1970. Across the drive from South Hall are the two annex units, now abandoned. Extending north and east of the South Hall Annex structures are the cluster of eight garden-type apartment buildings. Five of these were opened in 1980, two more in 1987, and one in 1990. Each of these apartment units operates on a landlord-tenant basis, unlike the traditional dormitories.

latter now accounting for a slight majority of the student population. The local orientation of the student body had altered but little. Though the change to full state funding in 1977 eliminated the lower-tuition classification of Jasper County Junior College District residents, most students still came from Southwest Missouri and out-of-state students remained a small but increasing minority of approximately 5 percent. The student body continued to come largely from families with low or modest incomes, and this was reflected in the large number of enrollees receiving financial aid. In the fall of 1979 more than 2,500 of the approximately 3,700 students attending received some form of aid such as grants, loans, scholarships, or work on campus, totaling about $1.4 million.

With the college's growing enrollment, the number of graduates increased correspondingly. Though the degrees issued fluctuated in number from year to year, the overall trend was upward and the 1978 graduating class of 561 almost exactly doubled that of the first four-year class of 1969. Total degrees granted averaged 499 per year in the period 1976–1982, while the average had been 397 for the 1969–1975 time period.

Within these overall totals, the old associate degree program showed surprising vitality. Though overshadowed from the beginning by the size of the baccalaureate offerings, the number of associate degree graduates increased steadily. In the seven years, 1969–1975, the associate degree recipients had averaged 84 per year, but in the 1976–1982 time period the average rose to 121. An attractive selection of job-oriented programs in the fields of Computer Science, Nursing, Dental Hygiene, Medical Technology, and Law Enforcement made this increase possible.

The baccalaureate degree programs also showed a steady increase. The number of these degrees issued rose from an average of 313 per year in the 1969–1975 period to a 1976–1982 average of 378. As in the associate degree programs, the most significant growth in the various baccalaureate offerings came in those fields that prepared students for immediate job prospects in the local economy. The bachelor of science in education degree had best fulfilled this demand in the years 1969–1975, but in the face of an oversupply of teachers the number of B.S.E. degrees granted actually declined slightly from a yearly average of 156 in the 1969–1975 time period to 152 in the 1976–1982 era. The bachelor of science in business administration degree, though a smaller program than the B.S.E. prior to 1982, was rapidly overtaking the latter. B.S.B.A. degrees granted averaged 116 yearly in the 1976–1982 time period, up from an annual average of 76 in the years 1969–1975. In 1982 some 146 B.S.B.A. degrees were issued, accounting for 39 percent of the total baccalaureate degrees granted that year. This total, for the first time, exceeded the number of B.S.E. degrees issued in any given year, in spite of the latter's broader base that encompassed several majors. Other bachelor of science programs such as Biology, Criminal Justice, Mathematics, Medical Technology, Psychology, and Sociology also held up well or were growing. The bachelor of arts programs, offered in a broad area of majors mostly for the benefit of students planning on entering graduate level training in certain professions, remained rather static and actually declined overall from an average of 55 degrees granted yearly between 1969 and 1975 to only 46 annually in the 1976–1982 time period. A bachelor of general studies curriculum, tailored for those students interested principally in academic enrichment, fared poorly and turned out only 30 graduates in the entire 1976–1982 era. By 1982, the School of Business Administration, with its job-oriented majors, had clearly emerged as the dominant academic division on campus.

The period 1976–1982 witnessed a steady enrichment of the curriculum that significantly upgraded the academic standing of Missouri Southern. While the process had been going on since the advent of the four-year college, as the faculty grew in numbers and in professionalism older courses were enriched and new ones added that gave added depth to the disciplines. The General Education requirements were at the heart of the college's growing academic attainments. These structured requirements remained basically intact and assured that all graduates would receive a broad grounding in the liberal arts, while the individual disciplines modernized and expanded their offerings.

Much of the growth of the 1976–1982 period occurred in the established academic divisions. Significant changes in the School of Arts and Sciences involved establishing a new job-oriented bachelor of science degree in Sociology and the addition of a new paralegal minor in the Political Science area in 1977. The paralegal program prepared students for careers as legal assistants or secretaries in law offices. An even more important change in the Arts and Sciences Division involved splitting the old Language and Literature Department into separate departments of English and Communications. Effective in 1980, the new arrangement left the English Department in charge of English Composition and Literature while the new communications area encompassed the fields of Journalism, Speech, and Foreign Languages. Communications, under its new department head, Richard Massa, became one of the most rapidly growing departments in the 1980s.

The rapidly growing School of Business Administration also underwent important changes in the 1976–1982 time period. Dr. Julio Leon replaced Dr. Keith Larimore as dean in 1976 when Larimore, who had headed the division since its founding ten years before, returned to teaching. Leon worked to establish a Small Business Institute (SBI) and a Bureau of Business Research. The SBI utilized students to help clients solve their business organization problems and was subsidized in this work by the federal Small Business Administration. The Bureau of Business Research put out a quarterly publication that provided local businesses with useful statistical information on the area's economy. Starting in 1980, the School of Business Administration worked with the Missouri Southern Foundation to sponsor a yearly series of lectures on business and economics.

The School of Education and Psychology continued to be one of the most

James R. Spradling, a part-time Political Science instructor, 1969–1982, is shown participating in the 1986 Phon-A-Thon fund-raising drive. Spradling, a Carthage attorney and important benefactor of Southern, helped establish the Paralegal program in 1978, and was the first instructor in that area. His sister, the late Helen S. Boylan, has supported the annual symposiums on women in politics. Sponsored by the Social Science Department, the symposiums are funded by the Helen S. Boylan Foundation.

The happy recipient of a bachelor of science degree in Accounting, Rob Reeser, a blind student, is assisted by an unidentified fellow graduate at the 1982 commencement ceremony. While active in extracurricular affairs as well as with his studies, Reeser still managed to graduate with a perfect 4.0 grade point average. His blind wife, Julie, also attended Southern and while enrolled at MSSC a son, with normal eyesight, was born to the couple. Reeser later attended the Oklahoma City Law School, but his declining health forced him to withdraw. He died in 1985 at the age of thirty-three.

Grace C. Mitchell is pictured here at the time of her retirement in 1982 after twenty-four years of service. Possessing a master's degree from Pennsylvania State University, Mitchell was much praised by students in her English classes for her helpful attitude and enthusiastic grasp of her subject. She became, in 1980, MSSC's first recipient of the Outstanding Teacher of a Freshman Class Award. After her retirement, Ms. Mitchell was honored by being named emeritus professor.

Members of the Biology faculty gathered around the departmental "Mr. Skeleton" for this 1978–1979 school year photograph. Pictured are, from left, front row*: Dr. Vonnie R. Prentice, 1972; and Dr. James R. Jackson, 1976. Back row: David L. Tillman, 1975; Art Boyt, 1978–1979; Dr. Orty E. Orr, 1966–1986; Wayne E. Stebbins, 1969; and Dr. William L. Ferron, 1971–1983.

Members of the department at this time, not pictured, were: Dr. E. Sam Gibson, 1967; and Dr. Gerald E. Elick, 1969–1988. Elick died in 1990.

Ferron, Orr, and Prentice are former department heads, with Ferron holding the position at the time this photograph was taken.

Orr is the department's only retired faculty member.

Prentice received the Outstanding Teacher Award in 1981; Jackson received the Outstanding Teacher of a Freshman Class Award in 1983.

*Names are followed by dates of employment—a single date if still on the staff.

important on campus though no longer growing rapidly or occupying the dominant position in the college's curriculum that it once held. An administrative reorganization split the school into separate departments of Education and Psychology in 1980, with Dr. Edward P. Merryman becoming head of Education and two years later dean of the entire school.

The School of Technology, under the direction of Dean James K. Maupin, continued to grow in the 1976–1982 time period with a number of new degree programs being added. By 1982 the school offered an extensive assortment of associate degree programs in Automotive Technology, Computer Science, Dental Hygiene, Drafting and Design, Law Enforcement, Machine Technology, Medical Technology, Nursing, and Radiologic Technology. Also, an important non-degree Military Science program was maintained for training ROTC recruits. To further augment its offerings, Technology, once an exclusive domain of associate degrees, added baccalaureate degree programs in Criminal Justice and Industrial Arts Education in this period. While most of the fields in Technology were growing, the most extensive areas of change were in Law Enforcement and Criminal Justice, and in Computer Science.

Though the established academic divisions generated most of the growth in this 1976–1982 period, expansion also took place in the auxiliary programs. The Division of Continuing Education, created in 1974, had grown steadily with its offerings of noncurriculum and mostly noncredit courses. Starting in 1980, in an effort to better serve students in distant towns, Continuing Education was upgraded to include all off-campus regular, college-credit courses.

Another, completely new, area of expansion involved graduate-level studies. Though precluded by state law from establishing a graduate degree program, Southern could invite another college to offer such a program on the MSSC campus. Administrators found a willing partner for this in Southwest Missouri State University at Springfield. A master's in education program started in January 1979 with all instruction being conducted by professors from SMSU, but the Missouri Coordinating Board of Higher Education rejected a similar plan for a master's in business administration on grounds that Drury College was already conducting such a program in Joplin. The next year, Drury phased out this operation on grounds of a lack of demand. This move then cleared the way for Southwest Missouri State to established an MBA program on the Southern campus.

Though neither program has produced large numbers of graduates, the Education degree program has enjoyed a steady demand that justifies its

continuation; but the MBA was discontinued in 1991 at least in part because of low enrollment. While these master's degrees are issued by SMSU, not MSSC, they do provide a service to local students and, importantly, they establish a precedent that could, in the future, lead to Southern having its own graduate program.

The addition of new student organizations slowed in the 1976–1982 period. After the flood of new clubs that came with the advent of the four-year college, this development is not surprising. The absence of any new Greek organizations being formed was particularly notable. The existing two fraternities and three sororities, with combined memberships hovering around one hundred, were struggling to stay alive. The strong commuter orientation and a lack of venerable traditions in the student body hampered the Greeks' growth.

Student organizations in other areas showed more strength. Five new academic clubs were formed that included Pershing Rifles for the new ROTC program in Technology, Students in Free Enterprise in the Business Administration Division, and Lambda Epsilon Chi for the new Paralegal program in the Social Science Department. Three new honor societies were formed: Pi Kappa Delta in Forensics, Pi Omega Pi in Business, and Sigma Tau Delta in English. Three new religious societies formed, Fellowship of Christian Athletes, Newman Community, and Chi Alpha, that reinforced the already existing church organizations. New general and service organizations included the Panhellenic Council, the Residence Hall Association, and the Film Society, which had existed since 1962 as an activity of the Spiva Art Center.

By 1982, Southern had a well-developed network of student organizations, but many were weak and occasionally lapsed into periods of inactivity. The most fertile period of development in such organizations lay in the next decade.

In this 1978–1979 photograph, members of the Chemistry staff, one of the oldest and most stable faculty groups at Southern, gather behind some of their laboratory equipment. Pictured are, from left*: Dr. Lawrence R. Albright II, 1969; Dr. Melvyn W. Mosher, 1974; Dr. Vernon D. Baiamonte, 1967; Dr. Phillip R. Whittle, 1970; and Harrison M. Kash, 1958.

Baiamonte has been head of the Department of Physical Sciences, which includes Chemistry, since it was established in 1970.

Whittle is also director of the Regional Crime Laboratory and Mosher is assistant director.

Members of the Mathematics faculty posed for this photograph during the 1978–1979 school year. Pictured are, from left*: Dr. P. D. Subramanian, 1970–1986; Rochelle L. Boehning, 1967–1983; Jack D. Jolly, 1968; Mary A. Elick, 1974; Dr. J. Larry Martin, 1965; William R. Livingston, 1968; Dr. Gerald E. Suchan, 1978–1982; and Dr. Gary R. Mulkey, 1977.

In 1980, Martin became the first MSSC faculty member to receive the Outstanding Teacher Award.

Boehning was Mathematics' original department head, 1970–1973, and since that time, Martin has held the post.

*Names are followed by dates of employment—a single date if still on the staff.

Business Administration had grown into such a large division by the 1978–1979 school year that the photographer broke the faculty into two groups. Pictured are, from left, front row*: Edith M. Compton, 1967–1992; Larry W. Goode, 1968; June M. Freund, 1978–1982; and Dr. Robert G. Price, 1973–1980. Back row: Terry D. Marion, 1976; Dr. Hilda J. Turner, 1977–1980; Dr. Julio S. Leon, 1969; Kathleen G. Grim, 1975–1991; and Dr. Charles E. Leitle, 1970.

Ms. Compton died in 1992. Ms. Grim is retired.

Dr. Leon was dean of the Division of Business Administration at this time; in 1982 he became president of MSSC.

Leitle received the Outstanding Teacher Award for 1984 and Goode received the same award in 1986; Marion received the Outstanding Teacher of a Freshman Class Award for 1990.

The other half of the Business Administration faculty in 1978–1979 posed for this photograph near the mansion. Pictured are, from left*: William H. Paapanen, 1976; Dr. John W. Tiede, 1968; Bernard A. Johnson, 1974; Dr. Carl A. Finke, 1970–1993; Robert J. Miller, 1968; Dr. Jasbir S. Jaswal, 1977; Dr. L. Keith Larimore, 1966–1988; Carolyn E. Cunningham, 1978; and Brent L. England, 1976–1979.

Tiede served as dean of Business Administration, 1982–1987. Finke retired in 1993.

Johnson was elected to the Joplin Municipal Council in 1988 and became mayor in 1992.

Larimore, the original head of Business Administration, served as dean of that division, 1966–1976. After teaching Business and Economics courses, 1976–1988, Larimore left to accept a position at Radford University.

*Names are followed by dates of employment—a single date if still on the staff.

Southern's student newspaper, *The Chart*, with its lackluster performance of the early 1970s well behind it, matured into one of Missouri's best college newspapers in the 1976–1982 time period. *The Chart* delved heavily into social issues in the late 1970s. In-depth stories appeared regularly on such subjects as alcoholism, cults, homosexuality, rape, and other issues of a sociological bent.

To better accommodate its growing news coverage, changes were made in *The Chart*'s format and production. In 1976–1977, the full-size broadsheet was adopted and two years later, the college purchased some $25,000 in new equipment that included an advanced phototypesetter. These machines cut costs, saved time, and gave students valuable experience in layout work, but actual printing was still contracted out.

Though *The Chart* moved heavily into the larger political, economic, and social issues, it did not sacrifice coverage of school events. In 1980–1981, *The Chart* gave extensive coverage to growing faculty unrest over the evaluation process and, in 1982, it published an unusual summer edition devoted to President Darnton's resignation.

The Chart, by 1982, had emerged as a college newspaper of considerable stature and special awards became more common. In the Missouri College Newspaper Association (MCNA) competition at Columbia, *The Chart* won five Best in State, in Class B, awards for 1975 through 1978 and in 1982. Numerous individual awards were gleaned by staff members including the MCNA's prestigious Collegiate Journalist of the Year, which was won by Tim Dry in 1976; Liz DeMarice in 1977; and Clark Swanson in 1979.

Missouri Southern State College entered the 1976–1982 time period with an already well-established varsity sports program and finally gained membership in a regional conference. Though no more national championships were won in this period, the various sports did gain a number of conference and NAIA District 16 titles. Women's teams, which had just emerged from their 1972–1975 incubation period, blossomed into first-rate intercollegiate sports contenders.

The administration upgraded the stature of varsity sports in the college's curriculum when, in 1980, the coaches' teaching schedules were cut in half. Prior to that time, they had been teaching twelve credit hours or more and it did not leave them with enough time to recruit quality players. Poor recruitment was seen as the cause of some of the teams' bad performances during the 1978–1979 season.

The festering problem of joining a regional athletic conference was finally resolved in 1976. At this time, the Great Plains Athletic Conference broke up when two Colorado colleges withdrew. The five remaining members consisting of the Kansas colleges of Emporia State, Fort Hays State, Pittsburg State, and Washburn University, plus Kearney (Nebraska) State College, invited Missouri Southern, her sister institution Missouri Western at St. Joseph, and Wayne (Nebraska) State College to join.

The member colleges agreed that they would abide by a common set of rules, that both men's and women's teams would be admitted, and that the colleges would maintain mem-

Ross C. Snyder (left) served as director of the Educational Media Center from 1968 until he retired in 1984. With a master's degree from Ball State University, Snyder was once a musician and had his own band before turning to education.

Elmer E. Rodgers, (right) a native of Youngstown, Ohio, came to Southern in 1968 as head librarian for the new four-year college and held that post until 1984, retiring the next year. Rodgers died in 1987.

Ten members of the Education faculty, plus the departmental secretary, gathered for this photograph during the 1978–1979 school year. Pictured are, from left*: Bea Moss, secretary; Harvey Walthall, 1978–1979; Hilda E. Richardson, 1972–1981; Dr. Robert O. Highland, 1968–1990; Dr. Leland D. Easterday, 1967–1987; Edward W. Wuch, 1969; Dr. James V. Sandrin, 1969; Ross C. Snyder, 1968–1984; Dr. Michael E. Banks, 1975; Dr. Robert C. Wiley, 1969; and Dr. Bob F. Steere, 1969–1991.

Easterday, Highland, Richardson, Snyder, and Steere are now retired. Sandrin is currently head of the Education Department.

*Names are followed by dates of employment—a single date if still on the staff.

Jack Dawson, a 1972 MSSC graduate, is shown receiving the Outstanding Alumnus Award for 1978 from Alumni Association President Glen Barnett during Homecoming festivities for that year. An artist and teacher at the Webb City High School, Dawson created the Praying Hands *and* Kneeling Miner *statues and a large mural for Webb City. His works have been featured in various exhibitions.*

Barnett received the Outstanding Alumnus Award in 1987.

Robert D. Carpenter (right), the first director of the Computer Center, and assistant instructor Kenneth L. Fore are shown working in the center during the 1969–1970 school year. These machines soon became obsolete due to rapid developments in the field of computer technology.

Computer Science, founded in the fall of 1967, was one of the early technical programs established under Dean Maupin's guidance. Offered initially as an associate degree curriculum, the new program grew rapidly.

James Gray replaced Carpenter as director of the center in 1973. Fore left in 1971 after three years as an instructor.

Dudley Stegge is pictured examining a money tree designed by Charles Moss, manager of the College Bookstore, and presented to him at a retirement ceremony in his honor.

Hired in 1951, Stegge's twenty-nine-year tenure encompassed several positions and, at the time of his retirement in June 1980, he was director of the Billingsly Student Center. In 1993, Stegge was named posthumously to the Letterman's Alumni Association Hall of Fame, the first player or coach from the Joplin Junior College to receive this honor. He died in 1992 at the age of sixty-eight.

bership in the National Association of Intercollegiate Athletics (NAIA) which Southern had joined in 1968. Finally the members agreed that the organization would be renamed as the Central States Intercollegiate Conference (CSIC), reflecting its more eastward geographical orientation.

President Billingsly liked the new three-state, eight-member conference. He pointed out that the colleges were compatible in size and philosophy, and that all gave limited aid to their athletes. On his recommendation, the Board of Regents accepted it.

Though unable to duplicate their great national championship performance of 1972, Coach James Frazier's football Lions established a creditable record in the 1976–1982 time period, experiencing only one losing season. It was also a time when a number of the college's most memorable football stars played and when numerous long-enduring statistical records were established.

In 1976, the football Lions experienced a heartening first season in the new

(Above left) Members of the Kappa Alpha fraternity are shown at their annual "Old South Ball" in the spring of 1974. In keeping with the fraternity's southern roots, these balls are a KA tradition. Members wear Confederate attire while the ladies dress as southern belles.

Formed on campus in early 1969 as Pi Beta Lambda, a local fraternity, the chapter received a Kappa Alpha charter in 1971, thus becoming the first nationally affiliated Greek organization on the MSC campus. A decline in membership forced the KA to relinquish its charter in 1988, but it reformed and in 1991–1992 members regained their national charter.

Members of the Beta Beta Beta club pose with the Biology Department's "Mr. Skeleton" in this 1976–1977 photograph. Pictured are from left: Doug Hardy, Steve McGuire, Kent Findley, Bob Turner, Steve Vinyard, Jeanne Casperson, Pam Lankford, Susan Compton, Rhonda Gess, Teresa Dougan, Lydia Jackson, and Peyton Jackson. "Mr. Skeleton" has his arms around Tri-Beta secretary, Pam Lankford.

Tri-Beta, a nationally chartered honorary society for Biology students dating from 1973, was supplanted in the late 1980s by the more popularly oriented Biology Club.

Central States Intercollegiate Conference, ending with a triple tie for first place. Overall, they ranked 8–2.

The next year, with a team weakened by a loss of players, the Lions experienced a lackluster season and continued their mediocre performances in 1978 and 1979. In fact, in the latter of these years, Coach Frazier suffered his first losing season in six years, ending up 5–6 overall.

The three years 1980–1982 saw the football Lions recover from their indifferent performances of the previous three years and emerge as a strong contender in the CSIC. A respectable showing in the 1981

(Top) Terri Anderson, 1978–1979 Varsity Rifle Team member, aims her rifle at the "bullseye" in this photograph. Other members of the team were Diane Davis, captain; Kevin Cornell; and Terry Thompson. The team picked up honors ranging from first to eighth place in the five tournaments in which they competed. The next year, the organization became the Pershing Rifles, oriented toward the ROTC program.

(Bottom) Baptist Student Union members from left, Terri Carter, president; Willie Williams; Bob Davis; and Steve Myers are pictured attending a meeting in 1976–1977. The BSU was one of the first student religious clubs to form on the new Mission Hills campus.

Willie Williams, one of Southern's most memorable football players, attended MSSC, 1973–1976. A native of St. Louis, the 245-pound offensive guard is one of only five football Lions to ever be named First Team All-American by the NAIA or the Football Gazette. *He also received many other honors. A very religious man, Williams has followed a career in the ministry and is now a chaplain with the Marines.*

season was clouded by a controversy over the Lions inadvertently playing an ineligible player in a game against Evangel College. The NAIA ruled that Southern had to forfeit their Evangel victory, leaving the Lions with a second place finish in the CSIC. The troubled 1981 season was sparked by the impressive performance of freshman tailback Harold Noirfalise who led the conference in rushing with 919 yards.

With an exceptionally strong team, the 1982 Lions, 7–2–1 overall, almost equalled their performance of 1976. The team had the satisfaction of crushing Evangel College 68–24 and the winning score still stands as the highest in MSSC's history as a senior college, though the Lions only placed third in CSIC play. Numerous honors were showered on the talented Lions. Frazier was selected as conference co-coach of the year and seven players were named to the CSIC All-Conference First Team. Offensive lineman Joel Tupper also received the prestigious honor of being named to the NAIA All-American First Team, an honor previously received by only two players.

The 1982 team's sparkling performance closed out the 1976–1982 time period on a high note, much as they had begun it six years before. It helped solidify the football Lions growing reputation as a major contender in conference and district play.

The basketball Lions, in the 1976–1977 through the 1982–1983 seasons, were a stronger team than statistics seem to indicate. Though the Lions lost or tied in four of the seven seasons, the three winning years were memorable ones that focused much attention on Southern's growing stature as a four-year college.

The opening year of this period, 1976–1977, under a new coach, Gary Garner, witnessed another mediocre performance. The team gleaned a 15–15 tie for the year, but found its 5–9 first foray into CSIC competition particularly galling. Garner resigned after one season to accept another position.

Tillman D. "Chuck" Williams became the new head basketball coach for the 1977–1978 school year. Williams, who established an impressive record over the next decade, proceeded to build a strong team for his first season that took the conference and district titles before moving into the NAIA national tournament at Kansas City. The inspired Lions lasted through the first two rounds of the tournament before losing. Reportedly there were more MSSC students at Kansas City watching the games than remained on campus. It was the Lions' first foray into this national tournament since 1973 and nine more years would elapse before they returned.

In December 1977, MSSC held the first of the Lionbacker Holiday Classic Basketball Tournaments in what was to become an annual event. The Lions won the championship in this first contest.

After the team's championship performances, Coach Williams experienced two losing seasons as he struggled to rebuild his team which had lost many of its best players through graduation. The Lions did gain one memorable victory, in December 1978, when they defeated Arkansas Baptist College 128–59, netting the most points ever scored in Southern's senior college basketball history.

For the 1980–1981 season, Coach Williams had again built a strong team, scoring 23–10 overall and winning the CSIC championship 12–2 only to be stymied in the District 16 playoffs by their old nemesis, the Drury College Panthers. But earlier the Lions had had the satisfaction of twice defeating the Fort Hays State Tigers, a NAIA top-ranked team. In the second game, the MSSC cagers won 84–77, overcoming a 21-point halftime deficit and snapping the Tigers' 26-game home-court winning streak. Williams again received the CSIC Coach of the Year honor.

The next year, with the usual loss of graduating players, mentor Williams' team slipped back to a mediocre 15–15 tie performance, but in the following season, 1982–1983, the Lions bounced back with a 20–9 overall record. Earning a third-place tie in CSIC competition, they advanced into the NAIA District 16 playoffs where they were again checked by their traditional rival, Drury College.

Two notable basketball players, Willie Rogers and Carl Tyler, emerged during the 1980–1984 period. Rogers, who played three years at MSSC, was a six-foot seven-inch forward. He was named to the CSIC All Conference First Team for 1982–1983. Tyler, a four-year MSSC letterman, received NAIA All District 16 First Team honors for the three years 1981–1984. He finished his career in 1984 with a then all-time scoring record of 1,902 points. His record of 49 points scored in one game still stands as an all-time high. Both Rogers and Tyler were later named to the 1968–1992 Silver Anniversary Commemorative Team.

Coach Chuck Williams had gained national recognition for the basketball Lions since he became coach in 1977. It was not only a noteworthy accomplishment in a highly competitive sport, but it also made the recruiting of talented players more effective and further enhanced the college's prestige.

Missouri Southern's soccer program developed into a mature sport in the years 1976–1982. In its four years of intercollegiate competition prior to 1976, Coach Harold Bodon, founder of the program, had struggled to find quality players and to obtain adequate college funding. This effort bore fruit in the spring of 1976 when, with the entire team in attendance, the Board of Regents/Trustees granted the soccer Lions full recognition and funding as a varsity sport. This move gave the soccer team membership in the NAIA District 16 and made them eligible to compete for the district champi-

Members of Rho Epsilon Chi, also known as the Physical Education Club, are shown here during the 1975–1976 school year. Pictured are, from left, front row: Terri Dresh, Allison Griggs, and Valle Matthews. Back row: Venus Yount, sponsor; and Bob Baker. Terri Dresh was named Outstanding Female Athlete of the Year in 1977. Venus Yount came to JJC in 1959 at a time when the college had only one teacher of Women's Physical Education. A native of Galena, Kansas, she retired in 1979.

Executive officers of the Student Senate for the 1977–1978 school year are pictured here, from left: Becky Morgan, treasurer; Sarah Frost, secretary; William Renner, vice president; and Steve Graves, president.

The Senate was reorganized in 1982 to consist of four executive officers and nine senators from each class. Since 1981, the Student Senate had been appointing a liaison to attend Board of Regents meetings. A new state statute in 1984 made this an official student position, appointed by the governor from a list of three nominees submitted by the Student Senate. Tim Eastin became the first student regent under this new law.

Pictured are members of the Newman Community Club as they gathered for one of their meetings during the 1979–1980 school year. From the left are, front row: Sheri Peasel; Dorsey Taylor; Liz Tonsi; Dr. James Jackson, sponsor; and Ann Johnson. Second row: Dianner Roles; Therese Roles; Kim Freeborn; Brenda Jackson; and Father Fergus. Back row: Mary Lemasters; John Taylor; Mark Ruzicka; Rick Ruzicka; Kathy McEntee; Cindy Taylor; and Tim Vinyard.

The Newman Community was organized in 1978 to serve the needs of Catholic students and faculty after the Ecumenical Campus Ministry dissolved the year before.

Girls from the flag, rifle, and dance section of the Lion Pride Marching Band are shown working on a routine for an upcoming football halftime presentation during the fall of 1982. Pete Havely, director of the 67-piece band, was able to put on more elaborate programs with the aid of these performers than when the band depended largely on marchers and twirlers for variety.

The Society for the Advancement of Management's 1975 Homecoming campus display set high standards for good taste and attractiveness at a time when many organizations' displays were crude in execution and concept. SAM's candidate for Homecoming Queen that year was Karen Shipman.

onship, but participation in the Central States Intercollegiate Conference remained in limbo because too few member schools had soccer teams.

The soccer Lions produced winning teams in six of the years in this period and reached a tie in the seventh, 1977. Still struggling to build strong teams out of inexperienced players, Coach Bodon was unable to win a NAIA District 16 championship, but his teams did reach the playoffs in three of these years.

The soccer seasons, 1979 and 1980, are the most significant of the 1976–1982 period with the teams attaining records of 16–3–1 and 15–4–1 in the two years respectively.

The year 1982 is memorable for the team's spectacular 0–0 overtime tie with the Rockhurst College Hawks, an outcome that considerably brightened the soccer Lions' image. Rockhurst's dominance of NAIA District 16 soccer had become almost legendary. They had claimed the championship for eleven years in a row and had won all of their regular season District 16 games for the past sixteen years. While the Lions did not defeat the Hawks, they did dim the Kansas City team's aurora of invincibility.

By 1982, Coach Bodon's Lions formed a well-established team that commanded considerable respect in District 16. On the other hand, soccer was still not a popular spectator sport with the public. Home games were ordinarily played in the vast expanses of Turkey Creek valley with the playing field marked by portable goals and a section or two of moveable bleachers. Most talented young athletes still preferred to go into one of the prestigious sports like football, basketball, or baseball.

In the 1976–1982 era, baseball, like soccer and the women's teams, was a relatively new varsity sport. By 1976 the baseball Lions, under Coach Ed Wuch, had established a very credible four-year record. In the next seven years, they experienced four winning seasons, two losing years, and one tie. Like soccer, baseball played under NAIA rules, but had no conference ties with the CSIC.

Ed Wuch retired from coaching, after five years, to become a professor in the Education Department and Warren Turner replaced him as head baseball coach and assistant football coach. Turner spent the year of 1977 strengthening his squad and entered the 1978 season with a team of much potential, but which developed slowly. Ending the regular season 15–14, they seemed a mediocre group, but suddenly in the postseason playoffs the Lions exploded into a squad of championship caliber. They captured first place in the District 16 playoffs at Springfield, then journeyed to Oshkosh, Wisconsin, where they took the Area Four title, and finally to St. Joseph for the NAIA Baseball World Series where the team lost to the Emporia State Hornets in the final game for the national championship. Amazingly the Lions had lost only one of the ten games played in these tournaments.

Though doing well overall, Coach Turner could not sustain the caliber of his 1978 team in the remaining four years of this time period. But he and his predecessor, Coach Wuch, had built MSSC baseball into a respectable power in NAIA District 16 competition, and one that lent prestige and substance to MSSC's growing reputation as a college of merit.

MSSC cheerleaders form a five-tier pyramid during festivities at the Homecoming pep rally and cookout in the fall of 1979. These activities, held at noon on the Friday before the Homecoming football game, have become a traditional part of Southern's Homecoming celebration, replacing the evening bonfire rallies associated with the junior college.

The 1976 Lions football team gathered in the Fred Hughes Stadium for this photograph. Pictured are, from left, front row: W. Williams, J. La Blank, R. Simpson, R. Green, D. Collins, B. Hayles, D. Clines, B. Patterson, J. Thompson, T. Cox, R. Brittan, H. Derrick, C. Chickering, and K. Howard. Second row: K. Conway, L. Lewis, R. Hamm, M. O'Brien, C. Cawyer, R. Jones, M. Keith, J. Page, G. Embry, J. Ristau, J. Manuel, B. Bland, L. Barnes, W. Donson, and R. Kungle. Third row: R. Barlett, J. Cupp, K. Newby, B. Richmond, L. Bolding, R. Rome, K. Jeanson, D. Wommack, J. Zingrich, S. Teeple, B. Mayberry, R. Shelley, D. Campbell, and K. Gundy. Fourth row: T. Hartsell, J. Cawyer, G. Days, M. Merryfield, M. Dake, R. Klos, J. Cole, D. Campbell, B. Neely, B. Brickey, D. Durham, L. Walker, and J. Gauntz. Fifth row: B. Winch, G. Shoemaker, S. Butler, D. Keith, R. Thomas, E. Sarduk, V. Featherson, M. Sims, and J. Wright. Back row; coaching staff: J. Frazier, B. Lentz, W. Turner, D. Gaddis, T. Calwhite, K. Sutton, T. Warron, and J. Strong.

Playing in the new Central States Intercollegiate Conference, the Lions gained a triple tie for first place and ranked 8–2 overall, their best year since 1972 and the best they would experience prior to 1983. The team was outstanding for its large number of talented players. Seven of the twenty-five players named to the 1968–1992 Silver Anniversary Commemorative Team served on this squad: Larry Barnes, Kenric Conway, Harvey Derrick, Gary Embry, Vincent Featherson, Marty O'Brian, and Willie Williams. Also, two, Vincent Featherson and Willie Williams, received Humphrey Awards, while Williams, Dean Collins, Tom Cox, and Rusty Shelley were named to the Letterman's Alumni Association Hall of Fame. Jim Strong later became head football coach at the University of Nevada, Las Vegas.

Cager Paul Merrifield demonstrates the advantages of height during this game against the Fort Hays (Kansas) State College Tigers during the 1979–1980 season. The Lions won the tightly contested game, 73–69.

The award-winning 1977–1978 basketball team is shown in this photograph. Pictured are, from left, front row: S. Shulte, J. Cochran, B. Corn, S. Brown, J. Sportsman, B. Brewster, and S. Coleman. Second row: Coach C. Williams, C. Cromer, S. McGuire, M. Dixon, R. Bland, T. Maxwell, R. Martin, and Assistant Coach R. Ellis.

The 1977–1978 basketball year began with a new coach, Tillman D. "Chuck" Williams, who was unusual for a coach in that he had a doctor of philosophy degree, earned at Indiana University. He coached the basketball Lions over the next twelve years, leading his teams into the national playoffs twice and winning Coach of the Year honors twice.

Though new, Coach Williams fielded one of the most successful basketball teams in Southern's history. The overall record of 27–9 still stands as the most ever wins. The team swept the CSIC and the NAIA District 16 championships and lasted into the quarter finals at the NAIA National Tournament before being defeated. Many honors were bestowed on team members. Russell Bland was named to the NAIA All-American First Team, the only basketball Lion to ever receive this honor. In addition, Bland, Roland Martin, and Scott Shulte received other important awards. Another notable player, Robert Corn, became MSSC's head basketball coach in 1989. Coach Williams earned the CSIC Coach of the Year Award.

Coach Harold W. Bodon's 1979 soccer team is shown lined up on the playing field. Pictured are, from left, front row: T. Johnson, J. Cindrich, W. Ticachek, J. Hatfield, J. Osborn, S. Holtz, G. Major, D. Morrison, K. Mulholland, K. Syberg, R. Chaves, J. Macken, and C. Bernheimer. Back row: Coach H. Bodon, C. Womack, S. Reeb, T. Hantak, J. Angeles, J. Murray, K. Burkeholder, R. Lonigro, R. Behnen, M. Ruzicka, T. Behmen, R. Ruzicka, A. Escobar, C. Dudley, S. Emery, and Trainer D. Smith.

This memorable team's 16–3–1 overall record, producing a .825 percent winning average, has never been exceeded in MSSC's soccer history. Its 17–1 victory over the Baptist Bible College, also set a scoring record that still stands. Many honors were showered on the team's players. George Major, the team's outstanding goalie, gained NAIA All-American First Team honors for two years in a row and received MSSC's Humphrey Award.

The men's minor sports, track and field, tennis, and golf, enjoyed little status in the 1976–1982 time period. Golf, alone of the three areas, still enjoyed some success under veteran coach Douglas Landrith.

The tennis program still functioned, but under amateur, part-time coaches. Interest declined and President Darnton cancelled it in 1982. The track and field program, with little support, lost its varsity standing in 1977 and was not revived as an effective sport until the late 1980s.

Foundations for a women's varsity sports program had been laid in the period 1974–1975, but much more needed to be done. The programs of volleyball, basketball, softball, tennis, and track remained underfunded, understaffed, and underdeveloped. In the next seven years these sports "grew up" and gained a maturity that placed them alongside men's sports and Southern's academic programs.

While the rudimentary women's sports program had functioned since 1974, mandates set by the Federal Education Act of 1972 required a further strengthening of the program in 1976. In that year, ten athletic scholarships were created for the benefit of women, the first ever offered to female athletes. Coach Sallie (Roper) Beard, who had initiated the women's sports program, was promoted to the new position of women's athletic director, a job in which she continues. Beard also coached the women's basketball and tennis teams through the 1976–1977 school year, after that she limited her coaching duties to the track team until 1983.

Several changes occurred in the staff in the next few years. G. I. Willoughby provided a net addition to the program in 1977 when she replaced Beard as basketball and tennis coach. The next year, with the departure of Geraldine H. Albins, Celia (Ce Ce) Chamberlin became volleyball and tennis coach while Willoughby took over the softball team. It was not until the 1981–1982 year that the women's coaching staff attained a measure of stability with James Phillips replacing Willoughby and Patsy Lipira taking over from Chamberlin. A major factor in Willoughby's resignation had been the burden of coaching both basketball and softball and steps were taken to lighten the coaching loads.

The affiliation of women's teams with regional and national associations underwent changes in the 1976–1982 period that brought them into line with men's athletics. Southern's entry into the Central States Intercollegiate Conference in 1976, also initially included the women's basketball and volleyball teams and was later expanded as the other sports developed. Since its inception, MSSC women's athletics had held membership in the national Association of Intercollegiate Athletics for Women (AIAW) and its Missouri affiliate the MAIAW which held a state tournament each year in which the Lady Lions competed. But when that league collapsed, the Lady Lions were brought into Southern's national affiliate, the NAIA, for the 1980–1981 school year and from that time on the women's teams competed under the NAIA District 16 umbrella along with men's athletics.

Basketball and volleyball were the Lady Lions leading varsity sports. In the

(Top) The 1978 "World Series" baseball team that placed second in the NAIA national championship contest is shown here with their new coach, Warren F. Turner. Pictured are, from left, front row: R. Roberson, B. Coggins, R. Koenig, and S. Sanders. Second row: R. O'Dell, L. Snider, R. Morris, J. Siel, D. Smith, J. Coleman, B. Jenkins, M. Allen, and T. Cox. Back row: Assistant Coach J. Eberhard, T. VanBrunt, R. Cable, B. McAffee, D. Miller, R. Dreier, G. Curran, D. Selbe, R. Jackson, C. Valentine, M. Massey, S. Spatz, K. Heimsoth, and Coach W. Turner.

Turner, beginning a long career as MSSC baseball coach, won NAIA National Coach of the Year honors for this year. In the five times that Turner has led his teams into National World Series playoffs, he has also won other Coach of the Year Awards.

Mike Swidler is shown scoring a hit for the baseball Lions at Joe Becker stadium in this 1989 photograph.

Since 1977 this city-owned stadium at Third and High streets has been the baseball Lions' home field. MSSC pays no fee for its use, but the baseball team assumes the costs of maintenance and repair. At an earlier time it was the home of the Joplin Miners which once served as a "farm team" for the New York Yankees. Some of baseball's greats, like Mickey Mantle and Stan Musial, have played on this field.

1976–1981 period the basketball team enjoyed only a modicum of success and won no important championships. All the basketball teams had a small cadre of outstanding players, but, as in the other women's sports, they lacked talent in depth. The 1978–1979 team finished the year 21–11 overall, but they failed to win first place in any major competitions.

The 1981–1982 season marked a significant turning point in the basketball Lady Lions' fortunes. The teams had performed poorly in the prior two years though Pam Brisby, Mary Carter, and Lisa Gardner had played brilliantly. Jim Phillips, the new coach, came too late to do much recruiting, but he found in the demoralized previous year's returnees a reservoir of underdeveloped talent. Phillips' team seemed to grow stronger as the season progressed. For the first time, they won the NAIA District 16 championship. Next the triumphant Lady Lions emerged victorious from the Area 4 playoffs and then moved on to Kansas City for the NAIA National Tournament. There the Southern team won the first two rounds only to lose in the finals, thus placing second in their bid for a national championship. The Lady Lions basked in the national spotlight for the first time. Many honors were showered on individual team members and Coach Phillips was named NAIA District 16 Women's Coach of the Year.

With many of the team's strongest players lost through graduation, the 1982–1983 season became one of rebuilding in which the Lady Lions experienced a 12–14 losing year, but the foundations were laid for a much stronger team in the next three years.

The volleyball teams enjoyed winning seasons in four of the seven years in the 1976–1982 time period, but never won any important championships. Coach Geraldine (Gerry) Albins, who organized the first women's volleyball team in the fall of 1975, continued to coach the teams through the next two years with winning seasons in both. She established a vigorous regimen of conditioning the players by requiring them to run the hill between Hearnes Hall and the Spiva Library ten times, three times a week, do pushups and lift weights.

Ce Ce Chamberlin coached the volleyball Lady Lions for the 1978 through 1980 seasons, followed by Patsy Lipira in the next two years. Chamberlin's 1979 team placed third in regular CSIC play, the best conference performance yet for the volleyball Lady Lions. Some of the college's outstanding women athletes, Barbara Lawson, Leah Williams, Patti Killian, Mary Carter, Dina Hein, and Joanna Swearengin played under her.

Lipira experienced a 22–18–5 season in her first year, 1981, but gained a more impressive 33–11–5 success the following year. In the newly instituted NAIA District 16 playoffs, her team placed second in both years. Players receiving honors were Lisa Cunningham, Teresa Gutherie, and Joanna Swearengin.

The softball program languished in its first four years under Coaches Beard and Albins. Little in the way of resources, either human or monetary, were put into the sport. A lack of talented players plagued the program and the absence of a suitable playing field posed another problem. At the beginning of the 1978 season, Coach Albins forfeited the first game for lack of a suitable diamond, before finding a home in Henson Park's Little League field. In the spring of 1979, Coach G. I. Willoughby took over the team. With six years experience as a college softball coach, she began to strengthen the neglected sport. In the first season of her three-year tenure, Willoughby fielded a winning 22–13 team, but in the next two seasons fell back into the loser's bracket by a narrow margin. Pat Lipira replaced Willoughby as head softball coach for the 1982 season, but with little time to rebuild the team, she too plunged into a losing 14–20 season.

The minor sports in the women's program, tennis and track, enjoyed an

With eyes dead on the ball, Tom Cox demonstrates proper batting technique during the 1977–1978 college year. Cox was outstanding in both baseball and football and he played on the baseball Lions memorable "World Series" team of 1978.

intermittent success in this period. They always suffered from a lack of student interest and from a scarcity of resources being devoted to them. Coach Beard directed the tennis team through the spring of 1977 season and enjoyed a 9–1 winning season that year. Terri Dresh was the team's outstanding star. In the next four years, tennis, coached first by Willoughby for one year and then by Chamberlin, continued to do well. In 1980, the team placed first in CSIC play and second in the MAIAW. From that time on the program deteriorated and in the spring of 1982 President Darnton reported that women's tennis had "died a natural death" for lack of student support.

When Sallie Beard became director of Women's Athletics in 1976, she dropped, one by one, her coaching duties except for track. Students exhibited little interest in the program until 1978 when Beard was able to field a team of seven who played in informal meets. It was a modest start, but in the next four years, interest grew and the college's more talented athletes began to participate in regular meets which featured such activities as the 100- and 200-meter dash, hurdles, javelin and discus throwing, as well as the shot put. Patty Vavra was named MSSC's "Outstanding Track Performer" for 1979. Beard was named Women's Track and Field Coach of the year for 1981 and 1983. After this the program was temporarily discontinued and she devoted full time to being director of Women's Athletics.

By 1982, women's sports had established themselves and became an integral part of the college's educational program. Equally important, they had gained an identity of their own. Though lacking the funding, size, and attendance-drawing power of men's varsity sports—women had no equivalent of men's football—they had demonstrated that there were many talented women athletes who could play with an athletic finesse, in their own areas of competition, that put them on a plane with men. The girls had established a fact, not fully recognized in 1974, that women's sports parallel and complement men's athletic activities, but do not necessarily compete with them. Debbie Phillips, voted the volleyball team's Outstanding Player for the 1976 season, emphasized this point. "We aren't trying to imitate men," she said. "We're Lady Lions out there playing volleyball . . . we're not trying to be men."

Members of Coach Douglas Landrith's 1981 golf team pose with their clubs in this photograph. Pictured, from left, are: Steve Schwartz, Steve Arnold, Scott Phillips, Geo Surprise, Tim Huffine, Doug Harvey, Steve Kelley, Jeff Walster, Rick Cupps, and Coach Douglas Landrith.

This was Landrith's last year as golf coach and he again fielded a strong team, finishing second in both CSIC and NAIA District 16 competition. The next year, the Board of Regents, faced with severe budgetary problems, seriously curtailed the golfing program, but allowed it to continue under part-time coaches. Landrith retired in 1983. His twenty-four years of service gives him the longest tenure of any head coach in Southern's history.

When the state legislature created Missouri Southern as a state-supported two-year senior college resting on top of a locally supported junior college an implicit obligation was created that sometime in the future the hybrid institution would become fully state funded. Prior to 1971 the issue lay dormant. The Missouri Commission on Higher Education in 1966 had called for a ten-year moratorium on adding any new state colleges and in fact had never at any time recommended full four-year funding for Southern or its hybrid twin, Missouri Western College. Furthermore, the college initially had only provisional accreditation and it was not until March 31, 1971, that the North Central Association granted Southern full accreditation.

The year 1971 marked the beginning of a five-year legislative

Coach G. I. Willoughby's 1978–1979 Lady Lions basketball team is shown in this photograph. Pictured are, from left, front row: A. Maloney, B. Johnson, P. Maples, D. Peters, L. White, P. Killian, M. Carter, B. Pitts, D. Swisher, K. Gordon, and S. Beeler. Back row: Coach G. Willoughby, D. Jantz, B. Lawson, S. Kelley, C. Kuklentz, P. Brisby, L. Gardner, L. Knoll, P. Vavra, and N. Robertson.

With a 21–11 overall record, this was the basketball Lady Lion's best season up to this time. Award winning players on this team were Pam Brisby, Mary Carter, Lisa Gardner, Karen Gordon, Patti Killian, Cherie Kuklentz, Barbara Lawson, and Brenda Pitts. Barbara (Lawson) Cowherd and Patty Vavra were inducted into the Letterman's Alumni Association Hall of Fame in 1993.

Pam Brisby, the Lady Lions leading player on the 1981–1982 basketball team is shown shooting a basket. A late-blooming squad, the 1981–1982 team's regular season performance was less than brilliant, but as they moved into the postseason playoffs, under the direction of new Head Coach James Phillips, the team found themselves and came within one game of winning a national championship. Pam Brisby and Linda Castillon were star performers, but most honors went to Brisby. Among other recognitions, she received the NAIA All-American First Team Award. Brisby's career total of 1,720 points scored stood as a new high for four years and her record of 775 points scored in one season still stands as an all-time high for a MSSC player, female or male. At Southern, she received the Humphrey Award and in 1993 was inducted into the Letterman's Alumni Association Hall of Fame.

The 1977 tennis team is shown in this photograph with their coach, Sallie (Roper) Beard. Kneeling are, from left: Vali Mathews, Kim Cummings, Deb Van Alman, and Kayla Sill. Standing are: Coach Sallie (Roper) Beard, Georgina Garrison, Julie Alford, and Dee Kassab.

In her last year as tennis coach, Beard led this team to an outstanding 9–1 season. Freshmen Georgina Garrison was an emerging star who sparked the teams to three more successful seasons. In 1980, the team finished 15–1 for first place in the CSIC.

Georgina (Garrison) Bodine, a Webb City native, received the Lionbacker's Award of Excellence in her senior year of 1980. Since the fall of 1989, she has coached the women's tennis team at Southern.

(Below) The 1980 Lady Lions softball team is shown in this photograph with their coach, G. I. Willoughby. Pictured are, from left, front row: K. Dozier, K. Castillon, B. Pitts, A. Henson, and S. Periman. Second row: G. Hunter, M. Carter, P. Killian, G. Bradford, D. Cole, and G. Grey. Back row: T. Guthrie, L. Gardner, A. Maloney, S. Payne, C. Pearcy, E. Rakowiecki, and Coach G. Willoughby.

The softball Lady Lions experienced few winning seasons prior to 1983 and this team's 20–23 overall performance was no exception, but five of Southern's outstanding lady athletes played on this team: Mary Carter, Kim Castillon, Lisa Gardner, Patti Killian, and Brenda Pitts. Carter, from Carthage, played basketball, softball, tennis, and volleyball. In her senior year, 1980–1981, she became the first Lady Lion to receive a CSIC All-Conference Academic award in basketball, was named MSSC's Women's Athlete of the Year, and received the Lionbackers' Award of Excellence.

struggle to gain full state funding for the two colleges. The legislative climate had changed little since 1965. Opposition to the funding bill was mild in the House of Representatives, but in the upper house a cadre of powerful senators strongly opposed the new colleges which they saw as rivals to long-established state colleges.

Senator Richard Webster and his fellow Carthagenian, the veteran Representative Robert Ellis Young, led the fight for Missouri Southern. Webster, after nearly ten years in the Senate, had become a powerful figure in Missouri state government and a skilled legislative infighter. He needed all his skill. The two new colleges' most vocal opponent was Senator Earl Blackwell, from Hillsboro. In leading the fight to kill the 1973 funding bill, Blackwell charged that Southern and Missouri Western had "completely loused up higher education in Missouri," and that instead of full state funding they should have their support for the third and fourth years withdrawn altogether.

Board President Fred Hughes and MSSC President Leon Billingsly presented strong arguments in favor of full state funding in testimony before legislative committees and in public speeches. They pointed, in particular, to the growing local burden of the system. As the college expanded and more students came from outside the junior college district, local taxpayers had to largely support the first two years of their schooling and provide the physical plant for their upper two years. They also pointed to the administrative complexity of two overlapping systems and the potential for friction between the two boards.

Pending passage of the funding legislation, the Board and President Billingsly decided to formally change the college's name from Missouri Southern to Missouri Southern State College. The former was in reality the name of the junior college while the latter was by law the name of the senior college, but had been little used up to this time. The 1972–1973 catalog was the first to reflect this change.

The move toward full state funding finally bore fruit in 1975. A new Coordinating Board of Higher Education (CBHE) withdrew opposition to the funding bill and Governor Christopher Bond then threw his strong support behind passage. The earlier move, promoted by Joplin and St. Joseph legislators, that gave university status to the four older state colleges helped to erode opposition and the bill passed the Senate by a surprising margin of 24–9 and the House by a vote of 85–68. Watching from the House gallery when the final vote was tallied were President Billingsly and Regents Thomas Taylor and Norval Matthews. To them it was the culmination of a dream.

Provisions of the new full funding act, slated to become effective July 1, 1977, provided for a six-member Board of Regents appointed by the governor for six-year terms. The existing Boards of Trustees were required to transfer all properties to the state as of the effective date of the act and were to continue to be responsible for retiring all existing bonded indebtedness, but would have no other duties or authority. MSSC and MWSC were restricted to offering only undergraduate degrees and were required to continue and to expand their technical-vocational associate degree and one-year certificate programs. On the other hand, the state was to assume all tax supported costs of operations and capital improvements of the two colleges, after the effective date of the act.

Governor Bond signed the full-funding act, June 26, 1975, but implementation of the act still lay two years in the future. No ceremony was held on July 1, 1977, when the act became fully operative, yet it was significant because it marked the end of the forty-year-old junior college as a functioning unit.

The 1977 Lady Lions volleyball team is shown here in an informal pose during the playing season. Pictured are, from left, front, seated: C. Dickerson. Second row, seated; L. Williams, M. Carr, M. Carter, P. Killian, and B. Lawson. Third row: L. Hansen, C. Yust, B. Knust, and L. Binns. Standing: K. O'Daniels, P. Crane, Coach G. Albins, and C. Pearcy.

This was Coach Albins' last and best year as a volleyball coach. The team posted a 25–16–1 overall record, their strongest performance in the seven-year period prior to 1982. Barbara Lawson, Becky Knust, Lindy Binns, and Leah Williams received CSIC All-Conference honors.

Locally, area residents had mixed feelings toward the new full state college status. They realized the bill would enhance MSSC's prestige by giving it more of a regional and statewide image. Taxpayers appreciated the legislation's more equitable spread of the tax burden and indeed 1976 became the last year in which the thirty-cent property tax for college operations was levied on district residents. On the other hand, some residents sensed that they were losing a stake in the college that local tax support had entailed. It was becoming less "our college," something they had always been fiercely proud of. Then, too, some local people felt the state was exacting a heavy price. An inventory showed that the Jasper County Junior College District was turning over to the state assets—buildings, land, and equipment—that had cost $17,502,073, but the local taxpayers were left with the burden of paying off the remaining $2,005,000 of bonded indebtedness incurred in purchasing those assets. Some critics maintained that, at a minimum, the state should assume the debt along with the assets.

Veteran members of the Board of Regents and Trustees were immensely proud of the college's new status and saw it as a necessary milestone in the college's development. This was especially true of Board President Fred Hughes who had played such a strong leadership role in gaining the college. For College President Leon Billingsly, then nearing the end of his life, it proved to be the crowning achievement in his dream of building a quality institution of higher learning that could open new windows of opportunity for local youth of limited financial means.

Governor Joseph Teasdale had the duty of appointing the new six-member Board of Regents when the full-funding act became effective July 1, 1977. Appointed were: Jerry Wells, Joplin; Carolyn Rogers McKee, Carthage; Fred Hughes, Joplin; William Schwab, Joplin; Ray Grace, Carthage; and Don Roderique, Webb City. The appointments, as required in the statute, ranged from one to six years and were made in the respective order shown. The first three were incumbents while the others were new appointments. Mills Anderson of Carthage, then serving in an interim position, became the only member of the old five-seat board to be eliminated. A fifth member of the Board, Norval Matthews, had died shortly before the restructuring. Further restructuring of the Board occurred when the new members met. Fred Hughes was reelected president, a position he had held throughout the twelve-year history of the Regents, but with the stipulation that henceforth presidents would serve only one-year rotating terms. A new post of president-elect was created and Jerry Wells, who received this appointment, moved up to become the Regent's second president in July 1978.

Full funding had left the old Board of Trustees with one last official duty before fading into memory; namely that of levying the necessary taxes to pay off the remaining bonded indebtedness. This was not accomplished without some controversy. The debt service tax levy had been eleven cents on July

Governor Christopher "Kit" Bond is shown signing the historic full-funding bill that turned Southern into a full-fledged state college. Standing are Boards of Trustees/Regents members, from left: Dr. Donald Patterson, Thomas Taylor, Elvin Ummel, Fred Hughes, Mills Anderson, Norval Matthews, Jerry Wells, and Carolyn McKee.

Only about one hundred spectators were present for the ceremony held on a hot summer afternoon, June 26, 1975, in front of the College Union. Representative Robert Ellis Young, Carthage, leader of the House floor fight, delivered the keynote address, terming the legislation "a beautiful bargain."

Earlier in the day, Governor Bond in a similar ceremony at St. Joseph, had affixed his first name and middle initial to the legislation. At this time, he added his last name, using several pens which provided souvenirs for the dignitaries present.

148

l, 1977, the proceeds of which, deposited in the bond sinking fund and with accumulated interest, was deemed sufficient to meet the required payments until the full debt was retired in 1986. A sharp rise in interest rates, which caused a surplus to begin to build up, upset this plan. Periodically the Board of Trustees lowered the tax levy rate and by July 1983 it had fallen to five cents. In September the state Attorney General sounded an alarm. He pointed out that the junior college district had $985,000 in outstanding obligations and $1,534,513 in the sinking fund and suggested that, with this surplus, a continuation of the tax might be illegal. The Trustees immediately dropped the tax in the interest of maintaining public confidence. They did not regard the tax as illegal and had hoped to retain the minimal levy until 1986 as a way of creating a building fund for the college. But interest income continued to build on the accumulated funds and when the final bond payment was made on February 15, 1986, approximately $1 million was left to transfer to the building fund. After this final act, the Board of Trustees existed only as an honorary body.

Missouri Southern reached a crucial transitional point with the death of President Leon C. Billingsly on Saturday, November 25, 1978, at the age of fifty-three. Billingsly had attended a reception at 4:00 P.M. for visiting coaches who were in Joplin for the annual Lionbackers Holiday Basketball Tournament. Shortly after returning home, he suffered a fatal heart attack. The suddenness of his death shocked students, faculty and administrators. Classes were dismissed for the following Monday and Tuesday. Funeral services were held in Taylor Auditorium with about one thousand mourners in attendance. A mark of the respect and high esteem accorded him was shown when a group of his former colleagues and friends flew in from Michigan where he had been director of the Kellogg Community College for only one year, some fourteen years before.

In the flood of comments that followed Billingsly's death, he was eulogized as the prime leader in transforming the old junior college into a full-fledged state institution. Sometimes pictured as a "brick and mortar" president with the implication that he neglected academics, in reality Southern was academically strong at the time of his death. Billingsly tried to strike a balance between the pressing need for new physical facilities and the need to maintain a strong academic program, but, on the eve of his death, he realized that priorities were shifting and that, with an adequate physical plant in place, more resources should be routed into academics.

Much has been written about Billingsly's qualities of leadership. That he was a forceful leader none would deny. He was physically a large man who projected a commanding presence in any gathering, yet he was friendly and outgoing. Billingsly had the quality of decisiveness as all strong executives do. Some criticized him for being unyielding and dictatorial, but none faulted him for equivocating on important issues. He did not hesitate to make weighty decisions. A superb administrator with a great mind for detail, Billingsly's knowledge of campus events was legendary, but in later years he sadly remarked that the college was growing too large for him to keep up with everything.

The late president was a highly effective spokesman for the college in the state legislature. In a sense, state college presidents are lobbyists for their institutions in seeking appropriations from the legislature. Though Billingsly

The Theatre Department staff pose informally in this 1978–1979 photograph. Pictured are, from left*: G. Joyce Bowman, 1967–1989; Milton W. Brietzke, 1956–1987; Duane L. Hunt, 1963; Samuel L. Claussen, 1977, and Trij Brietzke. Trij, Milton's wife, was a part-time instructor who taught, acted, and wrote theatre plays from time-to-time.

Milton Brietzke had been the only director of the Theatre Department up to the time of his retirement.

Claussen and Brietzke were recipients of MSSC's Outstanding Teacher of a Freshman Class Award in 1985 and 1987 respectively. Bowman received the Outstanding Teacher Award in 1988.

Bowman and Brietzke are both retired.

*Names are followed by dates of employment—a single date if still on the staff.

149

never liked that term, he probably enjoyed a closer relationship with the legislature than any of the other state college presidents of his era.

A considerate and caring individual, Billingsly carefully avoided humiliating faculty or staff members. Subordinates were given a chance to make their own decisions and to try out their own ideas. Students found him willing to listen to their problems. On snowy days he checked the roads and when tornadoes threatened he went to nearby mobile home parks to warn the students.

Billingsly was also honest and loyal. He practiced strict honesty so that no fog of rumors ever gathered around him involving the misuse of public funds, nor were his personal morals ever called into question. Pettiness and underhandedness were not part of his makeup. Loyal to his subordinates, they found he would back them in their decisions unless wrongdoing or manifest incompetence was involved. Some of his most agonizing decisions involved wrongdoing among valued associates. Yet, inwardly Billingsly was a very private person. He avoided "self glorification" and no plaque appeared on his door saying "president." He put the college before himself and generally avoided interviews or attempts to "saturate the media" with his own name.

The shock of President Billingsly's sudden passing left the Board of Regents in a quandary. Obviously leadership was needed immediately, but selection of a new president required careful consideration. The board then appointed Floyd E. Belk, vice president for Academic Affairs, as interim president and Paul R. Shipman, vice president for Business Affairs, as interim executive vice president. An eleven-member Search and Screening Committee was formed to conduct a nationwide search for a new president. Some 237 candidates applied and 10 were eventually interviewed.

By late April 1979 the regents had picked Dr. Donald C. Darnton as the new president. Darnton, age forty-seven, was a native of Detroit, Michigan, and had a strong academic background, with a doctorate in economics and twenty years experience as a professor and as a college administrator. Darnton initially received a salary of $46,000 per year ($1,000 more than Billingsly) plus use of the college-owned president's home.

A man of considerable analytical ability, Darnton, from the beginning of his presidency, promoted the twin goals of an enriched academic program and administrative reorganization. He called for "a change in direction," and at his first faculty workshop, stated, "Since our establishment as a four-year college, we have focused on numbers: more students, more buildings, more faculty. The time is here to turn our attention to quality."

President Darnton launched immediately into a series of changes that in the three years of his presidency made extensive administrative modifications and that brought new strength to the academic programs. In the area of administrative changes the Divisions of Arts and Sciences, Education and Psychology, Business Administration, and Technology were renamed as schools in what amounted to a largely cosmetic, but permanent change. New administrative offices created were Academic Services, assistant to the president, associate vice president, and director of Development. Student Services were reorganized with the posts of dean of men and dean of women eliminated and the positions of dean of students, assistant dean of students, and director of Academic Development created. Continuing Education was upgraded. In the Academic area, a post of assistant dean of Technology was added and new Departments of Communications and Education were established. Many of these administrative changes were extensively modified in the post-Darnton era, but changes in the academic area proved more lasting.

Darnton soon issued a new mission statement for the college which aimed to give more precise focus to his announced goal of enriching academics. The statement reiterated Southern's mission "to serve the people of southwest Mis-

Letterman's Club officers, from left: Dean Collins, president; Tom Cox, secretary; Mike Goodpaster, treasurer; Bill Patterson, vice president; and John Zingrich, sergeant-at-arms, posed for this picture during the 1976–1977 school year. The Letterman's Club was established in 1969 to honor varsity letter winners.

Cox and Collins, both outstanding in football, were named to the Letterman's Alumni Association Hall of Fame in 1988 and 1990 respectively.

souri" and confirmed its role as an undergraduate institution. On the recommendation of the North Central Association accrediting review team, Darnton set up a Long Range Planning Committee "to turn the mission statement into reality."

Darnton also took other steps to enrich Southern's academic programs. A system of Outstanding Teacher Awards were set up that granted $1,000 each to the outstanding teacher and the outstanding teacher of a freshman class each year. A business lecture series was established on a continuing basis, and a system of grants for faculty development were added. To support these programs, he turned to the newly reorganized Missouri Southern Foundation and in 1982, for the first time, the Foundation undertook a limited fund-raising drive.

Darnton's new administration had begun with high expectations. His program of administrative reform and academic enrichment seemed to herald a new era, but problems soon became evident. Measuring up to the late President Billingsly's image would have been difficult for any successor, but it soon became evident Darnton could not match Billingsly's strong leadership qualities. Though a friendly and articulate man who could present ideas in a masterful way, Darnton lacked Billingsly's decisiveness in dealing with vexing problems. He also fell short of the late president's understanding and diplomatic skills in dealing with personnel. As a consequence, he never established the rapport with the Board of Regents, administrators, staff, faculty, or students that the late president had maintained. This lack of finesse in dealing with people soon became evident in Jefferson City, where he failed to maintain the close liaison with powerful legislative committees that Billingsly had enjoyed, thus causing MSSC to lose some support.

Darnton also suffered from a budgetary crisis not of his making. Shortly after he became president, the nation, already torn by high inflation, slid into a severe economic recession that lasted on into 1982. The climax came when Southern's 1981–1982 state appropriation was reduced to $5,645,321, creating a $1,026,439 shortfall from the previous year. Student incidental fees were raised from $220 to $255 per semester and other steps were taken to partially offset the deficit, but drastic spending cuts also became necessary. The budgetary crisis greatly complicated a number of Darnton's other problems.

Another troublesome issue for Darnton was that of growing faculty unrest over the evaluation system. Though a problem he inherited from the Billingsly era, it proved the most damaging to his prestige.

The controversy grew out of an evaluation system installed in the mid-1970s that had two facets many faculty found objectionable: namely, student evaluations and merit pay. In a sense, the system of professorial ranks, established with the advent of the four-year college, was a merit system in that it provided for advancement in rank and salary based on outstanding work and training, but, at this time, administrators and the Board of Regents determined to reinforce it with a system providing for more frequent review based primarily on classroom performance.

The college-wide practice of having students evaluate faculty began in-

Assembled here are five members of the Board of Regents/Trustees in 1977. Pictured are, from left: Jerry E. Wells, Carolyn D. McKee, Fred G. Hughes, Arthur Kungle, and Elvin Ummel.

Wells, a Joplin lawyer, served on the Board of Trustees from 1968 until it ceased to function in 1986 and on the Regents from 1968 to 1985.

McKee, a Carthage businesswoman, served on the Board of Regents from 1974 to 1979 and on the Trustees from 1976 to 1986. She was the first woman appointed to the Board of Regents and the only woman ever to serve on the Board of Trustees. McKee died in 1991.

Hughes, a Joplin businessman and an original Trustee and Regent, was on the former board from 1964 to 1986, and the latter from 1965 to 1981.

Kungle, a Joplin businessman, served on the Board of Trustees from 1972 to 1986. He was never a Regent. Kungle died in 1990.

Ummel, a Jasper dairy farmer and a member of the original Board of Trustees served on that board from 1964 to 1986. He was appointed to the Board of Regents in 1991.

nocuously enough in 1974 when a survey showed that a majority of the faculty approved such evaluation "as a means of improving the college." Some departments had already been using them. The system tightened considerably in the 1975–1976 school year when the administration began requiring the usage in all classes of a uniform Student Instructor Report (SIR). These forms were supplied by the Education Testing Service and tabulated by them, scoring individual faculty against a national norm established for each discipline. Using the SIRs as a base, a complex 100-point system evolved for rating individual faculty. The SIRs accounted for 45 of these points. Individual faculty were rated from unsatisfactory to superior based on their total points.

Criticism of this highly structured system arose immediately. The SIRs, in particular, came under protest. Some felt they measured primarily popularity; others maintained they discriminated against teachers of lower-level courses, particularly the large General Education classes; while many maintained no uniform questionnaire like the SIR could be valid for all because of departmental variances. Other than the SIRs many felt the whole approach was invalid, that the measure of teaching effectiveness was largely subjective and that any attempt to reduce it to a mathematical formula was artificial. Soon bitter comments about "playing the point game" became commonplace.

Deep-seated dissatisfaction mounted year by year. In the spring of 1978, President Billingsly warned the Board of Regents that the evaluation system was causing low faculty morale, but the Regents, no longer as subservient to the forceful Billingsly as they once had been, insisted on continuing the system. In the faculty meeting that spring, Billingsly asked for suggestions and that fall the Faculty Senate set up an ad hoc committee to study the matter, but it came up with no suggestions for substantial reforms. Distrust again intensified in the summer of 1979 when investigation revealed that SIR forms had been altered in a way that considerably lowered the scores of two faculty members.

President Billingsly, had he lived, might have resolved the evaluation grievances, but the task fell to his successor. When Darnton became president, the Board of Trustees pointedly reaffirmed its commitment to faculty evaluation and merit pay, but, "given the ill-repute of the present system, recognized some review and revision might be necessary." During the summer of 1979 still another Senate ad hoc committee labored at solving the evaluation enigma. This committee presented an astute analysis of the problem, but only its recommendation for a new campus-designed student evaluation form, the Instructor Course Evaluation System (ICES) to replace the old SIR was accepted by the administration. Many faculty saw the change as largely cosmetic, but this fundamentally unchanged system became the basis for setting the fateful 1980–1981 salary schedule. In the meantime, President Darnton appointed his own committee to have yet another go at reforming the evaluation morass.

As the decade of the 1980s dawned, most of MSSC's faculty, finding their salaries ravaged by high inflation, looked upon the merit pay system as particularly galling. Unrest intensified. Many of those who benefitted most from the merit pay raises also objected to the system, which they saw as unfair and demeaning. But warnings that a serious morale problem threatened went unheeded.

In the fall of 1980 faculty unrest reached a boiling point. Attempts at reforming the evaluation system had been ineffectual, and both the administration and Board of Regents, bent on a rigid merit system, seemed insensitive to their grievances. Two events caused the pot to boil over. Just before school opened administration officials announced the new pay schedule for 1980–1981. The governor had recommended pay raises of 9.5 percent for state

Maureen McCullough as Maid Marian and Zander Brietzke as Robin Hood appear in this scene from the children's theatre performance of Robin Hood *during the 1979–1980 school year. Zander Brietzke, the son of then MSSC theatre director Milton Brietzke, completed his doctorate in theatre at Stanford University and now teaches at Lehigh University.*

employees and MSSC's schedule followed this for noninstructional staff, but, in order to implement the merit system, some 61 percent of the faculty received raises ranging from 4 percent to 9.2 percent, while 39 percent, in the meritorious category, benefitted from an 11.2 percent increase. Many faculty in the 61 percent categories, though most fell in the 9.2 percent bracket, saw this arrangement as a direct affront. To them it seemed to imply a performance so poor that it did not measure up to that of the noninstructional staff or state employees in general, though the Board of Regents denied this. Compounding the growing unrest over this pay schedule was the fact merit raises were not bonuses, but had always been added to the recipient's permanent salary base. Adding merit raises as a percentage of the base had a considerable accumulative effect that over a period of years held the prospect of creating a minority of very well paid faculty with a majority whose salaries were mediocre. A second event involved Darnton's announcement that his committee had completed a new evaluation system for the coming year. Even more complex, it made no substantive changes, but was approved by the Regents without ever having been presented to the Faculty Senate. Adding more fuel to the growing controversy, this plan was destined never to be implemented.

At this time, the National Education Association (NEA), long active in organizing public school teachers, desired to expand their organization in the college field and they were also lobbying for passage of a Missouri collective bargaining law for public school and college teachers. NEA officials, regarded the MSSC evaluation system as being particularly egregious and saw in it an opportunity to promote their cause. A few members of the Southern faculty had been NEA members in past years, but at this time, national officials of the NEA moved to build a strong organization around this nucleus by sharply lowering yearly dues and by assigning field representatives from the national and regional offices.

The effort paid off and membership mushroomed as frustrated MSSC faculty saw in the NEA a fresh approach that might bring some adjustment of their grievances. Associate Professor Rochelle L. Boehning, president of the new MSSC-NEA chapter, soon found himself at the head of a strong organization. By October of 1980, membership reached 47 and by January it surpassed 90, thus well over one-half of Southern's 143 teaching faculty belonged.

In the early fall an MSSC-NEA "Crisis Committee" formed and began planning a strategy for dealing with the evaluation problem. The committee sent a letter directly to Board of Regents President William S. Schwab, Jr., stating that the existing evaluation system "must be discontinued immediately." Schwab brusquely replied that he had referred the letter to President Darnton and reminded Boehning that the established procedure called for such matters to be initiated through the administration.

The stage was set for a confrontation. The administration tried to downplay faculty support for the NEA, but a survey conducted by the Faculty Welfare Committee early in November showed an overwhelming majority of the faculty were opposed to the existing evaluation system. The old evaluation plan had lingered on for some five years seemingly becoming more harsh, and some administrators had reportedly told complaining faculty members that if they did not like the system they could find another job. The Board of Regents at this time reiterated that they were willing to consider changes and that they had the best interests of the faculty at heart, but statements from individual Regents indicating their determination to impose a rigid merit system on the faculty largely negated any expressions of compromise. Many faculty had come to the conclusion that neither the administration nor the Regents would initiate any meaningful reforms unless pressured to do so.

(Top) Milton Brietzke "stole the show" as he played the role of Lord Brockhurst in this rendition of The Boyfriend, presented during the 1979–1980 college year. Brenda Michael portrayed Dulcie in this musical comedy set in 1928. Brietzke and other members of the Theatre faculty occasionally took roles in the department's presentations as a way of keeping themselves better attuned to their discipline.

(Bottom) Members of the 1980–1981 championship debate team pose with their coach, Richard H. Finton, for this photograph. Pictured from left, are: Aria Beck, Jack Woody, John Meredith, Mitch Savage, Tarri Bays, Amy Wickwar, Michael Tosh, Julie Storm, and Coach Richard H. Finton.

Consisting of mostly freshmen, this team placed first in the state and third in the nation. Finton was a speech instructor and debate coach at Southern from 1977 to 1988.

These attentive members of the Art League posed on a stairway in the Art Department during the 1975–1976 school year. Pictured are, from left, front row: President Rick Nielsen and Gretchen Kissel. Row two: Lana Miller and Becky Batemen. Row three: Sharon Klein and Mike Buchanan. Row four: Kim Kissel, Mary McCann, and Roger Green. Row five: Carter Leffen, Kathy Long, and Rod Roberson. Row six: Karen Bradfield, Randy Wright, Sherry Probert, and Sam Lewis. Back row: Rex Chaney and Linda Tourtillot.

Of the new academic clubs that sprouted with the advent of the senior college, the Art League has been one of the most successful.

In the event of a rebuff, which was expected, the NEA planned to launch a publicity campaign against the Board of Regents. The NEA made one last effort to avoid a public confrontation when field representative Arnold Erickson telephoned Board President William Schwab asking for a meeting, but Schwab refused to confer with him. In the next few weeks, the NEA launched a barrage of publicity against the Board of Regents. Flyers were passed out and press releases proclaimed, "a crisis has developed. . . ." Regents faced a torrent of phone calls. Newspapers picked up the controversy and coverage extended as far away as Kansas City. It gave the college a bad image; area residents who had always strongly supported the college were dismayed and tended to see fault on both sides.

The besieged Board of Regents weighed their options carefully, but soon realized they would have to play a more active role in seeking a solution. Dealing with the demands of the NEA became their most immediate concern. The Board's lawyer advised the Regents that the faculty had a legal right to join the NEA and to present proposals to the board, or its designated representative, and the Regents or their representative had a duty to "meet and confer" with the NEA. On the other hand, the faculty had no right of collective bargaining or a right to strike, and the board had no legal authority to enter into a bargaining agreement with the NEA. Under this directive, the Regents took the position that the NEA could confer with President Darnton, but not with them. They would not attempt to abolish the NEA on campus or attempt to punish faculty members for belonging, but they would not recognize the NEA nor confer with any of its leaders.

The dispute began to slowly resolve itself in the next few months. NEA President Boehning made repeated requests to confer with the Regents, but these were always rejected. The Board finally agreed, at President Darnton's suggestion, to meet with members of the Faculty Senate and they further announced that any faculty member, if put on the agenda, could individually speak at a Regents' meeting. Finally Boehning received permission to speak to the Board, but under strict guidelines that he was speaking as an individual and not as NEA president. Darnton began a series of faculty dinner/discussion meetings to give rank and file faculty a chance to express their grievances. In January 1981, the Regents took the important step of suspending the existing evaluation system and directing President Darnton to draw up a new one. NEA leaders, increasingly frustrated by being frozen out of a voice in developing the new evaluation system, considered a faculty strike, but most members opposed such a drastic move. Instead the NEA conducted a vote of confidence on the college president and the two vice presidents. The vote of confidence, conducted by an independent certified public accountant, showed a strong lack of confidence in all three. However 42 percent of the ballots returned and marked did express confidence in President Darnton. While negative, the percentage was surprisingly large considering the controversy that had swirled around him. The vice presidents fared worse, with little more than 25 percent expressing confidence in them. This vote of confidence marked the NEA's last significant act as a champion of faculty rights. It had played a crucial role in getting the old evaluation system abolished. This was the NEA's great accomplishment. Lacking any official standing as an intermediary, legal or by recognition, it became more and more irrelevant to the ongoing negotiations over faculty welfare. This privilege rested in the body of the Faculty Senate and its subsidiaries.

By April 1981, faculty unrest was subsiding and both sides of the controversy were looking toward the future with a more constructive attitude. In that month a North Central Association examination team appeared on campus preparatory to reaccrediting the college; ten years had lapsed since the last review. The Board of Regents was justifiably worried, considering the campus turmoil over the past few months, but the report turned out surprisingly positive. The examining team listed several strengths and some minor weaknesses. Not surprisingly the team identified the major weakness as a breakdown of communication between the faculty and administrators. They also expressed concern about inadequate long-range planning, space needs in the Library, and ventilation problems in the Science Building. The examiners found strengths in the college's still strong ties with the community, President Darnton's "open administration," and, most significantly, it found all academic programs satisfactory and some outstanding. From a broader perspective, the report saw the college as suffering largely from transitional pains, but concern about faculty unrest led North Central to limit reaccreditation to seven years with a progress report required in three years. Further recommendations called for the Board of Regents to establish liaisons with the faculty and students and that long-range planning be improved. All parties could sigh with relief. But critics of the now defunct evaluation system maintained that the North Central findings vindicated their viewpoint that Southern had a quality, professional faculty and not a majority of substandard teachers as seemed to be implied in the old merit ratings.

By April 1981, a committee which had been working on a new evaluation system had completed its work. Finally, it faced the need for fundamental changes by abolishing the point system, the heavy emphasis on student evaluations, and merit pay raises tied to the salary base. The new system called for the department head or supervisor to write a narrative evaluation addressing three areas:

Dr. Donald C. Darnton and his wife Joyce are shown strolling on the MSSC oval at the time of his arrival to assume the MSSC presidency, July 1, 1979. The Darntons have two children.

Darnton has a strong academic background with a bachelor's degree from William and Mary College and master's and doctor of philosophy degrees in economics from the University of Michigan. Immediately before coming to Southern, Darnton was vice president of Academic Affairs, 1973–1977 and interim president, 1977–1979, of Mansfield, Pennsylvania, State College.

As MSSC president, Darnton launched a program to strengthen academics and reform the administration, but more and more became engrossed in the problems of budgetary cuts and faculty unrest. He resigned June 30, 1982.

MSSC President Donald C. Darnton is shown in a classroom discussing an issue with students. With fourteen years of experience as a professor of Economics, he brought excellent credentials to the classroom. Darnton felt administrators should teach an occasional class to "keep abreast of what is going on in the classroom."

classroom instruction or job performance, scholarly or creative activities, and college service. The plan still called for student evaluations, but questionnaires were to be developed by individual departments and tailored to their special characteristics, except that there was to be one focal question that addressed the overall effectiveness of the instructor. But student evaluations would not be a sole factor in rating teacher effectiveness. At least one other alternative, such as administrative or peer observation had to be factored in. Any merit remuneration was to be in the form of a bonus, but details of this were not worked out. The new system was to be used on a trial basis for the 1981–1982 year. With the college facing a threatened budgetary deficit, merit or percentage pay raises were out of the question. All faculty and staff were limited to $300 across-the-board pay increases. When approved by the Board of Regents, the new plan went far toward quieting faculty unrest. Though student evaluations and bonus pay were still a thorn to many, most faculty saw the new plan as essentially fair.

In the wake of the evaluation dispute both the faculty on one side and President Darnton and the Regents on the other claimed victory. Actually both had gained and both had made concessions. The faculty had brought about an elimination of the harsh evaluation system and the NEA could claim much credit for that accomplishment. However, the faculty had to accept the principle of accountability for their performances. The old days of freewheeling independence, a legacy of the teacher-shortage years, was over. On the other hand, the Regents' claim to have crushed the NEA was exaggerated. The NEA was defeated by the Missouri legislator's failure to pass a collective bargaining law. Without this, the NEA had little to offer once the evaluation crisis subsided. The Regents had reluctantly established links of communication with the faculty and students, something they would not have accepted earlier. If they had succeeded in enforcing an evaluation system on the faculty, they soon found that they had a responsibility to make it fair, that they too would be held to standards of accountability. Governor Bond, taking office in January 1981, announced a new general policy of not reappointing board members once their terms had expired, and none of the Regents serving at this time were ever reappointed.

As the evaluation crisis subsided in the early summer of 1981, Darnton entered his last year as president. It proved to be another year of troubles for the ill-starred leader. The college was in the grip of its most severe budgetary crisis. No one blamed Darnton for bringing on this crisis, and he generally handled the problem well, but he did get blamed for what seemed to be unnecessary expenditures: such as his expansion of the administrative staff and the spending of $88,000 to remodel administrative offices in Hearnes Hall. Actually he had undertaken these moves before the full severity of the monetary crisis struck.

Other events that tended to undermine Darnton's prestige during his last year were the new Faculty Senate's liaison with the Board of Regents which began inauspiciously when the Regents denied the Senate's liaison a right to speak because he was not on the agenda. Another controversy arose over a faculty member's dropping of a football player for nonattendance and causing the Lions to forfeit a victorious game. Darnton also came under fire for the rained-out commencement of May 1982 in Hughes Stadium which left in its wake wet and indignant Regents and faculty as well as wet and disappointed graduates who did not receive their diplomas in the ceremony.

Another factor that proved very damaging to President Darnton's standing with the Regents was a management audit which the Board had commissioned in the fall of 1980. The report, handed down in May 1981, severely criticized Darnton and called on him to "take decisive action," stating that "the time had come to lead, to make plans, and to make specific decisions." The team rated campus morale as "extremely low," and felt that the faculty needed to be treated more professionally. They also noted that faculty perceived the Regents as "remote, removed, and uninformed."

Early in June, Board members invited Darnton to a luncheon where they told him that the Board had "expressed a loss of confidence" in his performance and he was given an opportunity to resign. After some negotiations over salary, Darnton resigned effective as of June 30, 1982. No official reason was ever given for his dismissal and Darnton himself never discussed it. Probably there was no one reason but a series of shortcomings that fell under the category of weak leadership. Undoubtedly the upheaval over faculty evaluations was an important cause, though some Board members denied it. Darnton had sided with the Board during the controversy, but seems to have discredited himself with the Regents by letting the crisis reach the boiling point. On the other hand, Darnton lost credibility with the faculty for essentially the same reasons. Had he moved early enough to gain substantive reforms in the evaluation system, he would have had faculty support and might have saved his presidency.

Darnton's three-year presidency was not without merit. With a strong background as a college professor, he charted a new course of enriched academics for the college. His series of administrative reforms, which brought charges that he favored administrators over faculty, proved a mixed blessing, but much of his restructuring has stood the test of time. Darnton was a transitional figure in the college's history. He effectively slipped the college away from the anchors of the Billingsly era, but immediately ran into foul weather as the college experienced its most severe budgetary crisis and faculty unrest became turbulent. Though he did not bring on these storms, Darnton can be faulted for not keeping s skillful hand on the rudder. Good at promulgating ideas, he lacked administrative skills in implementing what he proposed and in dealing with concrete problems.

In its 1981 report, the North Central accrediting team had concluded that Southern was "a maturing institution and in a state of transition." This statement succinctly summarized the events of the 1976–1982 time period. Enrollment continued to grow and the campus continued to build, but at a reduced pace. The faculty, while numbers stabilized, grew in maturity and teaching effectiveness. Athletics gained new standing in college sports. Full state funding gave the college new stability and acceptance. President Billingsly's death marked a watershed in the college's development. He will always remain a towering figure in the college's history and was in no sense a hindrance to progress, but his passing did clear the way for an infusion of new ideas and more emphasis on academics. President Darnton was a true transitional figure in the college's reorientation. His mission statement of 1979 charted a new course for the college by emphasizing strengthened academics while maintaining the college's traditional ties to the local area. The mission statement's call for MSSC "to become the best undergraduate college that we can be" set the tone for the next decade and beyond.

Rochelle L. Boehning, associate professor of Mathematics, is shown at his desk in this 1973 photograph. A native of Seneca, Boehning was the first head of the Mathematics Department. His strong leadership as president of the MSSC-National Education Association in 1980–1981 helped bring about substantive reforms in the faculty evaluation system.

Boehning left Southern to complete his doctorate at the University of Missouri, Rolla. Currently, he teaches computer science at the San Marcos, California State University.

This letter from Rochelle Boehning, president of the MSSC–National Education Association, to William Schwab, Jr., president of the Board of Regents, brought the long-simmering unrest over faculty evaluation to a boiling point.

The Regents rejected out-of-hand any meeting between themselves and representatives of the NEA, thus setting the stage for the worst confrontation between faculty and the administration in MSSC's history.

October 27, 1980

William Schwab Jr., President
MSSC Board of Regents
2700 East 15th Street
Joplin, Missouri 64801

Dear Mr. Schwab,

The NEA Chapter of Missouri Southern State College has met and after careful consideration has determined that use of the present faculty evaluation system must be discontinued immediately. We can no longer accept the concept of such an evaluation system being attached to pay.

Insofar as we no longer accept such a system and since past salary adjustments have been woefully inadequate in terms of inflation, it is our position that next year's salary adjustment for all faculty members shall not be less than the rate of increase in the cost of living.

We are willing and ready to meet with you concerning this matter. Because of the critical nature of this issue we shall expect your response by Monday, November 10, 1980. If a satisfactory response has not been received by this date, we shall call a meeting to discuss further action.

Sincerely yours,

MSSC-NEA
Rochelle Boehning
President

cc: Members Board of Regents
     MSSC Faculty

YOUR COLLEGE NEEDS

A CRISIS HAS DEVELOPED AT MSSC. THE CURRENT EVALUATION CREATED THE CRISIS.
IT FORCES THE STUDENTS TO EVALUATE THE FACULTY, WHICH IN TURN DETERMINES THE
SALARY WHICH FACULTY MEMBERS RECEIVE. THIS IS AN ADMINISTRATIVE JOB THAT
SHOULD NOT BE DELEGATED TO STUDENTS. WE NEED YOUR HELP TO GET THIS SYSTEM
STOPPED AND INSTEAD LET THE PROFESSORS CONCENTRATE ON EXCELLENCE IN TEACHING.

YOUR

IF YOU FEEL AS WE DO, CALL ONE OF YOUR REGENTS AND TELL HIM TO DROP THIS
EVALUATION SYSTEM:

IN JOPLIN:

WILLIAM SCHWAB, PRESIDENT	FRED HUGHES	JERRY WELLS	GLENN WILSON
623-8865	623-1633	623-7752	623-5392

IN CARTHAGE:	IN SARCOXIE:
RAY GRACE	LOREN OLSON
358-4669	548-2710

HELP

PLEASE DO NOT LITTER   DISTRIBUTED BY MSSC-NEA

This flyer distributed at parking lots and other public places in December 1980 was part of a publicity campaign to pressure the Board of Regents into reforming the faculty evaluation system. Press releases were also used to gain publicity. The publicity resulted in the Regents being plagued with a rash of phone calls.

CHAPTER V
TO BECOME THE BEST UNDERGRADUATE COLLEGE THAT WE CAN BE

I n the decade after Dr. Donald C. Darnton's presidency, Missouri Southern entered an era of stability and progress under a new president. Possessed of a new sense of purpose, the college moved on to achieve that degree of academic excellence that Darnton had articulated but was never able to implement. Most of the faculty morale problems were resolved. The budgetary crisis ended as prosperity returned, and the college entered a period of sustained growth that exceeded expectations.

The Board of Regents appointed Dr. Julio S. Leon interim president after Darnton's departure. Leon, dean of the School of Business Administration since 1976, had an outstanding record as an administrator. The Board also set up a Presidential Search and Screening Committee to look for a permanent replacement. After receiving 149 applications, the committee selected Leon. The committee liked his sense of direction for the college and his long record at MSSC which gave him a familiarity with the college's operations and the structure of Missouri higher education in general. Board members liked his business orientation. Ray Grace, president of the Board of Regents commented, "He has a studied interest in business affairs tempered by an academic overview."

The new president, Leon, did not undertake any fundamental restructuring of the college's goals. He perceived an immediate need to restore confidence in the college's public support that had eroded somewhat and to improve the low faculty morale resulting from the budgetary and evaluation crises. The college also needed to regain its sense of direction. Leon saw no need for an all-new mission statement. The college had been a four-year undergraduate institution with a strong two-year program since 1967 and it should remain that, though there was growing talk about MSSC becoming a university. "We need to reaffirm what we are and to concentrate on being an excellent four-year college," Leon noted; "better to be a good undergraduate college than a mediocre university." Thus Leon accepted the fundamentals of former President Darnton's mission statement, but he had a clearer perception of how to achieve them. Leon felt that the stature of the college was ultimately dependent on what happened in the classroom and that if Southern moved forward in that respect then other things like increased enrollment, an adequate building program, and enhanced prestige would follow in the wake of excellent academics. In the next decade, President Leon carried out this goal with a steady hand. A constant stream of new programs were implemented that enriched the academic offerings of the college, but initially there were budgetary and faculty morale problems to be resolved.

The severe budgetary problem that had so bedeviled former President Darnton began to ease shortly after Leon succeeded him. The economic recession lifted and the rest of the 1980s were marked with a sustained prosperity. Leon established good relations in Jefferson City with the Coordinating Board of Higher Education, the governor, and the legislature that helped in gaining favorable budgets. At this time, some 60 to 65 percent of the college's revenues came from state appropriations. By the end of the decade, MSSC's rapid growth outpaced budget increases as the state adopted a new

(Opposite) This crowd of more than one thousand students and faculty are looking toward the roof of the Billingsly Student Center, waving, and shouting "Good Morning America," as cameramen from the ABC-TV program of that name record the scene. This August 31 event and other activities that day marked the beginning of Southern's Fiftieth Anniversary festivities for the 1987–1988 school year.

The "Good Morning America" episode was telecast nationally on September 9, 1987.

161

Dr. Julio S. Leon is shown in December 1982 with his wife, Vivian, at the time he officially became president of Southern. Earlier he had served as interim president while a screening committee conducted a search for a successor to former President Darnton.

A native of Chile, Leon received his undergraduate degree there and taught elementary school a few years before coming to the United States on a track scholarship. In this country, he earned a master's degree from North Texas State University and a doctorate from the University of Arkansas. Leon joined MSSC's faculty in 1969 and became dean of the Division of Business Administration in 1976. The Leons have one son, Nathan.

budgeting formula that gave priority to factors other then increased enrollment. In the early 1990s a sluggish economy began, once again, to erode the state budget, but MSSC's administrative efficiency and higher student tuition rates helped prevent a major fiscal crisis.

President Leon realized that faculty evaluations was one of the most sensitive problems facing him. Yet the issue had to be resolved for the 1982–1983 school year. Fortunately the new plan, introduced in the spring of 1981, had been quietly accepted by the faculty and seemed to offer promise. Based on narrative evaluations by department heads, this system was continued with no fundamental changes for the new school year. The principal difference was that the awarding of merit bonuses, only mentioned in the 1981 plan because of the budgetary crisis, was now worked out in detail. Funds for these awards, which could vary from year to year, would be allocated to the departments according to a formula. The department head would be responsible for awarding the bonuses. The allocation could be divided between more than one recipient, but not to all members of the department. This system, with its greater flexibility, less weight on student evaluations, and more departmental control, seemed to resolve the evaluation controversy and has been continued with minor modifications.

As the budgetary and faculty morale problems began to be recede, President Leon began instituting a series of innovative new programs that stressed academic excellence. One of the first was an Honors program. Prior to this the college had offered remedial programs for students at the lower end of the scholastic scale, but Dr. Leon felt Southern needed a program to attract and hold highly talented students, many of whom had been bypassing MSSC in favor of colleges that offered stronger incentives to academically advanced students. The Honors program started in the fall of 1984 with Dr. Steven Gale as its director. Thirty students were initially signed up in special honors sections of three General Education courses. Students were admitted by invitation and were required to have ACT scores of 27 or above—later 28—and a grade point average of 3.5 or above. Financial incentives were also given. A solid success, the program has enhanced Southern's academic image.

However, the Honors program did not mean that students with special problems were neglected. A Return to Learn program was instituted for nontraditional students. These students, age twenty-five and over, were apprehensive about seeking a college education, but usually proved to be strong students. This program aimed to orient these students to the college routine by familiarizing them with campus facilities and reviewing communication and study skills. Closely related to this was a "60-plus" program under which Missouri residents, age sixty or over, could enroll tuition-free in any regularly scheduled class in which space was available.

The remedial and special help programs were organized into a Learning Center in the fall of 1984. Coordinated by Myrna Dolence, as had been the Return to Learn program, the Learning Center provided remedial work for students in reading, composition, and mathematics. The Learning Center

Anna Miller, a Southern Honors student and senior Biology major is shown at the governor's office in Jefferson City where she was honored on "Anna Miller Day." To her right is state representative Mark Elliott and on her left, Governor John Ashcroft.

Miller was one of twenty selected nationwide for USA Today's *All-USA Academic First Team. Active in extracurricular affairs, Miller maintained a perfect 4.0 grade point average. President Leon accompanied her to Washington, D.C., where she received the award and $2,500 in cash.*

Miller graduated in May 1990 and was accepted as a medical student by the Uniformed Services University.

has proved a solid addition in shoring up the lower end of the college's academic spectrum.

Admissions requirements was another area in which President Leon moved to improve Southern's academics. Traditionally MSSC had followed an "open-door" admissions policy—a legacy of its junior college origins—in which anyone with a valid high school diploma could enroll. While seemingly democratic, it could prove traumatic when a student, ill-prepared to deal with the academic rigors of college courses, failed. It also caused financial resources to be shifted to counseling and remedial courses that could better be spend on an enriched curriculum for the academically prepared students. Starting in 1986, mild restrictions were imposed on entering freshmen and since then they have tightened. Beginning in the fall of 1991 entering freshmen were required to have a minimum enhanced ACT composite score of 17 or rank in the upper two-thirds of their high school graduating classes. A change to require completion of a sixteen-unit high school core curriculum as a condition for admission has been approved as has other requirements that as of 1994–1995 will place Southern in the "moderately selective" classification as to entrance requirements. The overall effect of these new entrance requirements has been to bring in a body of entering freshmen who are better prepared and to raise the overall academic image of the college, while effects on enrollment have been minimal.

Two new programs, Oxford University Studies and Student Research Grants, were set up to help individual students enrich their academic work through independent studies. The Oxford program began in the summer of 1987 in cooperation with Florida State University and Oxford University. It gives students an unique opportunity to participate in several seminars at one of the world's most prestigious universities and to experience British culture during their three-week stay. Scholarships of $1,000 each are granted to fifteen students each summer to help defray costs. Faculty are also eligible to go. This program has proven popular with full complements of fifteen or more students going each summer.

The Student Research Grant program was established in the fall of 1989, at the suggestion of President Leon. Dr. Richard LaNear became grant committee chairman. It awards grants to top scholars to fund in-depth research on significant topics in their respective disciplines. Over fifteen students have taken advantage of it in each of the years that it has been offered.

A revision of the General Education requirements has been one of the most important steps of the 1980s in promoting academic excellence. First formulated in 1967 for the new baccalaureate degree program and drawing on the old junior college format, these requirements had undergone only minimal modifications in the following years. In 1969, the total credit hours required dropped from forty-eight to forty-six, with a modification of the United States history requirement, and remained unchanged for the next twenty years. These requirements formed a specific program, structured in the traditional mode so that students would be exposed to the basic liberal arts, long considered the mark of a college educated person. Yet the late 1960s and 1970s were a time of student restlessness when many colleges and universities shifted to a less structured format that allowed many electives. By retaining the traditional structure, Southern assured that its graduates would receive a thorough academic grounding in the basic liberal arts and it was the bedrock of the college's emerging reputation as an excellent undergraduate four-year college.

Interest in revising the General Education requirements began to build in the 1980s. An important change came in 1981 with the substitution of American Economic Systems for a three-hour elective course, but the overall

(Top) Dennis Weaver is shown signing autographs for students in the Lions' Den during his visit to Southern in April 1986. He came to deliver the principal address at the Lantern Society banquet.

As was usual during visits to his hometown, the veteran actor made several appearances around Joplin and visited with students at MSSC, his alma mater.

(Bottom) Sue Billingsly, widow of the late President Billingsly, became director of the Missouri Southern Foundation in 1979. With both bachelor's and master's degrees, she taught in public schools for several years. The couple have one daughter, Connie Sue.

The Foundation has become a much more active fund-raising organization under Billingsly's directorship through the annual Phon-A-Thon and the Lantern Society. The former has been highly successful in appealing to donors among the general public and the latter has given special recognition to large contributors.

Students are shown using a temporary ramp to gain entrance to Reynolds Hall during construction, completed in 1988, that added twenty-six thousand square feet to the front of the building. The rapid increase in enrollment during the 1980s once again strained the capacity of the still fairly new campus.

This aerial view centers on the new Richard M. Webster Communications and Social Science Hall completed in August 1992. Encompassing 69,090 square feet, it is second in size only to the expanded Matthews Hall among Southern's classroom buildings.
   Facing westward at the intersection of Newman and Duquesne roads, Webster Hall is highly visible, and its expanses of semi-reflecting glass and its arched entry-way give it a singular appearance among Southern's older buildings.

requirement of forty-six credit hours remained. In 1987, an ad hoc General Education Committee was set up to consider a general revision of the twenty-year-old requirements, which assumed the new title of Core Curriculum at this time. Two developments seemed to dictate important changes: The nation's culture and economy had become much more internationalized and many felt this international element needed more emphasis. Secondly, officials felt that with rapid technological changes, the Core Curriculum needed to be enriched, that it had become increasingly important as students more and more needed to prepare for a possible lifetime of changing careers.

The committee labored for the next two years mapping out changes that considerably enriched the Core Curriculum requirements for baccalaureate degrees; corresponding changes were also made in the associate degree programs. The new baccalaureate Core Curriculum established requirements in five areas: Basic Requirements, Humanities and Fine Arts, Natural and Behavioral Sciences, American Cultural Studies, and International Cultural Studies. The modifications added 6 credit hours to the Core Curriculum. Changes in the American Cultural Studies area doubled the United States History requirement to 6 credit hours thereby restoring the principle, abandoned in 1969, of requiring students to study the full span of this nation's history. The dropping of one hour from the Physical Education activities requirement left a net addition of five credit hours to the Core Curriculum. Total Core Curriculum requirements rose from 46 to 51 credit hours. Credit hours for a baccalaureate degree increased from 124 to 128 and from 62 to 64 for an associate degree.

Revision of the Core Curriculum provided an important step in enhancing Southern's reputation for an excellent academic program and it tied in with the revised mission statement which stated that the college has "a strong commitment to the liberal arts, to professional and pre-professional programs, and the complementary relationship that must exist between liberal and professional education in order to prepare individuals for success in careers and lifelong learning."

Other new programs in the 1983–1992 era that reinforced MSSC's academics were requirements in Computer Literacy and Writing Competency. The Computer Literacy program, added in 1985, grew out of the growing importance of computers as tools of learning and for use in the work place. The 1985–1987 catalog specified that all students were to receive computer instruction to a level "necessary for them to function as members of society and to a level of skills sufficient to use the computer for problem solving within their discipline." Specific requirements were left to the individual departments.

The Writing Competency requirement addressed a need for college graduates to be able to express themselves clearly, concisely, and cogently with the written word. No additional courses were added, but students were required to take five courses with writing complements so that they would be taking courses with structured writing requirements throughout their four-year college careers.

The Computer Literacy and Writing Competency requirements were im-

Canadian geese are shown swimming in the Biology pond on the MSSC campus. The geese, virtual year-around inhabitants of a pond on a nearby estate, like to come onto the Southern campus in the late summer to browse on the well-watered lawns.

portant additions in the movement toward academic enrichment. Though not a part of the Core Curriculum, they complemented it.

Concurrent with restructuring the Core Curriculum, MSSC instituted an Outcomes Assessment program. Conscious of the growing public and governmental clamor for greater "accountability" on the part of education for its poor performance, President Leon moved to set up this program in 1986. He stressed "the need for us to know how well we are doing our job—we have no systematic way of knowing." Outcomes Assessment aims to measure how well Southern is doing in educating students in the areas of the Core Curriculum and individual majors.

MSSC and Northeast Missouri State University led in establishing such programs among Missouri's state colleges and universities, but Governor John Ashcroft soon asked the other state institutions of higher learning to establish similar programs.

The program began with ACT-COMP tests (College Outcomes Measures Program) being given to entering freshmen in the fall of 1986. A similar test would then be given to them as exiting seniors four years later to provide a measure of the Core Curriculum's effectiveness. As an experiment, ACT-COMP Tests were given on a voluntary basis to graduating seniors in the spring of 1987, but the inconclusive results led the Board of Regents to require all graduating seniors to complete a departmental exit examination.

Assessment of majors posed a more complex problem. Adequate standardized tests and national norms did not exist in several areas when testing began in 1988 and many departments found it necessary to formulate their own testing devices. Still in its formative state, Outcomes Assessment promises to provide another anchor for a strong academic program.

Another outgrowth of the college's commitment to academics has been the formalizing of a program aimed at retaining students and facilitating their academic growth and development. Central to the new effort is an Office of Retention, directed by Dr. Elaine Freeman, which coordinates existing efforts by the departments, the Learning Center, and Student Services. The new program aims to help not only those on academic probation, but also those with personal problems which may be interfering with their academic progress.

A significant change of direction for Southern came with President Leon's announcement of an added international emphasis to the college's mission as an undergraduate institution. Approved by the Board of Regents in June 1990, it placed MSSC in the forefront of a national trend and gave Southern a unique distinction among undergraduate colleges in the state and region. President Leon's announcement reflected the growing trend toward interna-

Glenn D. Dolence, vice president for Student Services, came to Southern in 1969 as dean of men. Later this position grew into the post of dean of Student Services, and in 1985 it was was raised to the status of a vice presidency.

Dolence, who has a doctorate in education from the University of Arkansas, held coaching, teaching, and administrative positions at the Neosho High School before coming to MSSC.

tionalism that had been recognized earlier in the International Cultural Studies area of the revised Core Curriculum.

The new program began with a series of activities that emphasized the goal of preparing students for life in a global community. As a part of the Foreign Language Field Day in April 1991, Southern officials announced that up to ten one-year scholarships, covering tuition, would be made available to high school seniors who agreed to attend MSSC and major or minor in a foreign language. In the first year, some eight faculty members attended international seminars or made foreign junkets in addition to the already existing Oxford program. Also, in the spring of 1992, Southern hosted an international piano competition, the first since 1990.

President Leon found funds to help support his new academic programs through the Missouri Southern Foundation. Dating from 1967, it had operated in a desultory fashion, receiving and managing monetary gifts to the college. Early in 1979, the Board of Regents upgraded it by enlarging its board and hiring Sue Billingsly as a full-time director. Officials saw a more active Foundation as a way to promote special projects that could not be funded out of the regular budget or, as Mrs. Billingsly so succinctly phrased it, "It helped Southern maintain a margin of excellence not otherwise possible."

As it developed more fully, the Missouri Southern Foundation carried on two major fund-raising activities: the Phon-A-Thon and the Southern Lantern Society. The former consists of an annual fund-raising drive aimed primarily at numerous small donors. Organized in 1983, with the help of outside consultants, it is managed by Mrs. Billingsly and the alumni director, Dr. Kreta Gladden. Each spring a temporary organization, consisting of numerous volunteers, make thousands of phone calls soliciting funds from prospective donors. A huge success, the Phon-A-Thon has exceeded its goals in most years and in the nine-year period 1983–1991 approximately $1,100,000 was raised. Much of the money has been expended on numerous projects that promote academic development such as scholarships, internships, faculty and student development support, outstanding teacher awards, and business lectures.

The Southern Lantern Society grew out of a five-year capital funds drive, established in December 1984, to raise approximately $5.5 million for endowments, scholarships, and general activities. This drive aimed at gaining sizeable contributions and the Lantern Society was set up to recognize these substantial donors. Membership is initially gained with donations of $500 by an individual or $1,000 by a corporation and an annual banquet honors the members. Though not altogether successful, the capital funds drive did raise nearly $1 million in its five-year life span and the foundation has also been the recipient of more than $2 million from the estates of deceased persons.

Though emphasis shifted to expanding academics in the decade of 1983–1992, the rapid increase in enrollment dictated that growth of the physical plant would remain important. Most of the construction in this period took the form of additions to existing structures, but one major classroom building and three residence apartment halls were completed.

The press of student enrollment brought about the expansion of both Matthews and Reynolds halls. The

The English Department faculty gathered for this photograph during the 1982–1983 school year. From left, front row, are*: Dr. Arthur M. Saltzman, 1981; Dr. Doris A. Walters, 1983; Bobbie Z. Short, 1965–1987; Dr. Ann M. Marlowe, 1971; Dr. Elliott A. Denniston, 1974. Back row: Dr. Steven H. Gale, 1980–1988; Dr. Steve C. Atkinson, 1981–1986; Dr. Joseph P. Lambert, 1970; George C. Greenlee, 1970; Dr. Dale W. Simpson, 1979; Dr. Harry E. Preble, 1968; Dr. Jimmy C. Couch, 1970; Dr. Henry G. Morgan, 1971; Dr. Henry L. Harder, 1970; and Dr. David L. Ackiss, 1981.

Dr. Gale was department head at this time. Drs. Harder, Lambert, and Preble are former department heads. Morgan (1986) and Simpson (1991) received Outstanding Teacher of a Freshman Class awards. Saltzman (1992) received the Outstanding Teacher Award.

*Names are followed by dates of employment—a single date if still on the staff.

Matthews addition provided a new home for the rapidly growing School of Business Administration. The Social Science and Communications departments then moved into Business' old quarters in the mansion and mansion annex. The Reynolds Hall expansion provided badly needed space for the Biology, Chemistry, Physics, and Mathematics departments that were already there.

Another important expansion of the late 1980s involved Gene Taylor Hall which was enlarged primarily to create space for a Child-Care Center, but which also added an elevator, television and computer laboratories, and offices for the School of Education and Psychology.

The most important single construction project of the decade ending in 1992 involved the new Richard M. Webster Communications and Social Science Hall. Built at a time of stringent budgetary restrictions, Webster Hall was constructed in stages over a three-year period as the state legislature made funds available. The death of Senator Richard Webster in March 1990 accelerated the building's completion with the state legislature promoting it as a memorial to their departed colleague and even taking the unusual step of naming the building. A loan from a consortium of banks made it possible to finish the building without further delay. Webster Hall opened with the fall semester of 1992.

The rapid growth in enrollment also made it necessary to expand the college's residence hall complex. The five residence apartment units which opened in 1980 had been considered minimal to meet the needs at the time and the growth of freshmen waiting lists for campus housing in the next few years made an expansion necessary. Since students seemed to like the apartment-style living introduced in the 1980 units, future construction followed that pattern. Three more of these units were opened by 1990 giving Southern a housing capacity of over 650 students. Even more housing is now needed to attract students living beyond commuting distance of the college.

Other construction projects of the 1983–1992 era mostly involved modifications of existing buildings. The Hughes Stadium football field and track

Jean Campbell and Dean Ray A. Malzahn are shown in 1990 trying a new recipe on the "Jean Campbell Showcase," a MSTV variety program conducted by Ms. Campbell. The dean is an accomplished amateur cook.

Dr. Malzahn, dean of Arts and Sciences since coming to Southern in 1980, became interim vice president for Academic Affairs in 1993. With a doctorate in Chemistry from the University of Maryland, Dr. Malzahn regularly teaches a course in that subject at MSSC.

Ms. Campbell is an outstanding example of a nontraditional student. With a husband, four daughters, and grandchildren, she managed to graduate from Southern in 1986 as an honor student. She remained at MSSC after graduation as a staff assistant in charge of special projects for the Communications Department. Among her numerous duties, Campbell is now adviser to the Crossroads *and Telecommunications Promotion Director.*

were resurfaced in 1988. Other notable additions to the campus included the Lea Kungle Softball Field, the Stults Memorial Garden, and the Veterans Memorial.

Looking to the future, three new construction projects have the highest priority: a multipurpose arena, a new library, and an addition to the Anderson Police Academy. The most pressing need is for an arena that could provide a meeting place for college and community events as well as more space for the Athletic Department. The acquisition in 1989 of 16.744 acres of land at the southeast corner of Newman and Duquesne roads, adjacent to Fred Hughes Stadium, has made an excellent site available, but a proposed $25 million arena complex, to be financed by a Jasper County sales tax, was rejected by the voters in 1992.

The cumulative effect of the last decade's building, and even more extensive construction of the previous fifteen years, has been to give Southern a very modern campus of impressive proportions. The campus consists of thirty-eight buildings totaling approximately 773,000 square feet of floor space and located on nearly 340 acres of grounds. Thirty of the buildings were completed in the period 1967–1992, either in whole or as major additions to older structures. The North Central Association accrediting team of 1987, commenting on the relative newness of the campus, noted that it "creates a pleasant, efficient learning environment."

Enrollment growth provided the most significant development in the 1983–1992 period. Actually the surge in student population spanned the entire decade of the 1980s; and was the greatest since the unparalleled tripling of enrollment in the 1960s. The student count increased by slightly over 10 percent in the three-year period 1980–1982 inclusive and then, in the next ten years, enrollment jumped by nearly 37 percent with the heart of the increase coming in the four years 1986–1989 when the student population grew by a full 28 percent. Dips came in 1983 and at the end of the period in 1991 and 1992. A drop of one student in 1991 was insignificant, but the slightly over 2 percent decline in 1992 may herald an era of slower growth for Southern.

The strong growth of enrollment in the 1980s was not due to any one reason,

In this view, the upper section of a 160-foot microwave tower is being swung into position while two men wait precariously on the base to bolt it into place. Constructed to increase the range of Southern's new television station, K57DR, the tower, completed in January 1988, beams programs to the main transmitter located on the roof of the Mercantile Bank some four miles away in downtown Joplin. Larry Meacham photo

Missouri Southern's Board of Regents gathered for this photograph in 1990. From the left, front row, are: Sara Woods; Russell Smith, president; and John O. "Pat" Phelps. Back row: Gilbert Roper; Douglas Crandall; Julio Leon, MSSC president; Frank S. Dunaway; and Cynthia Schwab.

Woods, Student Senate president for the 1989–1990 academic year, also served as student regent for that year. Smith, a Joplin businessman, served as regent from 1985 to 1990. Phelps, a Carthage banker, served from 1985 to 1992. Roper, a Joplin businessman, served from 1986 and as of early 1993 had not been replaced. He is the father of Sallie Roper Beard, director of Women's Athletics. Crandall, a Carthage lawyer, Dunaway, a Carthage businessman, and Schwab, a Joplin civic benefactor, were appointed in 1989, 1897, and 1989, respectively. Their terms are unexpired. Schwab is the second woman to serve as a regent.

but several strong factors do stand out. Low tuition contributed strongly. A College Board survey over two consecutive years listed Southern as being among the ten least expensive public colleges in the nation. A similar finding by *USA Today* in 1987 gave MSSC even more national exposure. *USA Today* determined that total fixed charges for tuition, fees, room, and board of just $2,846 per year, made Southern the eighth least expensive public college in the nation.

Another strong factor boosting enrollment was MSSC's growing reputation for academic excellence. By the 1980s, the college had a strong teaching staff who assured that students received quality tutoring in their particular majors. Beyond this, Southern's structured Core Curriculum was taught by professors, unlike many large universities where many such courses were taught by graduate assistants. Altogether, the MSSC approach assured that graduates ranked favorably with those from prestigious colleges and universities, and the performance of those who went into graduate-level professional programs demonstrated this.

An additional factor boosting the student population was the influx of nontraditional students, age twenty-five or over, many of whom were women. By 1990, this nontraditional group made up some 40 percent of MSSC's enrollment, whereas, at an earlier time, they had accounted for less than 10 percent of the student body. These were mature people who returned to college, or entered for the first time, because they sensed the need for additional education to further their careers or for self-satisfaction. Averaging thirty-six years of age, this group gave a more mature cast to MSSC's student body as well as boosting enrollment.

Other factors stimulating the growth in enrollment were the efficient recruitment programs and the transfer of upper division enrollees from larger universities. Many of these transferees came because of the closer contact they could have with their professors and because of the college's growing reputation for quality academics.

One segment of the student population that showed no significant growth in the decade 1983–1992 was that of minorities. Overall minority enrollment hovered near the 3 percent mark at this time, with that of blacks accounting for slightly under 1 percent. Most of the black students were males of whom many were athletes; sometimes they complained about the shortage of black females for dating purposes. These percentages reflected closely the racial composition of Joplin and the surrounding area. Though no systematic program for recruiting minorities existed, there were no restrictions on their admission and they were generally well accepted. No serious incidents marred Southern's history of race relations.

Southern's enrollment growth in the 1980s came in spite of a drop in high school graduates. Statewide figures show that the number of graduates peaked in 1980 at a little over sixty thousand, but the yearly average for the rest of the 1980s was near the fifty-one thousand mark. Projections for the early 1990s showed a further drop to near the forty-seven thousand level before enrollment begins to rise again in 1995. This drop in high school graduates has already helped to slow MSSC's growth, but can be offset by more vigorous recruitment and better retention.

Not surprisingly the number of graduates, though subject to yearly fluctuations, increased steadily in the 1983–1992 time period as overall student enrollment grew. In 1989 the total graduates reached six hundred for the first time and three years later the figure surpassed the seven hundred mark.

Baccalaureate degree programs remained the heart of the college's offerings as they had been since 1967. The bachelor of science in business administration remained as MSSC's leading degree, growing proportionately as the number of graduates increased. This highly popular program accounted for approximately one-third of the 4,574 baccalaureate degrees issued, 1983 through 1992. Biology, Computer Science, and Criminal Justice were also leading bachelor of science offerings though collectively they still accounted for fewer majors than the B.S.B.A.

The bachelor of science in education degree continued as the second most important baccalaureate program. Though it had declined some in importance, dropping from approximately 40 percent of the baccalaureate degrees issued in 1976–1982 to 29 percent in 1983–1992 as the job opportunities in teaching tightened, it remained the mainstay of majors in such liberal art disciplines as English and History as well as Physical Education.

Dean John W. Tiede is shown in his office during the 1985–1986 school year. A member of the Southern Business faculty since 1968, Tiede has a juris doctorate from the University of Missouri.

Turning from teaching to administrative work, Tiede served as an assistant to former President Darnton. From 1982 to 1986 he held the post of dean of the School of Business Administration. At the latter date, he became vice president for Business Affairs and, in 1990, was elevated to the new post of senior vice president.

Robert C. Brown became dean of the School of Business Administration in 1987. With a doctorate from Louisana State University, Brown had several years of experience in administration and as a professor of Economics at McMurry College and at Hardin-Simmons University in Abilene, Texas.

In 1990, Brown replaced Floyd E. Belk who had retired as vice president for Academic Affairs. Brown resigned in the spring of 1993 to assume the presidency of Arkansas Tech University at Russellville.

The bachelor of general studies degree never became more than a minor program appealing mostly to those who were interested in a college degree as a work of cultural attainment. Graduates averaged only about nine per year in the 1983–1992 time period.

Bachelor of arts degrees, the classical programs of the liberal arts, remained fairly static in numbers of graduates generated, but of declining importance relatively as enrollment increased. B.A.'s accounted for about 10 percent of the baccalaureate degrees issued, 1983–1992. Communications, because of its more direct job orientation, had the most vigorous B.A. program and accounted for more such graduates than any other single discipline.

The associate degree program provided a mixed picture in the 1983–1992 period though it still remained an important part of the college's curriculum. Associate degrees granted averaged 111 per year for this period, down almost 10 percent from the 1976–1982 era. Much of the decline was due to the introduction of baccalaureate programs in Computer Science and Criminal Justice. While associate degrees were still offered in these two fields, most students preferred to bypass them in favor of the B.S. degree. Nursing remained the most important associate degree in spite of its very popular baccalaureate program because the associate degree remained a prerequisite for working on the four-year degree. Drafting and Design and Dental Hygiene, areas where baccalaureate degrees were not available, remained strong associate programs.

Graduates in the 1983–1992 period reflected a trend that had been evident since the beginning of the four-year college, if not before. Namely, Southern students leaned heavily toward those programs that seemed to prepare them for immediate job opportunities. Those attending college principally for cultural enrichment were few, and those looking to careers in the advanced professions that required extensive graduate-level training formed a significant core but still a minority.

James W. Gray, a native of Iowa, has a master's degree from the University of Arkansas, plus certification as a Certified Systems Professional.

Coming to Southern in 1969, Gray has taught in Business Administration and Computer Science, except for a three-year stint in private business. He served briefly as assistant dean and then as interim dean before becoming full dean of the School of Business Administration in 1990.

(Top) Edward P. Merryman, with a doctor of philosophy degree from Ball State University, came to MSSC in 1980 as head of the new Department of Education. Three years later he assumed the post of dean of the School of Education and Psychology. He has presided over the school through a decade in which enrollment has expanded, and educational requirements have become more complex.

(Bottom) Donald L. Seneker came to Southern in 1971. He took over the newly developing Law Enforcement program and under his guidance it grew into a full Department of Criminal Justice. Seneker, who has a master's degree from Central Missouri State University, received the Outstanding Teacher Award for 1982 and five years later became the first faculty member to deliver a commencement address. In 1990–1992, he served as assistant dean and then as interim dean of Technology. Seneker retired in 1993.

The rapid increase in enrollment during the 1983–1992 era came in spite of the heaviest student tuition increases in the college's history. Caught between low state budget appropriations that did not keep pace with the growth in enrollment and with continued inflation, the Board of Regents had no recourse but to cover the budgetary shortfalls with added student assessments. The basic tuition for a full-time student, carrying a fifteen credit hour load, more than doubled in this ten-year period, from $350 in 1983–1984 to $842 in 1992–1993.

In the years 1983–1992, Southern continued to utilize a series of programs, in addition to sports and cultural events, to honor students and to improve college life as well as to provide educational events for public school students.

The long-established honors convocations to recognize student academic achievements were continued. At these assemblies, held in the spring of each year, awards are passed out for exceptional achievement in the academic disciplines and for other special merits. The Alumni Association selects an outstanding graduate each year and Bartlett Respect Awards are passed out each year to four students showing outstanding qualities of character and citizenship.

Always solicitous of the welfare of students, the college, in this period, put special emphasis on protecting the individual's health environment. Though substance abuse had never been a serious problem on campus, the college, in 1986, instituted an "awareness program" to discourage the use of drugs and alcohol and to promote individual responsibility. Mostly educational in its approach, the program spotlighted athletes for special attention and, with the cooperation of the Athletic Department, a drug-testing program was instituted; counseling was also made available to individuals with severe problems.

Closely related to substance abuse was a growing concern over the health hazards of breathing secondary tobacco smoke in the confines of crowded campus buildings. Mounting criticism led the Board of Regents in 1991 to ban all smoking in campus buildings except for a few designated areas in the residence halls. Though some smokers protested the prohibition as being too extreme, it reflected a growing public concern about the health hazards of tobacco smoke and compliance with the order did not prove to be a problem. Smoking was not restricted on the campus grounds.

Another new program that developed at this time was the Child-Care Center. It grew out of the increasing enrollment of nontraditional students, many of whom had young children and a need to find a convenient place to "park" them while attending classes. The program began in January 1985 when the college took over operation of the old Sunshine Corner Child-Care Center in the Ecumenical Campus Ministry Building. A temporary arrangement, this location was replaced by an extension of Gene Taylor Hall that opened during the 1986–1987 school year. A self-supporting service, the Child-Care Center has a capacity of about fifty and gives first priority to children of students. It also provides a facility for the training of teachers in early childhood education.

Programs continued to be developed and older ones expanded for public school students. Not only were these events an educational service, but they formed a recruiting tool by bringing in young people and familiarizing them with the campus. The Southern Plus program, developed in 1985 by Erin Ray of the Education Department, provided an example of this. Southern Plus offers a variety of three-week courses each June to elementary and junior high school pupils, grades three through eight. A solid success, Southern Plus provides one hundred or more youngsters with a constructive summertime experience as well as familiarizing them with the campus. In addition, well-established programs for public school students were continued such as Children's Theatre, History Day, Foreign Language Field Day and other programs in Communications, Mathematics, Music, and English.

In the 1983–1992 time period, all the academic departments and areas within the Schools of Arts and Sciences, Business Administration, Education and Psychology, and Technology experienced growth and a steady improvement in their programs, but the Communications Department in the School of Arts and Sciences, newly created in 1980, provided the most outstanding example of growth and academic enrichment in this period.

Communications, encompassing the areas of Foreign Languages, Journalism, and Speech, found in Broadcasting, which was a logical extension of the latter two areas, a field that could prepare students for immediate job opportunities in radio and television.

The initial entry into Broadcasting involved the installation in 1984 of a television studio at a cost of $150,000. Its programs were carried on Channel 18 to the 8,600 homes in Joplin, Webb City, and Carterville that had cable connections. Programming consisted of student productions and a Learning Channel that featured commercial television courses.

A major expansion came two years later when KOZK, a Springfield, Missouri public television station, established a Joplin satellite, KOZJ. Though principally a station for the public television network, the Communications Department was allotted approximately seven hours of programming time each week, which greatly expanded the range of MSTV for part of its productions.

The department's next step in television programming was the establishment its own broadcasting station in 1988. Licensed by the Federal Communications Commission as station K57DR, its low power gave it a range of little more than the city limits of Joplin, but it extended MSTV coverage to homes without cable connections thereby reaching approximately 20,800 homes.

Radio station KXMS rounded out the Communications Department's curriculum in broadcasting. Established in 1986, with Dr. Robert Clark as general manager, KXMS aired classical music on a 24-hour-per-day schedule. Students did the programming except for an occasional satellite pickup of an opera broadcast or other special event. In 1988, the antenna was raised and power increased to give the station more regional range.

Like other departments or schools, Business Administration, the college's largest division, sought ways to better serve student and community needs. A series of new programs, some initiated prior to 1983, led to the creation of a Small Business Development Center (SBDC) that functioned in conjunction with the Small Business Administration. The SBDC encompasses the following areas: The *Southern Business and Economic Review* journal, Small Business Institute, Business and Economic lecture series, Management Development Institute, and the Center for Entrepreneurship.

Another significant new offering was a bachelor of science degree in Management Technology with an emphasis in Computer Integrated Manufacturing (CIM). Though a baccalaureate degree in Management Technology, based on an associate degree in one of the technical fields, had been offered since the early 1970s, this new program aimed to ground students on the revolution in management technology as evidenced in the latest advances in the business field and the new CADD/CAM program in the School of Technology.

The Education Department maintained a progressive program in the 1983–1992 time period, meeting new Missouri state requirements on the certification of teachers and monitoring their later progress on the job, but

These enthusiastic members of the Nursing faculty posed for this photograph during the 1982–1983 school year. From the left, front row are: *Marilyn J. Jacobs, 1974; Doris T. Elgin, 1971; and Retha Ketchum, 1970. Back row: Mary G. Ross, 1979; Celia A. Allman, 1982–1984; Dr. Betty Ipock, 1978–1988; and Christine B. Eller, 1981.

Dr. Ipock, as director of Nursing, was instrumental in setting up a baccalaureate degree program. Dr. Barbara Box succeeded her as director. Jacobs (1981) and Elgin (1987) received Outstanding Teacher of a Freshman Class Awards.

* Names are followed by dates of employment—a single date if still on the staff.

The historic Barn Theatre was gutted by fire in the early morning hours of Thanksgiving Day, November 22, 1990, making it necessary to raze the structure. Investigators ruled that the fire was set by an arsonist, but no suspect has been apprehended.

Veteran theatre people, with nostalgic memories of the plays presented in the crowded confines of the 63-year old structure, were dismayed. An ongoing move to raise money to build a new Barn Theatre began almost immediately. Some $400,000 of the approximately $600,000 necessary to build a new theatre has been raised from donations and an insurance payment, but a state appropriation of the additional $200,000 needed has not been forthcoming because of a budgetary crisis.

experienced considerable difficulty in meeting the tough standards set by the National Council for the Accreditation of Teacher Education (NCATE).

In 1983, the Education program underwent a reaccreditation examination by NCATE for the first time in ten years. The department failed this screening in spite of its strong teaching staff and reputation for turning out well-prepared teachers. The NCATE team cited shortcomings in governance, objectives, multicultural education, and long-term evaluation of graduates. The college appealed this obviously unfair ruling and was granted a re-examination the next year which the department passed with positive marks in all major areas and its accreditation was restored.

In 1991 the Education Department underwent another NCATE accreditation examination. Though the NCATE team found the program generally strong and a renewal of accreditation was granted, the department was faulted for its lack of minorities in the Teacher-Training program. In the fall of 1991, only 2 blacks, 13 Native Americans, and 1 Hispanic were enrolled in education out of a total of 835. There were no black instructors and out of a total student population of approximately 6,000 only 66 were blacks. No black had graduated with a teaching degree since 1983, the worst record of all of Missouri's state colleges.

The lack of a sizeable minority population in Southern's service area has handicapped the Education Department's efforts to recruit minority students and to provide teacher trainees with experience in dealing with minorities in a classroom setting. Arrangements are being instituted to transport student teachers to larger population centers where they can experience some contact with minority pupils.

The School of Technology in the decade 1983–1992 remained strong overall, but presented a mixed picture of growth and decline. Its established programs in Computer Science, Law Enforcement and Criminal Justice, Nursing, and Dental Hygiene remained the most vigorous. Medical Technology; Radiologic Technology; and the Reserve Officers Training Corps (ROTC), taught by military officers; remained as stable, basic programs. Drafting and Design and Machine Technology, long-established basic programs, emerged as the technologically most progressive areas in this period. The application of computers has changed these programs fundamentally.

The trend toward baccalaureate degree programs in the School of Technology, that had started earlier with Criminal Justice and Industrial Arts, continued in the 1983–1992 period with the addition of four-year degrees in Computer Science and Nursing. The bachelor of science degree in Computer Science program began in the fall of 1983 and soon overshadowed the associate degree offering. One year later, Southern added a bachelor of science degree program in Nursing to fill a growing need for more highly trained nurses. This offering also grew rapidly but preserved the associate degree as a prerequisite. MSSC's associate program in Nursing continued to be one of the strongest in the state, with 100 percent of the graduates in most years passing the Missouri State Board examinations for certification as registered nurses.

Not all developments in the School of Technology at this time were progressive. An earlier attempt at establishing an associate degree in Cosmetology faltered in its formative stages, but in this period three established programs were discontinued. A certificate program in Dental Assisting was dropped from the 1987–1989 catalog because of low demand. Local dentists did not feel specialized training was needed for these jobs. More serious was the collapse of the Automotive Technology program in 1987 after twenty-one years of operation. Once a strong program, a decline in enrollment developed principally because manufacturers began to establish centers to give mechanics specialized training in dealing with the technical complexities of their own products. A third casualty was the bachelor of science in Education degree program in Industrial Arts. Established in 1976 it aimed at training industrial arts teachers for the public schools, an area of perceived shortage, but there were few enrollees and the program was cancelled at the end of the 1989–1990 school year.

Certain lessons were evident from the School of Technology's experience in the 1980s. One was that though the school, a product of junior college origins, remained a vital part of the institution's curriculum, the increasing complexity of technology had tended to blur the distinction between junior college and senior college programs. Also it became clear that great care needed to be exercised in instituting expensive new programs and that the college's resources were best utilized in developing a few programs in which MSSC could clearly serve a public need without wasteful competition with neighboring colleges.

Southern's students continued to turn out some outstanding publications in the decade 1983–1992, with the excellence of *The Chart* being particularly notable. *The Chart* had won many awards for its professionalism in the past, but it was not until the late 1980s that it emerged as one of the state's leading small, four-year college newspapers, outstanding for its aggressive coverage of college events, local and state news, and in-depth studies of special events. By 1983 it was a full broadsheet newspaper, publishing approximately twenty-five

Kevin Babbitt and Susan Thomas are shown playing the roles of Pinocchio and Margo, respectively, in the children's play Pinocchio. *Presented in the Taylor Auditorium on a Saturday afternoon during the Christmas season of 1985, the performance drew a crowd of over twelve hundred, the largest audience ever for a children's play.*

Appearing in this dramatic scene from The Diviners *are, from left: Jeremy W. Aumen, James D. Carter, Beth Ames, and Douglas Hill. Staged in November 1989,* The Diviners *was the last major production in the Barn Theatre. In February 1990, Joplin fire safety inspectors condemned the structure as a hazard and it was closed.*

Members of the 1991–1992 International Club appearing in this photograph are, from left, front row: Eddie Lyons: Irma Ranliar; Annie Wu; Sandra Wilke; Toni Chou Moorman; and Michelle Moorman. Second row: Patrick Day; Ann Day; Leta Wilson; Holly Carnine; Arvin Coonfield; and Joanna Chau Lu Yang. Back row: Allen Merriam, faculty; Judy Bastian, faculty; Pamela Chong; Timothy Majors; Ann Allman, adviser; and Pallavi Pate.

Though an old organization, dating from the mid-1970s, the International Club took on added importance in this period as the number of foreign students increased and as Southern implemented its new international mission. Pamela Chong, a native of Singapore, came to Southern as an Honors program student. Annie Wu, an artist and a nontraditional student, is a native of Taiwan.

issues during the school year. Richard W. Massa, whose creative guidance since 1972 had helped build *The Chart* into a publication of regional significance, stepped down as adviser in 1984 and was replaced by Chad D. Stebbins. Stebbins continued *The Chart*'s tradition of alert coverage of news while avoiding controversial editorializing.

Special supplements were published by *The Chart* from time to time. One of these, an April 1986 in-depth analysis of Missouri's farming crisis, won a second place award in the *Los Angeles Times* editorial leadership competition. The farm supplement was part of a 44-page issue, the largest edition in *The Chart*'s history. A supplement on AIDS, published in the spring of 1992, won a similar third-place award. In keeping with the college's new mission of adding an international emphasis, *The Chart* in 1990, added a "Global Viewpoint" section as a regular feature.

The Chart and its staff continued to win many awards in the Missouri College Newspaper Association's annual competition. For several years, *The Chart* received Best in State Awards for its division. At the 1991 MCNA Convention, *The Chart* gained twenty-one awards including Best Overall

Members of Students Achieving Greater Education (SAGE) appearing in this 1986–1987 photograph are, from left, front row: Terry Miksell, Marty Barlet, and Harold Krueger. Back row: Carol Cable; Sue Simmons; Gabe Wright; and Linda Davey, sponsor.

SAGE grew out of the rapidly increasing enrollment of nontraditional students during the 1980s. Most nontraditional students were women and SAGE's membership reflected this. SAGE members played an important role in gaining a Child-Care Center for Southern by conducting a survey that found sufficient demand existed to justify the facility.

Newspaper in Class 3A and captured the sweepstakes trophy. Staff members received many honors in various categories, but the top MCNA individual award, Collegiate Journalist of the Year, went to editor-in-chief Christopher Clark. Mark Ernstmann, in 1988, had also received this award and three staffers in the 1970s had received similar awards.

The Chart also became a recipient of the prestigious Regional Pacemaker Award issued by the Associated Collegiate Press. These awards were received in 1986 and in the five consecutive years 1988 through 1992. In 1991 Christopher Clark won $1,000 as first runner-up in the College Journalist of the Year ACP national competition.

The Crossroads, MSSC's yearbook, that had suffered from a lack of student interest ever since the founding of the four-year college, underwent another of its recurring crises in the 1980s. The problems were twofold: the office of public information found it increasingly difficult to find a staff of students to produce the yearly issues and the number of students buying the often late yearbook was so small that its production had to be heavily subsidized. In the 1983–1984 school year, a staff could not be assembled and the 1984 *Crossroads* was never produced, the first time this had happened since 1971. Eventually a sixteen-page supplement for 1984 was added to the next year's yearbook. The crisis was resolved by having the Communications Department, where a staff of journalism students could be assembled, take over production. The *Crossroads'* format was extensively revised under the new advisers, first Chad Stebbins and then Jean Campbell. Even with these improvements the yearbook might have faced extinction, but for the fact that students voted for a five dollar increase in their per semester activity fee to help underwrite production costs.

The *Winged Lion,* a joint publication of the Art and English departments since the early years of the four-year college, continued its long tenure as one of the college's leading student publications. In the 1980s it received a number of National Pacemaker and All-American Honor awards from the Associated Collegiate Press and the National Scholastic Press Association for its well-edited literary compositions and professional-looking art.

The Theatre Department continued to present a strong program of major plays in the fall and spring semesters of each year in the 1983–1992 time period. The ever popular children's theatre still attracted large audiences. Milton Brietzke, who had directed the theatre program for thirty-one years retired in 1987. Dr. Jay E. Fields replaced him as director.

The Music Department made an important addition to its program in 1987 with the institution of an International Piano Competition. Organized by Clive Swansbourne, assistant music professor, it was planned for every two years but was repeated in 1988 as part of the college's fiftieth anniversary festivities. The events were continued in 1990 and 1992 under the direction of Mrs. Vivian Leon and have become part of a general arts festival held on the MSSC campus. The International Piano Competition is a unique event with only a few colleges nationally holding similar contests. In keeping with the college's new international emphasis, it attracts distinguished pianists from all over the world and several thousand dollars in prizes are awarded.

The increase in enrollment and the enrichment of the curriculum in the years 1983–1992 led to a proliferation of new student organizations. Even the weak Greek fraternities and sororities began to show new signs of life. These societies had languished for years after a brief flurry of activity when the four-year college formed. Reaching a low ebb in the mid-1980s they began to capture renewed student interest toward the end of the decade. Both the Delta Gamma sorority and the Kappa Alpha fraternity lost their national charters because of a decline in membership in the 1985–1986 period. This left Southern with only two sororities, Lambda Beta Phi and Zeta Tau Alpha, and one fraternity, Sigma Nu. Some concerned alumni and students worked to strengthen the Greek system, fearing that a lack of strong Greek organizations was tarnishing the college's image and hurting enrollment. Supporters in 1989 suc-

Members of the 1988–1989 Black Collegiates appear in this photograph. From left, are: Keith Brown, president; Orlando Smith; James Galloway; Paul Brown; Craig Horace; Cheryl Williams; Greg Barnes; Renee Grayson; Reggie Jammal Mahone; Lance Williams; Marc Rollerson; and Eric Dulin.

The Black Collegiates, established in 1987 under the leadership of Keith "Beef" Brown, reflected a revival of interest in an organization for black students to replace the earlier, defunct, Afro-American Society. Since most of the small number of black students at Southern were from big cities, there was a felt need to help them orient to life at MSSC.

Members of Omicron Delta Epsilon posed for this photograph during the 1986–1987 school year. From left, front row, are: Felicia Rowe; Mary Davis; Steve Tipton; and Carl Atnip. Second row: Jennell Fredrick; Terri Honeyball; Joleen Murray; and Lee Martin. Back row: Charles Leitle, sponsor; Stephen Bryant; Michael Carter; Janet Watson; and J. S. Jaswal, sponsor. Omicron Delta Epsilon, an honorary Economics society founded on campus in 1976, continued to function in this period as one of the college's strongest honorary academic organizations. It regularly counted among its members some of MSSC's outstanding students such as Terri Honeyball, Student Senate president for 1987–1988, who also received many other honors, and Lee Martin, a 1987 graduate, who became the first Honors student to receive a diploma.

Emma Jo Walker, 1989 Homecoming Queen, is shown at the annual Homecoming cookout. Reflecting the growing importance of nontraditional students, she was the first member of this group to be chosen as Homecoming Queen. Walker, a Nursing student, was age thirty-eight at this time, had a family of three children, and her son, Brian, a sophomore, was one year ahead of her at MSSC. A resident of Webb City, she maintained a 3.9 grade point average.

ceeded in establishing a new national fraternity, Sigma Pi. Kappa Alpha was resurrected in 1990 as a local organization; two years later it regained its national charter. MSSC's status as a commuter college weakened the Greek movement. Working students or those living off campus were not good candidates for the movement. Some of the Greek societies established homes in old residences scattered about town, but no "Greek row" adjacent to the campus ever developed.

In most other areas the formation of new student organizations flourished. Some ten new clubs were formed in the academic area alone, with the Business Administration, Communications, Education, Physical Education, Social Science, and Technology areas sharing in these. Honorary scholastic societies grew nearly as fast with eight being formed, but half were nondepartmental, reflecting the administration's efforts to cast a broader, across campus, base for academic achievement. These included Alpha Chi, Omicrom Delta Kappa, Phi Eta Sigma, and Sigma Mu Epsilon. General and service organizations grew by seven, but four of these, the Rodeo, Rugby Football, Bicycle, and Camera clubs were sports or recreational oriented. Only Students Achieving Greater Education, the Black Collegiates, and a revival of the Circle K International were service organizations. In the religious area, only one new society, the Latter Day Saints Student Association, was formed in the 1983–1992 period, but seven older organizations still gave religious denominations strong representation on campus.

The increasing number of student organizations in the 1983–1992 period reflected above all the vigor of academic development. Most of the clubs gave depth and breath to the students' growth in their major fields, while other societies enriched the students' opportunities for social and recreational growth.

Southern's intercollegiate sports program was considerably strengthened in the 1983–1992 time period. Its move into a higher level of competition against more prestigious universities and its expanded reach for talented athletes paralleled the college's stronger academic program and added to MSSC's stature as an excellent undergraduate college.

The most significant development in Southern's athletic program came with the decision to join the National Collegiate Athletic Association (NCAA) Division II and the Missouri Intercollegiate Athletic Association (MIAA) conference. Southern had had a standing invitation since 1983 to make this

These attentive Psychology students are listening to a lecture in Dr. Brian Babbitt's Learning Memory, and Cognition class during the 1988–1989 year. Psychology produced a growing number of majors in this period as well as providing a support area for education, criminal justice, and the Core Curriculum. Melanie Hicks photo

change and join a conference with its sister Missouri state colleges and universities, but the more complex regulations and the additional costs of travel, recruitment, and expansion of programs made college officials hesitant to move. Their hands were forced when Missouri Western State College, Pittsburg State University, and Washburn University expressed an interest in joining the MIAA and it became clear the old Central States Intercollegiate Conference of the NAIA was breaking up. In 1992, the name Missouri was dropped from the MIAA and it became the Mid-America Intercollegiate Athletics Association in keeping with its expanded interstate status.

In April 1987 the Board of Regents approved Southern's move from the CSIC/NAIA to the MIAA and its prestigious national affiliate, the NCAA, Division II. Regulations required that the college go through a two-year probationary period before being officially admitted to NCAA/MIAA competition. In the meantime, plans began taking shape to budget funds for the more expensive new programs and for the new stiffer academic admissions standards for athletes that the NCAA required. Coaches were not unduly worried about stiffened competition in the new conference. They had played many of these teams in nonconference games and had two years in which to build up their teams. Administrators were pleased with the changes. They saw it as another step that would reinforce Southern's growing image as a significant four-year college.

The football team in the decade 1983–1992 mirrored the fortunes of the athletic program in general, suffering some reverses but overall turning in a strong performance. Jim Frazier, head football coach, maintained strong teams in the early 1980s, with such notable players as Glen Baker, Harold Noirfalise, Billy Jack Smith, and Joel Tupper performing brilliantly. The year 1983 was most memorable for the Lions ranking of 9–2 overall and for claiming a second in the Central States Intercollegiate Conference. This was the Lions best single performance in the twenty years after their 12–0 national championship of 1972, though the 1976 and 1991 seasons with 8–2 and 8–3 records were also impressive.

Frazier retired at the end of the 1985 season to devote full time to his position as men's athletic director. His impressive overall record of 97 wins, 52 losses, 5 ties and only 3 losing years, as well as a national championship, marks him as one of MSSC's most successful coaches. His fifteen-year tenure as a head football coach was the longest in Southern's history on either the junior or senior college level.

The next three years, 1986 through 1988, the football Lions experienced a dismal period, losing twenty-one games while winning only eight. Rod Giesselmann, a defensive coordinator for the Lions since 1979, replaced Frazier as head coach in 1986. In his short tenure Giesselmann suffered two disastrous years. His 2–7 overall record in 1986 was the worst in fifteen years and a 3–7 performance the next year was little better. Giesselmann suffered from problems recruiting and holding quality players, injuries plagued his

Sonny Glass, a Quapaw Indian, is shown in the Lions' Den discussing Indian folklore with students during Multicultural Week in 1987. This was his third annual appearance.

Multicultural Week, usually held each February or March, featured performances by various cultural groups and the cafeteria served a different ethnic food for each day of the event. It was terminated after 1989 as being too concentrated and its activities were spread out over the year.

Seated around the table are members of the Alumni Association Board of Directors for 1988–1989. In foreground and to left are: Pam Perkins George, president, Joplin; Dr. Kreta Gladden, director; Nancy Dymott, Carthage; Gloria Turner, Joplin; Gerald Hendren, Joplin; Dr. Charles Leitle, adviser. To right of table: Maxine Cullum, treasurer, Neosho; Dr. Patrick Thompson, Joplin; and Mike Gilpin, past president, Joplin.

The Alumni Association has been active in providing special gifts for the college, scholarships, and recognition for outstanding students and alumni, as well as providing a special link between the alumni and their alma mater. Larry Meacham photo

teams, and he was the victim of plain bad luck. Of his seven losses in 1987, three were by one point and two by two points.

Charles Wade replaced Giesselmann as head coach, but resigned less than two weeks before the first scheduled game of the 1988 season. William M. "Bill" Cooke, an assistant coach, replaced Wade as interim head, and the Lions suffered another 3–7 losing year. Cooke did not seek the position of head coach on a permanent basis, preferring to remain as an assistant, but he left his successor with a seasoned team, including senior quarterback Alan Brown who had broken or tied fourteen school records in 1988 and earned All-American Honorable Mention honors.

The new head coach, Jon Lantz, ushered in another era of improved performance on the part of the football Lions. Southern's entry into the tougher MIAA conference in 1989 made Coach Lantz's 6–4 winning season even more impressive. Lantz had built a strong team out of seasoned returnees and recruits, but it suffered a severe blow when four members of the team were involved in an automobile accident.

In the next three years, Coach Lantz's teams performed unevenly. The 1990 season ended on a losing 4–5 count, but the Lion's, with a more experienced team, came back strongly the next year. Sparked by the outstanding performances of Matt Cook, Rod Smith, and Jay Pride, the Lions posted an 8–3 winning season, the best since 1983. The year 1992 proved to be a frustrating one for the Lions. Entering the season with high

Members of the Class of 1940, JJC's second graduating class, posed for this photograph during the 1990 Homecoming. From the left are: Bob Galbraith, Carthage; Jack Guinee, Rogers, Arkansas; Ed Wyrick, Sharpsburg, Georgia; Paul Morrison, New Orleans, Louisiana; Kenneth McCaleb, Huntsville, Alabama; Margaret (Baughman) McCaleb, Huntsville, Alabama; Margaret McGregor, Kansas City; Imo Jean (Aggus) Bryson, Joplin: Alice Loue (Leonard) Ritter, Canyon, Texas; Joseph Filler, St. Louis; Mary Jane (Lang) Grundler, Columbia; Bob Hatley, England; Ed Farmer, Jr., Joplin; Ray Palmer, Sarcoxie; Ruth (Klinksick) Short, Churchville, Virginia; Oscar Short; Jack Swope, Bridgeton, Missouri; R. G. Sheppard, Smith Center, Kansas; Bill Owen, Joplin; J. Kenneth Smith, Roswell, New Mexico; and Mrs. Harry Gockel, Carthage.

Since Southern's fiftieth anniversary celebration, the Alumni Association has extended special Homecoming recognition each fall to the Joplin Junior College alumni as they reach their golden anniversary. Larry Meacham photo

hopes and a strong team, severe injuries early in the season effectively removed two of the team's leading players, Matt Cook and Rod Smith, and the disheartened squad ended up with a losing 4–6 year.

Looking back on the ten years, 1983–1992, the Lions could be pleased with their overall performance. Most mettlesome though has been the rivalry with Pittsburg State University, dating from the founding of the four-year college. In this 25-year rivalry, known as the "Miners Bowl" since 1986, the Lions have recorded a disappointing 8–16–1 record and have not won a game since 1984. In total, the football Lions had suffered some losses and some disappointments but overall had won 70 games while losing 57, and they had firmly established themselves in the tougher competition of the twelve-team MIAA conference. By 1992, the "gray" years of 1986–1988, in which the Lions had lost considerable prestige, were behind them and they could confidently look forward to the future.

Men's basketball in the 1983–1992 time period began on a strong note, went into a bad slump in the late 1980s, and then emerged again, but experienced difficulty in making the transition from CSIC to MIAA play. The basketball Lions never won first place in conference play in this period and, in fact, in their entire history of conference competition, 1976–1992, had won titles only in 1978 and 1981. The quest for a national title always eluded the cagers though they played in NAIA national tournaments in 1987 for this period and three times previously in the 1970s.

The Lions enjoyed three winning seasons in the four-year period 1983–1984 through 1986–1987. Two strong players, Carl Tyler and Greg Garton, dominated the team. In a January 1984 game against Missouri Western State College, Tyler's 49 points set a new all-time record. In his senior year, 1983–1984, Tyler established a new career scoring record of 1,902 points only to have it toppled two years later by Greg Garton. In November 1983, the Lions set a new winning margin record when they devastated a hapless Cardinal-Newman College 113–34. The MSSC cagers won berths in the NAIA District 16 playoffs in 1984 and 1986, but lost in the early rounds. The 1986–1987 Lions proved to be one of Southern's best basketball teams. The cagers gained the NAIA District 16 championship in a thrilling final round 85–84 victory over Drury College when Chris Tuggle sank a three-point floor shot in the closing seconds of the game. The Drury Panthers were so good that they had gained a berth in the NAIA national tournament five times in the past eight years, but this time it was the Lions who journeyed to Kansas City, though they lost in the first round of the tournament. The Lions further enhanced their prestige that spring of 1987 when they scored an 81–75 upset victory over Oklahoma State University at Stillwater, an NCAA Division I school. *Sports Illustrated* magazine gave the victory national coverage.

The next two years, 1987–1988 and 1988–1989, turned into near disasters for the basketball Lions. The veteran team that had fought its way to the national playoffs was largely gone through graduation or moving. Coach Williams had no returning starters, lettermen, or seniors. Dissention soon racked the rookie team. Williams was suspended from one game for making a racist remark to a black player. Five players left during the season, leaving only eight at the end of the season. The next season, with only three re-

President George Bush appeared on the Southern campus oval on Friday September 11, 1992, to address a Republican campaign rally. In this photograph, Governor John Ashcroft and Attorney General William Webster (concealed) are to the president's immediate left while Representative Mark Elliott and MSSC President Julio Leon (both partially concealed) stand to the president's right.

A crowd of several thousand assembled for the event, but proceedings were marred when Democratic placard carriers, a number of them MSSC Young Democrats, were confined in a roped-off area completely away from the rally. Charges of violating the protestors' civil rights have been brought against some members of the Jasper County Sheriff's Department by the American Civil Liberties Union and litigation is pending.

This was the first time a president of the United States has ever visited Southern, though Bush, while still vice president, and his vice presidential running mate, Daniel Quayle, made separate campaign appearances in 1988. Larry Meacham photo

turnees, Coach Williams headed another freshman team torn by low morale and just as ineffective. In the two seasons the Lions had won only 9 games and had lost 44. Coach Williams resigned at the end of the 1988–1989 season. As a freshmen coach he had led the basketball Lions to their best year as a senior college, now, twelve years later, he was leaving on a sad note.

Robert Corn, a Southern graduate and member of William's 1977–1978 championship team, replaced the latter as head basketball coach. He experienced two losing seasons building up his team and adjusting to the new stiffer MIAA competition. In 1991–1992 Corn fielded the strongest team since 1986–1987, and the Lions 21–8 overall performance and 10–6 in the MIAA was impressive, but failed to gain them a berth in the NCAA Division II national tournament. Thus the Lions ended the 1983–1992 era in a strong position but had found a national championship to be an elusive hope.

Soccer remained a strong sport through most of the 1983–1992 period, but went into a sharp decline the latter three of these years. Though a varsity sport since 1976, soccer had never been adequately funded, depending on amateur coaches who, with one exception, were full-time professors teaching in other disciplines. Nevertheless, up to 1990, soccer had had experienced coaches who coped with the shortcomings, but after that the weaknesses of the system tended to surface and the program went into a decline.

Harold Bodon, founder of the MSSC soccer program in 1972 and varsity coach since 1976, continued to field strong teams. His 1984 team made it to the NAIA District 16 playoffs but lost in the first round. The next summer, Bodon took his seventeen-member team on an unusual trip to Europe. There they played teams in Germany, Austria, and Switzerland, compiling an impres-

Terron Jackson (left) and John Thomas are shown reminiscing at the 1985 Homecoming football game. Both were honored at the festivities by being inducted into the MSSC Letterman's Alumni Association Hall of Fame.

Jackson, an offensive tackle, played at Southern, 1969–1973, and in 1972 became the first Lion to ever receive an NAIA All-American First Team Award. In 1982, he was named to MSSC's Silver Anniversary Commemorative Football Team. Jackson has followed a career in business since graduating from Southern. His son, Tony, played basketball on MSSC's 1992–1993 team.

Thomas, "Mr. Basketball" to fans, was a center for the Lions, 1969–1973. His records of 1,536 rebounds for a career and 445 for one season still stand as all-time highs. Thomas received NAIA All-American Honorable Mention honors for three years in succession, another unbroken record. In 1992, he was also named to MSSC's Silver Anniversary Commemorative Basketball Team. After graduating from MSSC, Thomas became an assistant basketball coach and remedial reading instructor at the Aliquippa (Pennsylvania) High School, his hometown.

This aerial view of a football game in progress at Fred Hughes Stadium during the fall of 1988 shows the newly reconditioned playing field and track to good advantage. The old surfaces were replaced with an innovative sand-filled artificial turf playing field and an all-weather, 400-meter, eight-lane polyurethane track for track and field competitions.

sive 6–1–2 record. Back at Southern that fall, Bodon's team managed only a 7–9–3 year, the only losing season in Bodon's twelve years as a varsity coach. Bodon had strong teams the next two years but he resigned at the end of the 1987 season, remarking, "It is time for a younger man to take over." He had coached Southern soccer for sixteen years, including the first four years when it was a club sport, and his overall sixteen-year record of 172–95–30 was exceptional for a part-time coach. Jack G. Spurlin, an assistant professor of Criminal Justice, succeeded Bodon as head coach.

Spurlin's 1988 squad became the first team in the Lion's soccer history to win a NAIA District 16 Championship, but the next year he faced NCAA Division II competition for the first time. Under this stiffer opposition, the Lions finished with an honorable 11–6–2 overall record, but Spurlin resigned at the end of the season.

Spurlin's impressive overall record of 25–10–5 for two seasons marked an end to the era of strong teams in MSSC soccer. The problems of a limited budget, part-time coaching, recruitment, travel, and training that had plagued Coach Bodon for years and bore down heavily on Spurlin, began to cut into the teams' effectiveness under their successors. Scott Poertner succeeded Spurlin as head coach for the 1990 season. Poertner, a Southern graduate who had played on Bodon's teams, left a high school teaching and coaching job to accept the part-time position as head soccer coach. Facing an increasingly difficult task, Poertner left after two seasons, leaving behind a losing overall record of 13–20–4. In 1992, George Greenlee, an assistant professor of English and active in junior league coaching, took over the weakened team and led them in a losing 3–13–0 season, the worst in MSSC's seventeen years of varsity soccer competition. Greenlee faces a difficult task rebuilding the team in the face of soccer's manifold problems.

Baseball emerged as one of Southern's strongest sports in the 1983–1992 time period. In its eleven years on campus, baseball had been heavily overshadowed by football and basketball as a varsity sport, but Coach Warren Turner successfully set about improving its image. In 1978, Turner first led his team into a NAIA world series playoff tournament. During the years 1983–1992, he guided four more of his teams into these national championship contests, including two attempts under the new NCAA Division II format. Though a national championship always evaded Turner, these journeys into the national spotlight added immensely to the baseball Lion's prestige.

Between 1983 and 1989, Southern's last seven years under the NAIA/CSIC umbrella, Coach Turner continued to build the strength of his teams with only two bad years. By 1986, and again the following year, they were strong enough to capture berths in the national playoffs. In both years, they won the NAIA District 16 and Area IV championships which entitled them to play in the NAIA world series tournaments at Lewiston, Idaho. There they placed seventh in 1986 and fifth the following year. Honors were bestowed on the Lions. In 1986 Joe Janiak, Chris Adams, and Tim Williams received honorable mention to the NAIA All-American team. The following year, Rick Berg received Southern's coveted E. O. Humphrey award, the first baseball Lion to be so honored. Turner, himself was named Coach of the Year on both the District 16 and Area IV levels. He experienced the fourth of his losing seasons in 1988, but District 16 honors were showered on Jody Hunt, Jim Baranoski, and Steve Carvejal. Carvejal also earned the dubious distinction of being hit by pitched balls fourteen times during the season, a new NAIA record. In 1989, the Lions bounced back with a 36–22 winning season, but were unable to capture any championships. Jim Baranoski, who led the team with 16 home runs, became the second baseball Lion to receive the Humphrey award.

Harold Noirfalise, Southern's star running back, is shown eluding an opponent in the Lions' 1982 Homecoming 23–14 win over the Kearney State Antelopes.

Noirfalise's four-year career record of 3,864 yards gained rushing still stands as does his career record of 43 touchdowns and 266 points scored. Among his many honors, Noirfalise gained NAIA All-American Honorable Mention Awards for the three years 1982 through 1984. In 1992 he was named to MSSC's Silver Anniversary Commemorative Team.

Because of its scheduling, the baseball team did not enter the new NCAA Division II/MIAA competition until the spring of 1990. This higher level of competition posed no serious problems for the baseball Lions. They were used to contesting NCAA Division I and II teams, and by their second year were again strong contenders for a national championship. In 1990, the Lions won the MIAA South Division championship, but could advance no further. The next two years they fielded the strongest teams in their history. In both years, the baseball Lions swept the MIAA conference and the NCAA Division II central region championships and moved on to the NCAA Division II championship tournaments in Montgomery, Alabama. In 1991, Turner's team narrowly missed the national championship, taking the runner-up trophy, and the next year, they again fell short.

By 1992, baseball was a solidly established sport that complemented the college's drive toward academic excellence. The program was soundly directed and its growing prestige tended to attract players who were not only talented athletes but also academically oriented individuals.

Women's varsity sports were well established by 1983, but in the next ten years they reached a new level of maturity and turned out some strong teams that ranked high in conference and regional standings, including one national championship. Basketball, volleyball, and softball remained the principal sports though competition in tennis and a modified track and field program were reintroduced toward the end of the period.

Lady Lions basketball, the most popular of the women's sports, proved strong with few exceptions, gaining six winning seasons in the nine-year period 1983–1984 through 1991–1992. On the other hand, they never advanced far enough to gain a berth in a national championship tournament as they had in 1981–1982. Still, under Coach Jim Phillips leadership, the Lady Lions, after their losing season in 1982–1983, came back strong in the next three years, placing first or second in Central States Intercollegiate Conference play, and ranking second for all three years in the NAIA District 16 championship tournaments. The 1984–1985 and 1985–1986 teams were exceptionally strong. In a November 1984 triumph over Harris-Stowe College, the winning score in the 108–43 victory was the largest ever attained by a Lady Lions basketball team.

With many strong players graduating, the Lady Lion's performance weakened in the next two years. In 1986–1987, the team still maintained a winning season, but the next year an even weaker team turned in a near disastrous 8–18 overall performance and a dismal 2–12 record in the CSIC that precluded them from gaining a berth in the District 16 playoffs for the first time since 1980–1981. Coach Phillips resigned as head women's basketball coach in July 1988 to take a similar position at Austin Peay State University.

Janet Gabriel, who replaced James Phillips as head women's basketball coach, began a two-year term in July 1988. Due to the lateness of her appointment she had to depend largely on the team already in place, but she did surprisingly well, finishing the season 17–12 overall and entering the NAIA championship contest where the Lady Lions placed fifth. The next year Southern entered into its new NCAA/MIAA Division II affiliation. Gabriel, faced with a tougher schedule and with a team plagued by injuries, soon saw her hopes turn to ashes. Finishing the season 9–18 overall and crushed 4–12 in the MIAA, the Lady Lions failed to qualify for the championship playoffs. Coach Gabriel resigned at the end of the season.

Scott Ballard, a successful coach from the Marshfield, Missouri High School, became the new head women's basketball coach in 1990–1991 and continued in the following years. Ballard, in his first year, suffered a losing, 12–15 overall season, but in 1991–1992 the Lady Lions sprang back to gain an 18–10 ranking and place third in conference play, but they failed to reach the national playoffs.

Honors passed out to players in 1990–1991 and 1991–1992 included academic honors gained by Diane Hoch, Caryn Schumaker, and Sandy Soeken. Terri Haynes, from Wheaton, the Lady Lion's leading three-point shot artist, gained All-MIAA and All-NCAA awards. Rolanda Gladen and Nancy Somers also received All-MIAA citations.

The basketball Lady Lions established a solid record in the 1983–1992 time period. Though they won no national championships, their performance compared favorably with that of other leading MSSC sports. Furthermore, the team gained recognition for the college throughout the region and helped establish it in women's sports, as in academics, as a leading regional undergraduate college.

Women's softball became one of Southern's most successful athletic programs in the years 1983–1992 under the leadership of Head Coach Patsy K. Lipira. Lipira in her first year, 1982, suffered a losing season, but thereafter she fielded winning teams every year. Her overall eleven-year record of 346–163 is impressive for any coach.

Lipira's victories mounted steadily. Each year from 1983 through 1992 her teams did well enough to gain entrance into the NAIA District 16—later the MIAA—playoff tournaments. In four of them the teams placed second, third, or fourth. In the other six they won championships which qualified them to compete for national titles, but the elusive national championship remained beyond their grasp until 1992.

Members of the 1991–1992 basketball team appearing here are, from left, front row: K. Allen; S. Williams; W. Bushnell; S. Hagel; R. Morris; and R. Joyner. Second row: R. Corn, head coach; M. Wilson, assistant coach; J. Starkweather, assistant coach; C. Tucker; M. Doman; B. Rhinehart, student trainer; J. Miller, student coach; and M. Conklin, head trainer. Back row: K. Simpson; N. Smith; J. Hill; M. Saulsberry; D. McCullough; T. Burell; and R. Ressel.

Under a new coach, Robert Corn, this squad proved to be the strongest team in five years. Their 21–8 overall record was impressive, but a 10–6 third-place finish in the MIAA conference ended the season for them.

The Lions most impressive player in the two-year period, 1990–1992, was Kenney Simpson. A forward from St. Louis, and a junior college transfer, he led the Lions in scoring and rebounds during his two years at MSSC. In 1992, Simpson received NCAA Division II All-American honors and that same year he received MSSC's Humphrey Award and was named to the Silver Anniversary Commemorative Team. Assistant Coach Jeff Starkweather, played at MSSC three years, 1984–1987.

Members of the 1988 soccer team posing in this photograph are, from left, front row: R. Geller, R. Gourd; C. Dikeman; S. Housner; D. Henkel; J. Burnes; and S. Reed. Second row: S. Watson; S. Hull; D. Kelly; C. Milliman; E. Mallory; K. Hooks; and B. Johnson. Third row: J. Spurlin, head coach; T. Davidson; B. Erwin; L. Stephenson; J. Malasek; K. Borucki; L. Stemmons; and D. Youst, assistant coach. Back row: T. Kohler; R. Fritz; L. Rollerson; B. Taffner; C. Mathis; M. Prater; and S. Owens.

Headed by a new coach, Jack G. Spurlin, the squad of mostly talented novices turned out to be Southern's most successful soccer team. With a 14–4–3 overall performance, the team established some important firsts. It finally defeated the Rockhurst College Hawks. Also, the team for the first time won a NAIA District 16 championship and then advanced into the Area IV playoffs before being defeated. Coach Spurlin received Coach of the Year honors and players Keith Borucki, Shawn Owens, Mike Prater, and Jeff Malasek received District 16 Honors.

Spurlin, a full-time Criminal Justice teacher, overwhelmed by the additional responsibilities of coaching, resigned at the end of the 1989 season, announcing that he could not "handle two full-time jobs at once." A fine teacher, he was named Outstanding Teacher of a Freshman Class for the 1988–1989 year. Later he became director of the Criminal Justice Department.

The baseball Lions outstanding 1991 team appear in this photograph. From left, front row, are: T. Casper; T. Tichy; T. Busch; D. Fisher; and S. Madden, student coach. Second row: R. Williams; D. Gaffney; R. Curry; M. McNew; B. Larson; R. McCoy; and J. Dill, student trainer. Third row: W. Turner, head coach; C. Wagner; O. Rhone; T. Casper; T. Luther; M. Zirngibl; and K. Luebber, assistant coach. Back row: M. Ashmore; M. Baker; K. Grundt; C. Pittman; J. Beres; D. Burns; and K. Koch.

This 1991 team's 48–13 overall record provided the best finish in MSSC's baseball history and its 44–13 performance the next year was second best. The 1991 team won second place in the national tournament, equaling their 1978 finish and the nearest the baseball Lions have ever come to a national championship.

Many honors were bestowed on Coach Turner and the team players. Turner received MIAA and NCAA Division II, Central Region, Coach of the Year Awards. Honors to individual players included NCAA Division II All-American awards to: David Fisher, First Team; Bryan Larson, Second Team; and Scott Madden, Third Team. Also, Division II regional awards went to many of the players.

Andrea Clarke, a native of Pinckneyville, Illinois, is shown pitching for the Lady Lions during the NCAA Division II national championship tournament in May 1992. Though only a sophomore, Clarke was a picture of intense concentration as she pitched all three games in the tournament, allowing only one run, a performance sufficient to win the national championship for the Lady Lions.

Clarke gained many honors. Her team voted her Most Valuable Player for the second straight year and she received the prestigious NCAA Division II All-American Second Team Award.

The softball Lady Lion's successful quest for a national championship in this period resulted from Coach Lipira's skillful leadership, college and community support, and a sequence of success building on success. The three years 1985 through 1987 proved to be the transitional period during which the Lady Lions emerged as significant competitors in midwest regional softball. The team's first trip to the NAIA national tournaments was in 1985, but it was repeated in the next two years with Coach Lipira's charges reaching a high of fourth place in the 1986 playoff at San Antonio, Texas. In that year, shortstop Renee Livell became the first softball Lady Lion to be named to the NAIA All-America First Team while pitcher Lana Baysinger and third baseplayer Kim House were Second Team choices. Baysinger had also received the Second Team award the year before. These appearances at national tournaments, and the honors bestowed on individual players, gave Southern widespread recognition and a growing reputation for having a top-notch softball team. In turn, the growing recognition helped immensly in the recruitment of quality players as did the new playing field.

The period 1989–1992 saw the softball Lady Lions take part in the college's planned switch to NCAA Division II/MIAA affiliation. Lipira, at this time, dropped her head coachship of the volleyball team to better concentrate on

In this interesting photograph, five players from the 1991 and 1992 baseball teams, who gained contracts with professional league teams, are shown with Pitching Coach Steve Luebber. From left, Luebber; infielders Tim Casper and David Fisher; and pitchers Tim Luther, Ken Grundt, and Chuck Pittman. Casper, Luther, and Grundt signed with the San Francisco Giants; Fisher with the Philadelphia Phillies; and Pittman with the St. Louis Cardinals. All five of these players were on the 1991 team that placed second in the nationals while Fisher and Pittman also played for the Lions the following year.

Luebber was once a pitcher for the Minnesota Twins. During the fall and winter he serves as pitching coach for the Lions. In the spring and summer of 1992 he was a minor league pitching coach for the Baltimore Orioles organization. Joplin Globe/Vince Rosati photo

One of the basketball Lady Lions most memorable teams, the 1985–1986 squad pose in this photograph. From left, seated: J. Phillips, head coach; D. Rogers, assistant coach; S. Sutton; G. Klenke; L. Wilson; K. Bowen; M. Main; and K. Barnett, manager. Standing: T. Wilson; S. Walton; A. Rank; A. Oberdieck; T. Hagan; M. Womack; and B. Fly.

This team racked up a 25–7 season overall, 25 being the second most games the basketball Lady Lions ever won in one year. The team ended their season by being defeated in the NAIA District 16 playoff finals.

Such Lady Lion greats as Becky Fly, Amy Oberdieck, Anita Rank, Suzanne Sutton, LaDonna and Trish Wilson, and Margaret Womack played on this team. Fly and Womack both earned NAIA All-American honors. Womack received the Humphrey Award in 1986 and held the career scoring record of 1,747 points for two years. The Wilson sisters, LaDonna and Trish, natives of Anderson, were not only outstanding players at MSSC, but also went on to establish careers as college coaches: LaDonna as head women's basketball coach at Austin Peay University and Trish as assistant coach at Morehead State University. The sisters compete with one another yearly in Ohio Valley Conference games.

softball. Competition in the new league posed no formidable problems for the softball team. In their first year, 1990, they grabbed the MIAA conference prize and the NCAA Division II Midwest Regional title before advancing into the NCAA Division II National tournament where they placed fourth. The next year they failed to gain a berth in the national playoffs though their 36–8 finish was slightly better than in the year before.

The 1992 season proved to be the softball Lady Lions' banner year. Coach Lipira entered the season with an experienced team of sixteen, including six seniors, four juniors, and only three freshmen. The season moved smoothly with the Lady Lions winning the MIAA South Division title for the third straight year, the MIAA championship tournament, and the NCAA Division II Midwest Regional playoffs. The team then traveled to Shawnee, Kansas, for the NCAA Division II national championship tournament. The Lady Lions ousted Saginaw Valley State University (Michigan) 8–1 on May 15, Bloomsburg University (Pennsylvania) 1–0 the next day, and on May 17 they faced California State University, Hayward, for the national title. Blessed with skilled pitchers and tough defenses on both sides, the two teams were held scoreless into the fifth inning when MSSC pinch-hitter Dana Presley drove a grounder to centerfield with the bases loaded, enabling centerfielder Carrie Carter to score. No more runs were gained and the game ended with a 1–0 victory for the Southern team. The whole Lady Lion squad had played with professional skill, but the star of the tournament was sophomore pitcher Andrea Clarke. The softball Lady Lions ended the season with a 50–7 overall record, a performance so impressive that it had never been even closely approached in their previous history. It was the first time an MSSC sport had won a NCAA national title and only the second time any national title has been won by a major senior college team.

Team members were the recipients of many awards, and a number of Coach-of-the-Year honors were showered on Coach Pat Lipira for her guidance in producing the 1992 national championship team and earlier winning squads. She received these Coach-of-the-Year awards from NAIA District 16 for 1985, 1986, 1987, and 1989; the MIAA for 1990 and 1992; the NCAA Central Region, 1990 and 1992; and the singular NCAA Division II national honor in 1992.

Volleyball, the third of the major women's varsity sports, has never enjoyed the popularity of women's basketball or shown the vitality of the softball program. Yet the volleyball teams have experienced few losing seasons and only three in the ten-year period 1983–1992. On the other hand, the spikers have won only one conference title and have never gained a NAIA District 16 or NCAA Division II Central Region championship. This record has also precluded them from ever having even entered a national championship tournament.

Coach Pat Lipira headed the volleyball teams from 1981 through 1987. These were the program's best years and the peak of this era was the four years, 1983–1986, when the spikers won 40 or more games in each of those years, a record never equaled before or since. With a cadre of seasoned players, Lipira's charges won a record 47 games in 1986 but again fell short of the championships. Lipira's final year as volleyball mentor was 1987. Though she had some talented players, like Shelly Hodges-Garr, the team went into a further slump, but still gained a winning season. Lipira chose to lighten her workload by dropping volleyball and concentrating on softball, a sport in which she had excelled in college. Nevertheless, her 264–90–11 MSSC volleyball career record is impressive.

Debra Traywick replaced Lipira as head volleyball coach in 1988. Faced with adjusting to a new situation, changes in the team, and tougher competition brought on by the shift to NCAA Division II/MIAA affiliation, Traywick suffered three consecutive losing years. The 19–31 loss in 1988 was the first in ten years and the 9–25 humiliation the following year was the worst setback in the volleyball program's history. Following an improved, but still losing year in 1990, the volleyball team bounced back the next year with a 32–11 season overall and a second place finish in the MIAA tournament. In 1992, the spikers finished the season 20–17 overall but lost out in the early rounds of the MIAA playoffs.

Southern's volleyball Lady Lions historically have enjoyed only modest, but respectable, successes. Their overall record of twelve winning years out of eighteen compares favorably with the other MSSC sports, yet because they have rarely competed above the level of regular conference play, they have never basked in the publicity or earned the prestige that has come to the other Southern sports that have competed on the higher levels.

The minor sports for both men and women, golf, tennis, and track and field remained weak in the 1983–1992 time period. Aside from golf, they had been largely abandoned at the beginning of this period and were not reinstituted until late in the decade. Men's track and field had been cancelled in 1977, but the women's portion of the program continued until the budgetary crisis of 1982–1983. Men and women's tennis also became a victim of this crisis and the former was never revived.

Golf, alone among the minor sports, escaped the budgetary ax largely because it was a low-budget sport and because it had a few dedicated supporters. Golf, under Coach Douglas Landrith, had long been surprisingly successful for a sport that attracted few athletes or fans and it continued to be so in this period under head coaches Randy Sohosky, 1983–1985, and Bill Cox, 1986–1992. In 1984 and again in 1987 and 1988, the MSSC golfers captured CSIC titles and gained berths in the NAIA national championship tournaments. Though they did not win, it was an impressive performance for the small team which sometimes amounted to no more than five players. The teams

Anita Rank, shown sinking another jump shot in a game against Fort Hays during the 1987–1988 season, demonstrates the graceful style that helped make her the basketball Lady Lions all-time leading scorer. A six-foot forward from Lincoln, Rank's career record of 1,842 points scored and her mark of 42 points netted in a single game both remain unbroken.

Rank gleaned many citations in her career. She twice received NAIA All-American Awards as well as NAIA and CSIC academic honors. Named MSSC's Outstanding Athlete of the Year for 1986–1987, Rank also became the third Lady Lion to receive the Humphrey Award.

Sheila Hunter is shown connecting for a base hit on the Lady Lions' new playing field during the 1986 softball season. The team's cause was advanced at this time by the completion of this new field, after coping with inadequate facilities for years. The new quarters, dedicated as Lea Kungle Softball Field, honored a civic benefactor by that name who died in 1985. Her husband, Arthur Kungle, a member of MSSC's Board of Trustees, donated the funds to build the diamond in her memory.

continued to perform impressively in the new MIAA conference.

The women's tennis program was revived in the spring of 1988 in anticipation of joining the MIAA, where Southern would be required to compete in four men's and four women's sports. The low-budget program ran into difficulty the next year when, through a misunderstanding, the coach violated MIAA rules. The MIAA reprimanded and imposed sanctions on the college for "providing benefits in excess of room and board or tuition. . . ." The coach resigned and the team was prohibited from participating in the spring of 1990 MIAA tournament. Georgina (Garrison) Bodine, the college's leading singles player in 1977–1980, took over as head coach. After recovering from the MIAA upheaval, Bodine's teams have posted winning seasons of 15–5 in 1991 and 11–6 the following year as well as gaining fifth and fourth places respectively in the MIAA tournaments. The leading players have been Adriana Rodriquez, Melissa Woods, and Diane Hoch. Hoch received the Most Valuable Player Award and a co-award of the Lionbackers' Award of Excellence in 1992 for her performance in softball and tennis.

The long neglected track and field competition was reinstated in the fall of 1989 and a new sport, cross country, was added to the program. Affiliation with the MIAA made possible the introduction of cross country competition. Held in the fall of the year, cross country activities involves distance running in open terrain as opposed to the more formal track contests, which were continued. Track and field events are concentrated in the spring semesters. Tom Rutledge was hired as head coach of the new programs for both men and women's teams. Serious competition did not begin until the 1990–1991 school year. Though the teams have won no MIAA tournaments or national events, the programs are growing. Leading runners have been Donna Boleski and Rhonda Cooper on the women's teams and Jason Riddle on the men's team.

Successes in athletics complemented the college's strengthened academics and overall growth in the decade, 1983–1992. The change to a NCAA Division II/MIAA affiliation moved athletics to a higher plane of competition in intercollegiate athletics and enhanced the stature of the college. All of the major varsity sports proved strong enough to gain added regional or national recognition. The softball Lady Lion's winning of MSSC's first NCAA Divsion II national championship symbolized the inherent strength of Southern's sports programs and how they can add to the college's reputation for educational excellence.

The school year of 1987–1988 at Missouri Southern is remembered for its many anniversary activities. Proclaimed the "Golden Anniversary Year," in reality it encompassed three anniversaries: Southern's fiftieth year as a college, its twentieth milestone as a four-year college, and the tenth year since it achieved full state funding.

A Fiftieth Anniversary Committee, chaired by Richard W. Massa, was formed to steer the projects. Jean Campbell, a staff assistant, was in charge of coordinating the many activities. In turn, two subcommittees were formed: an Honorary Steering Committee to which the

Members of the 1992 Lady Lions softball team, who won a NCAA Division II national championship, appear in this photograph. From left, front row: Andrea Mauk, trainer; Cindy Cole; Krissy Konkol; Cheryl Kopf; Sharla Snow; and Andrea Clarke. Second row: Amy Ladner, ball girl; Marcie Waters; Leah Ingram; Diane Miller; Carrie Carter; and Angie Hadley. Back row: Pat Lipira, head coach; Stacey Harter; Katrina Marshall; Jaki Staggs; Rene Weih; Dana Presley; Sharon Wright; and Dee Gerlach, assistant coach.

The team's 50–7 overall record and their clean sweep of the three-game national tournament were impressive and the numerous honors bestowed on individual players reflected this. Catcher Diane Miller and Andrea Clarke were the leading players and both received the NCAA Division II All-American Second Team Award, an award Miller had also received the previous year. MIAA All-Conference and NCAA Division II All-Central and All-Tournament awards also went to many of the players, Miller gained the Lionbackers Award of Excellence for 1992 and she had received the Humphrey Award the year before.

Members of the 1984 Lady Lions volleyball team shown here include, from left, front row: M. Stone; J. Rule; D. Cox; C. Lauth; T. Roberts; L. Cunningham; and L. Steenbergen. Back row: P. Lipira, head coach; S. Hodges; L. Hawthorne; K. Howard; B. Gettemeier; K. Greer; and B. Jennings, assistant coach.

This 1984 team gave MSSC volleyball its best individual year. Piling up a 42–6 overall record, they also captured the CSIC title, 12–2, the only time a volleyball team has won a conference championship. The team then swept into the NAIA District 16 playoffs where they placed second.

Kingpins of the Lady Lion's success were three seniors, Lisa Cunningham, Becky Gettemeier, and Tina Roberts. Both Roberts and Cunningham were NAIA All-American picks. All three, Gettemeier, Cunningham, and Roberts shared in All-CSIC and All-District 16 honors.

twenty living emeritus and retired faculty were named in recognition of the history that they embodied, and a Historical Resource Committee consisting of the twelve current faculty who had begun service in the junior college.

Many activities unfolded as the college moved through the year. Officially the calendar of events began with a July Fourth celebration in Hughes Stadium, sponsored by KSNF-TV. The real kickoff began that fall with a fiftieth anniversary celebration on August 31, 1987, held on the oval in front of the Billingsly Student Center. Several emeritus and retired faculty, who were present, received special recognition; emeritus Professor Cleetis Headlee addressed the crowd as did Senator Richard Webster. A major feature of the day was the filming of a greeting for the ABC-TV program *Good Morning America*. Other activities followed concluding with a barbecue picnic and the cutting of an anniversary cake.

Traditional Homecoming activities blended in with and gave emphasis to the anniversary celebration that fall. Festivities began with a pep rally and cookout on Thursday, October 1, at which Katrina Todd was crowned Homecoming Queen and Edith Lundien Mayes, first college queen, was recrowned. The honored received further recognition at Homecoming football game halftime ceremonies the following Saturday. A Golden Memories Ball provided another nostalgic occasion for the alumni.

Various special fiftieth anniversary events were arranged throughout the year. Three of these were the issuance of commemorative pewterware, a commemorative postal cancellation day, and a historical competition. The postal cancellation day began with a ceremony followed by the hand-stamping of commemorative mail. The historical competition was co-sponsored by the Joplin Historical Society and MSSC's Social Science Department.

Other events in the fall of 1987 that helped keep the anniversary spirit alive were a piano concert, a musical on the bicentennial of the U.S. Constitution, a salute to James K. Maupin, a Jasper County Development Association banquet, and the groundbreaking ceremony for a Veteran's Memorial. The fiftieth anniversary piano concert by Clive Swansbourne, MSSC assistant professor of music, was one of the first special programs of the fall cultural season. Dr. Allen Merriam, an MSSC associate professor of Communications, organized the musical commemorating the bicentennial of the Consti-

Gail Gilmore, a freshman member of the 1986 volleyball team, is shown waiting for a serve. The 1986 team won forty-seven games, an all-time high, but was unable to win any championships. Gilmore was strong in both volleyball and softball. A scholar with a 3.65 grade point average, she was named to the NAIA Academic All-American Team in 1989 and won the Lionbacker Award of Excellence.

Jason Riddle, No. 607, is shown competing with runners from Southwest Missouri State University in a Cross Country contest. An outstanding representative of MSSC's emerging Cross Country program, Riddle transferred to Southern from Northeastern Oklahoma A & M College at the beginning of his sophomore year. He placed high enough in regional events to qualify for entry into the NCAA national championship tournaments and earned All-American honors there in 1991, 1992, and 1993. In 1993 he received the Humphrey Award for his contribution to the Cross Country program.

tution, which coincided with Southern's anniversary celebration. The salute to James K. Maupin, dean of the School of Technology, on November 3 consisted of a surprise dinner and program honoring him on his sixty-fifth birthday and for his thirty-two years of service to the college. The Jasper County Development Association joined in the festivities with a banquet, on November 5, honoring Senators Richard Webster of Carthage and John E. Downs of St. Joseph and other legislative leaders who helped in bringing a four-year college to the region.

Another series of activities in the spring semester of 1988 helped the fiftieth anniversary celebration maintain its momentum. These included the encasement of a time capsule, a commemorative quilt, an anniversary cookbook, and a reunion of personnel from *The Chart*. The time capsule encasement aimed at establishing a link between the fiftieth and one hundredth anniversaries of the college. The commemorative quilt, produced by college secretaries, reflected a novel approach toward marking MSSC's fiftieth anniversary. In a similar project, several secretaries compiled an anniversary cookbook to raise money for a scholarship fund. *The Chart* reunion, a two-day affair, turned out to be one of the largest social gatherings of the anniversary year.

The yearlong anniversary activities ended with commencement exercises on Saturday, May 14, 1988. A doubly special occasion, this ceremony honored the fiftieth graduating class since the college's founding in 1939 and the twentieth since the first baccalaureate degrees were issued in 1969. On the eve of the commencement exercises, alumni who could not attend held "birthday parties" across the nation wherever a group could be brought together. Some eighteen of the alumni who could not attend any of the activities joined in the occasion through a long-distance telephone chat with President Leon on Friday evening. The Alumni Association also added to the uniqueness of the occasion by naming a record five graduates, Glen Barnett (1969), Jerry W. Cooper (1957), Dan H. Fiecker (1969), Eugene E. Langevin (1963), and Chuck Surface (1969) as the Outstanding Alumni of 1987.

The 1988 fiftieth anniversary commencement exercises came on a warm and windy day at Hughes Stadium, with an overflow crowd present. Several members of the 1939 and 1969 graduating classes attended and seven of the 1939 alumni led the procession of current graduates into the stadium. Some 530 received associate and baccalaureate degrees, a record number for the growing college. Special speakers were Joan Epperson Giles (1939), Lt. Colonel Barbara Blackford Bevins (1969), Terri Honeyball, Outstanding Graduate of 1988, and Betsy Griffin, president of the Faculty Senate. Giles enlightened the crowd with anecdotes on the beginnings of Southern traditions. In identifying her class of 1939 with the 1988 graduates before her, she concluded, borrowing a Shakespearian phrase, "'We few, we happy few' . . . we wish you well and I hope in fifty years many of you can come back and . . . say, 'We few, we happy few'. . . . " Seventh District Congressman Gene

Taylor, a member of the original Board of Trustees, delivered the keynote address, urging the graduates to "be builders."

The fiftieth anniversary celebration accented Southern's growing reputation for excellence in education. The activities were remarkable for their richness and variety as well as for the smooth efficiency with which they were carried out. They added to the college's prestige and provided a proper symbolic launching for the institution's next fifty years of progress.

In the decade since Julio Leon assumed the full title of president in 1983, the college has grown and has moved far toward meeting the then stated mission "To become the best undergraduate college that we can be." Discounting talk about gaining graduate level programs for Southern, Leon set as his goal the establishment of an excellent undergraduate college. Though he built on an already strong curriculum, his emphasis on upgrading and expanding the disciplines, adding new programs, and attracting superior students with incentives such as the Honors program, has greatly enriched the college's academics and given it an expanded regional recognition as a truly superior four-year college.

Missouri Southern is now well established and is accepted in the family of Missouri state colleges and universities as a progressive, growing institution. Gone are the years when area legislative leaders fought valiantly to found the college and then struggled to keep it from being strangled by rival legislators. Present-day legislators, while performing laudable service in seeing that MSSC receives its fair share of the tax dollars, no longer have to fight those elemental battles characteristic of the early years. One constant is the strong community support for Southern. Local people still look on it as a blessing; a genuine educational, cultural and economic asset to the area. Some unbiased people statewide, looking at the area's population base in the 1960s, viewed Southern's expansion into a four-year college as being of questionable merit, feeling that existing nearby state colleges could adequately serve the district's needs at less cost to the taxpayers. But time has justified the college's creation. As local residents foresaw, it has provided a developmental factor: that the college's growth and that of the region's economy and population have advanced hand-in-hand, but most importantly it has provided an educational opportunity to many low-income people who might otherwise have found the gates to a college education closed to them.

Southern's regional reputation as a college that offers a superior undergraduate education has been enhanced by the quality of its faculty. Boards of Trustees and Regents and the administration have consistently paid salaries sufficient to attract academically strong professors who are oriented toward classroom teaching. This tradition of staffing the college with faculty who set high standards, but who also take a personal interest in the students, had its origins in MSSC's junior college past. Also a legacy of the past is the policy of maintaining small class sizes taught by professional instructors, even for the beginning-level courses.

Another factor in creating MSSC's reputation for quality in undergraduate education has been the insistence on maintaining a structured Core Curriculum. This program assures that MSSC graduates leave with an excellent liberal arts background, truly a mark of quality education. An indicator of the quality of Southern's academic program is that in its first twenty years as a four-year college, some 86 percent of the graduates applying for entrance to professional schools were accepted. In many ways, Missouri Southern, in its quest for academic excellence, has come full circle from the years when JJC was considered one of Missouri's premier junior colleges

William "Bill" Grigsby, popular sportscaster for the Kansas City Chiefs football team, is shown introducing from left, Emeritus Professors Grace Mitchell, Julie Hughes, Cleetis Headlee, and Dorothy Stone during the fiftieth anniversary celebration, August 31, l987. Behind them is Student Senate President Terri Honeyball.

Grigsby, a 1947 graduate of Joplin Junior College and recipient of the 1984 Outstanding Alumnus Award, acted as master of ceremonies for this event and served as grand marshall of the Homecoming parade that fall. Larry Meacham photo

and one that attracted national attention for the quality of its academics.

Along with the quality of its educational offerings, Southern has always worked to keep tuition rates low. President Billingsly insisted on establishing this tradition because of the area's many young people from low-income families. Though rates have risen sharply in recent years, they are still low compared with similar state institutions. Moderate tuition rates coupled with Joplin's low cost of living has enabled MSSC to rank among the least expensive colleges in the United States.

As of 1992, Southern faces some problems, but none are of a critical nature. Enrollment and the budget are areas of some concern. Starting in 1989 the rapid rise in enrollment that had characterized the 1980s began to slow, peaking in 1990 with 6,012 students and dropping to 5,889 in the fall of 1992. Though a minor decrease and only the fourth in the senior college era, it does seemingly herald the beginning of a period of slow growth for the college. The number of students graduating from high school is in a decline and any significant growth in student population will have to come from increased retention and by recruiting from outside the college's service area. Neither factor is likely to fuel a boom in enrollment. Rapid growth is not a necessity for maintaining a quality educational program, and this is reflected in the administration's decision to raise admission standards. The budget problem is another factor that seems to dictate holding student enrollment near its present level. Growth has outpaced state appropriations for the college in recent years. President Leon has pointed out that Southern is essentially operating as an institution of 6,000 students on a budget that

would provide adequately over the long run for only 4,500 enrollees. MSSC is unable to put as much funding behind each student as do the other state colleges in Missouri.

The outlook for Missouri Southern's future remains bright. It does not have to grow significantly to remain an excellent college. The North Central Association of Colleges and Schools reaccreditation of MSSC in 1987–1988 found the college to be generally strong with only a few minor areas of weakness, and they granted reaccreditation for the maximum ten years. The examiners praised the college's performance in many different areas, but especially singled out the harmony between the faculty, administration, and the community. They concluded: "The team's assessment is that the college has a loyal faculty and staff who have the capacity to provide creative ways of meeting challenges of the future. The growth and expansion of the college is a good indicator of that creativity and continued community support. The college has the vision and commitment to maintain its tradition of service."

One area of possible expansion in Southern's academic program is the addition of graduate-level degrees, supplanting a program now offered on campus by Southwest Missouri State University. President Leon is not opposed to the proposal, which would require state enabling legislation. Though in the ten years of his administration he had consistently promoted Southern's mission as an undergraduate institution, he foresees the day when, with sufficient growth, the college will adopt a graduate program, but feels it should be innovative and different from the traditional offerings.

The fiftieth anniversary celebration, August 31, 1987, concluded with the unveiling of a large cake, baked in the form of the Missouri Southern logo, mounted on a trailer and pulled to the oval by a 1927 model American LaFrance firetruck. Julio Leon, college president, and Terri Honeyball, president of the Student Senate, are shown ceremonially cutting the cake; it was then served to those present. Larry Meacham photo

Katrina Todd, a senior elementary major from Branson, was crowned Homecoming Queen at the fiftieth anniversary pep rally and campus cookout in the fall of 1987. Todd is shown being escorted by her finance Don Fowler at halftime of the Homecoming game the next day. The Lions defeated Fort Hays, 38–13, in the game.

The calendar rolled back fifty years as Terri Honeyball, 1987–1988 Student Senate president, recrowned Edith Lundien Mayes of Webb City as 1937–1938 college queen. Looking on are (left) Mary Laird McClintock, Neosho, and Joan Epperson Giles, Claremont, California (right), her original attendants for the event. The ceremony took place at the annual Homecoming rally and cookout, October l, 1987, at the time of the crowning of the 1987 Homecoming Queen, Katrina Todd. Larry Meacham photo

J. R. Graue, Webb City, a retired businessman, is shown enjoying himself at the Golden Memories dance on October 2, 1987. Some five to six hundred persons, including many alumni, attended the special fiftieth anniversary event.

Held at the Hammons Trade Center, the hall was decorated in the image of a 1940s nightclub. Jim Lobbey, Class of 1962, served as master of ceremonies of the nostalgic gathering. Graue was a star halfback on JJC's first football team. His children are also Southern alumni. Larry Meacham photo

Richard W. Massa, chairman of the Fiftieth Anniversary Committee, presented this piece of commemorative pewterware to Mrs. Vivian Leon, wife of the president, in a ceremony on September 15, 1987. Mrs. Leon accepted the gift for the College Archives.

The committee selected pewterware to symbolize the college because of its lasting beauty and durability. Featuring the fiftieth anniversary logo on each piece, a set of five sold for $100. Larry Meacham photo

*In September 1987, the newly completed Stults Memorial Garden became the site of
a colorful ceremony honoring the two hundredth anniversary of the Constitution. The
beautiful garden, donated by Joplin businessman Jack Stults in memory of his daughter,
Tracy, a Southern freshman who was killed in an automobile accident, has become
a focal point of the campus for meetings, photography, and students seeking a quiet
moment of repose. Designed to appeal to the four senses, touch, smell, sight, and sound,
each plant is also labeled in Braille for the benefit of the blind. Larry Meacham photo*

Larry Meacham, writer/photographer for the Public Information Office, is shown addressing the audience at the dedication of the Veteran's Memorial on November 11, 1988. Standing behind Meacham, from left, are Harvey Derrick; Bernice Gockel; unidentified; Julio Leon, president; Terry James, regent; unidentified; unidentified; and Wallace Matthews.

Meacham and Matthews were co-chairmen of a Veterans Committee that promoted the project as a memorial to Southern's veterans. Mrs. Gockel, widow of the late MSSC professor, Harry Gockel, donated the 340 bricks—salvaged from the old junior college building at Fourth and Byers—that form an inset border on the low walls of the memorial. Harvey Derrick, an outstanding football player of the mid-1970s, sang his own original composition, "Let's Not Forget Our Veterans," at the ceremony.

This $8,500 brick and glass campus directory, located on the circle in front of the Billingsly Student Center, was the Alumni Association's gift to the college in recognition of its fiftieth anniversary. Shown at its dedication in 1990, from left: John "Pat" Phelps, Board of Regents president; Marilyn Ruestman, Alumni Directory chairperson; and Julio Leon, MSSC president.

It took two of Southern's huskiest employees, Richard Humphrey, (left) and Jack Spurlin, to lower this stainless steel time capsule into its vault in front of Reynolds Hall on May 2, 1988. Part of the fiftieth anniversary activities, the canister was sealed in a cement vault capped with a slab on which was bolted a bronze plaque directing that the vault be opened in the academic year 2037–2038 in honor of MSSC's one hundredth anniversary. Prepared for preservation by archivist Charles Nodler, the contents consisted of various mementos from the administration and the departments. Larry Meacham photo

Miriam Morgan and a group of over thirty other college secretaries spent their lunch hours in the fall of 1987 designing and sewing this green and gold, queen-size fiftieth anniversary quilt. It consists of thirty-five colorful blocks, all hand- designed and representing a departmental or anniversary theme.

Shown working on the project, from left, are: Karen Wilson, Arlene Nash, Pat Martin, Bertha Smith, Miriam Morgan, Dorothy Kolkmeyer, Patty Crane, and Linda Henderson. Ms. Smith, an expert quiltmaker, helped the secretaries with the project.

The quilt was raffled off with the money going toward establishing a scholarship fund for Secretarial Science majors. Connie Martin, a rural Joplin resident, won the quilt. Larry Meacham photo

H. Kenneth McCaleb, who named The Chart and served as its first editor, is shown conversing with senior Mark Ernstmann, the current editor-in-chief, during The Chart's fiftieth anniversary reunion.

McCaleb, a World War II veteran, chose a career in engineering rather than journalism and is now a retired mechanical engineer. He married fellow 1940 JJC graduate, Margaret Baughman.

Ernstmann, named "Collegiate Journalist of the Year" for 1988, also received a Spencer Bartlett Respect Award that same year.

The Chart reunion, held on April 22–23, 1988, was attended by over fifty former staffers. Festivities began with a reception on Friday followed by a picnic on Saturday and a special ceremony and banquet honoring Cleetis Headlee, longtime adviser to The Chart. Richard Massa, head of the Communications Department and former Chart adviser, was also honored. Larry Meacham photo

Lieutenant Colonel Barbara J. (Blackford) Bevins, Class of 1969, addressed the graduates at the 1988 fiftieth anniversary commencement exercises. Commenting on the growth of the college since its first four-year graduating class in 1969, she noted, "One of the places that Missouri Southern has not grown, is the fact that nowhere will you get a better education in a small classroom setting where you and the instructors get to know one another."

With a bachelor's degree in Sociology from Southern, Bevins joined the Air Force in 1971 and at the time of the 1988 commencement was commander of the 554th Combat Support Group, Nellis Air Force Base, Las Vegas, Nevada. She received the Alumni Association's Outstanding Alumnus Award for the year 1991.

A trip into nostalgia during the fiftieth anniversary celebration brought members of the 1939 graduating class back to sit on the sidewalk wall were they had once sat as junior college students fifty years before. Pictured are, from left, standing: Dale Palmer, Neosho; and Bayred Vermillion, Lillington, North Carolina. Sitting: Jim Corl, Webb City; Ellen Beasley Phelps, Carthage; Mary Laird McClintock, Neosho; and Joan Epperson Giles, Claremont, California. Kneeling: Jim Silliman, San Antonio, Texas; and Joe Van Pool, Bartlesville, Oklahoma.

The old college building at Fourth and Byers had been torn down in 1961–1962, but the grounds remained remarkably the same with the surrounding stone wall intact and even the sidewalks undisturbed. Larry Meacham photo

SOUTHERN'S FUTURE

S peaking of the American character, French statesman and author Alexis de Tocqueville said:

These Americans are peculiar people. If, in a local community, a citizen becomes aware of a human need which is not being met, he thereupon discusses the situation with his neighbors. Suddenly, a committee comes into existence. The committee thereupon begins to operate on behalf of the need and a new community function is established. It is like watching a miracle, because these citizens perform this act without a single reference to any bureaucracy, or any official agency.

In this pictorial history of Missouri Southern State College, Dr. G. K. Renner has depicted the same kind of American spirit and community determination noticed by de Tocqueville more than a century and a half ago. Because of the determination of citizens, Jasper County and the southwest Missouri area now are the proud supporters of a first-class four-year college. From its very beginning as Joplin Junior College and through its evolution as Jasper County Junior College, Missouri Southern College and Missouri Southern State College, the institution has enjoyed the love and support of the people of the area because it is "their" college. "They" saw the need for the college, got together, formed committees, and made it a reality.

During the celebration of the fiftieth anniversary of the college in 1987, much praise and recognition was given to the former Joplin Junior College, its wonderful faculty and the quality of its programs. Much deserved homage was also paid to those Jasper County citizens and legislators that labored so very hard for the legislation that created the senior college. And much was said about the tremendous academic progress Missouri Southern has made in the last twenty years.

The essence, the spirit, and the history of this institution has been magnificently captured by Dr. Renner in this book. As I read the book and reminisced about our college's beautiful past, I couldn't help but wonder about its future and what is in store for our beloved college. Now that we are about to step through the threshold that will separate the centuries and as we are faced with a sometimes dizzying pace of change, I wonder: "What kind of an institution is Missouri Southern going to be in the year 2037 when the college will celebrate its one hundredth anniversary? What are the citizens of the area, the college faculty and staff, the students, going to think of us and the Missouri Southern of the 1990s when they open the time capsule we buried in front of Reynolds Hall during the fiftieth anniversary celebration?"

I believe Missouri Southern will be a different institution than it is today. It will most likely be a university with graduate programs and professional schools. It will be, as it is today, an institution with a clear purpose and highly respected because of the quality of its faculty, staff and programs.

By then the reputation of the institution will be international in nature. The faculty will most likely make use of educational technologies not yet dreamed of today and our programs of instruction will reach by telecommunications many people all over the world. But above all, the Missouri Southern of the year 2037 will continue to be thought of by the people of the region as "their" college, as the college "they" made a reality when a need was seen as not being met, and committees were formed.

Then, as now, in celebration of the larger vision, the students and the citizens of the region will have a reason to repeat John Ruskin's words:

> *When we build . . . let it not be for personal delights*
>   *nor for present use alone.*
> *Let it be such work as our descendants will thank us for*
>   *and let us think . . .*
> *that a time is to come when these stones will be*
>   *held sacred because our hands have touched them,*
> *and that men will say as they look upon the labor,*
>   *and the wrought substance of them,*
> *"See! This our fathers did for us."*

Julio S. León

APPENDIX 1

Total Student Enrollment, Fall Semesters,
Full and Part Time, For Credit, 1937–1992

Junior College Era		Senior College Era	
1937	114	1967	2,411
1938	314	1968	2,864
1939	335	1969	3,120
1940	327	1970	3,185
1941	332	1971	3,158
1942	248	1972	3,062
1943	129	1973	3,067
1944	135	1974	3,289
1945	143	1975	3,610
1946	484	1976	3,748
1947	420	1977	3,774
1948	501	1978	3,900
1949	501	1979	3,790
1950	362	1980	4,013
1951	280	1981	4,330
1952	312	1982	4,478
1953	399	1983	4,305
1954	509	1984	4,323
1955	532	1985	4,529
1956	507	1986	4,610
1957	626	1987	4,926
1958	882	1988	5,404
1959	858	1989	5,901
1960	830	1990	6,012
1961	967	1991	6,011
1962	987	1992	5,889
1963	1,144		
1964	1,444		
1965	1,584		
1966	1,837		

APPENDIX 2

Total Degrees Granted, Associate and Baccalaureate
Junior and Senior College Eras
1939–1968 and 1969–1993 Respectively

Junior College Era		Senior College Era			
Year	Associate Degrees	Year	Baccalaureate Degrees	Associate Degrees	Total Degrees
1938–39	23	1968–69	198	88	286
1939–40	75	1969–70	298	52	350
1940–41	93	1970–71	321	74	395
1941–42	81	1971–72	346	82	428
1942–43	51	1972–73	361	84	445
1943–44	29	1973–74	321	95	416
1944–45	36	1974–75	348	114	462
1945–46	39	1975–76	332	118	450
1946–47	83	1976–77	359	128	487
1947–48	103	1977–78	433	128	561
1948–49	88	1978–79	363	115	478
1949–50	78	1979–80	419	123	542
1950–51	68	1980–81	367	131	498
1951–52	50	1981–82	371	103	474
1952–53	45	1982–83	392	126	518
1953–54	65	1983–84	385	124	509
1954–55	86	1984–85	389	103	492
1955–56	97	1985–86	437	85	522
1956–57	89	1986–87	401	97	498
1957–58	100	1987–88	440	90	530
1958–59	110	1988–89	505	95	600
1959–60	142	1989–90	507	100	607
1960–61	117	1990–91	542	135	677
1961–62	124	1991–92	576	151	727
1962–63	125	*1992–93	616	135	751
1963–64	143				
1964–65	149		10,027	2,676	12,703
1965–66	182				
1966–67	252				
1967–68	82				
	2,805				

*Approximate figures

APPENDIX 3

Student Senate Presidents, 1937–1938 to 1992–1993

Year	Name	Year	Name
1937–38	Kathleen Moyer	1965–66	Phil Wiland
1938–39	Dale Palmer	1966–67	Terry Helton
1939–40	Ed Farmer	1967–68	Dave Hokanson
1940–41	Kenton Slankard	1968–69	John "Jeb" Prince
1941–42	Robert Rice	1969–70	Rick Call
1942–43	Not available	1970–71	Gary Armstrong
1943–44	Bill Pinnell	1971–72	Roger Sisco
1944–45	Don Newby; Jean Farrar	1972–73	George Hosp
1945–46	O. B. Heck; Bill Wagner	1973–74	Scott Hickam
1946–47	Jack Parker	1974–75	Phil Clark
1947–48	Jack Short; John Kaplanis	1975–76	Phil Clark
1948–49	Dick Sayers	1976–77	Jim Cook
1949–50	Kenneth Priaulx	1977–78	Steve Graves
1950–51	James Chaney	1978–79	David Meadows
1951–52	Dick Rousselot	1979–80	Robert Mutrux
1952–53	Lloyd Reis	1980–81	Scott Rosenthal
1953–54	Walt James	1981–82	Linda Wilson
1954–55	Bill Agan	1982–83	Brian Atkinson
1955–56	Ron Richardson	1983–84	Lisa Funderburk
1956–57	Henry Baker	1984–85	Lisa Funderburk
1957–58	Dave Garrison	1985–86	Nick Harvill
1958–59	Not available	1986–87	Lance Adams
1959–60	Buddy Ball	1987–88	Terri Honeyball
1960–61	Bill Anderson	1988–89	Robert Stokes
1961–62	Bob Newberry	1989–90	Sara Woods
1962–63	Carl Gilmore	1990–91	Mary Hanewinkel
1963–64	Myron McKinney	1991–92	Bryan Vowels
1964–65	Jack Burke	1992–93	Larry Seneker

APPENDIX 4

Outstanding Graduate Awards, 1972–1973 to 1992–1993

1972–73	Jeffrey Dymott
1973–74	Kreta Cable Gladden
1974–75	Kevin D. Herd
1975–76	Kerry Anders
1976–77	James Kiser
1977–78	James I. Moeskau
1978–79	Kathy Lay
1979–80	Cherrie Dickerman Schulte
1980–81	Shawn De Graff
1981–82	Shelia Peters
1982–83	Richard Alan Gibbons
1983–84	Beth Barlet
1984–85	Sara Beth Rice; Suzanne Gallaghan; Todd Thelen
1985–86	Christie J. Amos
1986–87	John Nicolas Harvill
1987–88	Theresa Honeyball
1988–89	Susan Paulson; Scott Fields
1989–90	Anna Miller
1990–91	Jacquelyn Johnson
1991–92	Brian Vowels; Mary Hanewinkel
1992–93	Brian Nichols

Outstanding graduates are selected yearly by the Awards Committee of the Alumni Association from nominees presented by the faculty. The awards are conferred at the Honors Convocation in April of each year.

APPENDIX 5

Outstanding Alumni Awards, 1971–1992

Year of Award	Name	Year Graduated*
1971	Dennis Weaver	1943
1972	Vernon Lawson	1946
1973	Dr. Arrell Gibson	1941
1974	Robert Higgins	1942
1975	Dr. and Mrs. James Stephens	1948–1957
1976	Dr. Kenneth Bowman	1963
1977	None	
1978	Jack Dawson	1972
1979	Robert Moyer	1957
1980	Dr. Edwin Strong, Jr.	1956
1981	Dr. Ronald Lankford	1971
1982	None	
1983	Robert G. Sheppard, M.D.	1941
1984	Bill Grigsby	1947
1985	Dr. Larry J. Moore	1961
1986	Dr. Mark Claussen	1974
1987	Glen C. Barnett	1969
1987	Jerry W. Cooper	1957
1987	Dan H. Fieker, D.O.	1969
1987	Eugene E. Langevin, D.O.	1963
1987	Chuck Surface	1969
1988	Marion A. Ellis	1959
1988	Dr. Mary Jane Lang Grundler	1940
1988	Robert M. Headlee	1971
1989	Michael L. Storm	1969
1990	Dr. Cynthia Carter Haddock	1976
1990	Dr. Floyd E. Belk	1948
1991	Lt. Col. Barbara J. Bevins	1969
1992	L. Howard Hartley, M.D.	1954

* Last year attended if did not graduate

APPENDIX 6

Bartlett Respect Awards, 1969–1970 to 1992–1993

Year	Name	Name
1969–70	Miles R. Call	Helen H. Robertson
1970–71	Alfred E. Jenkins	Gloria Ann Baucom
1970–71	Patrick F. Kelly	Jerilyn Ann Farrar
1971–72	James Carter	Nancy Baggerly
1972–73	Jeff Dymott	Laura Schooler
1973–74	Richard G. Cook	Debra K. Dotson
1973–74	Charles H. Obermann	Deborah A. Hough
1974–75	Robert J. Mills	Candace J. Holz
1974–75	Jon M. Johnson	Penny S. Huff
1975–76	Mark A. Flanegin	Constance S. Thomas
1976–77	Gary M. Goodpaster	Suzanne H. Patterson
1976–77	Neal L. Ball	Karen S. Shipman
1977–78	Robert L. Corn	Sara J. Frost
1977–78	Russell R. Kemm	Gay L. Garrison
1978–79	Raymond S. Schulte	Georgiana L. Menapace
1978–79	Douglass C. Parker	Kathy Jo Lay
1979–80	Martin J. O'Brien	Cherrie L. Schulte
1979–80	Randy Lee Gilmore	Jill M. Morrison
1980–81	Jarrett C. Herrell	Julie M. Freeborn
1980–81	Samuel J. Starkey	Judith L. Willard
1981–82	Lyndell D. Scoles	Ivy Margaret Pugh
1981–82	Alexander K. Brietzke	Wilma Anne Waggoner
1982–83	Gregory D. Fisher	Dawn (Ellis) Martin
1982–83	Darrell L. Kern	Cynthia Sue Coale
1983–84	Stanley R. Lowery	Beth Barlet
1983–84	Kevin M. Moyer	Anne E. Nicolas
1984–85	Todd S. Thelen	Lori E. Rhoades
1984–85	Joseph G. Cole	Sara B. Rice
1985–86	Keith R. Aubele	Melissa C. Thelen
1985–86	Daniele L. Strubberg	Christie J. Amos
1986–87	J. Nicolas Harvill	Joann K. Freeborn
1986–87	Tedd M. Thelen	Mary E. Robinson
1987–88	Anthony A. Wilson	Lori R. LeBahn
1987–88	Mark J. Ernstmann	Theresa A. Honeyball

(Appendix 6 continued)

Year	Name	Name
1988–89	Charles Urban	Kathy Jones
1988–89	Robert Stokes	Marianne Fletcher
1989–90	Kenneth Reasoner	Letitia Winans
1990–91	Brad Hodson	Jane Reid Brown
1990–91	Philip Snow	Deborah Newby
1991–92	Mark Tedford	Michelle Carnine
1991–92	Bryan Vowels	Michelle Nader
1992–93	Keith Allen	Nancy Newby
1992–93	Russell Souza	Lori St. Clair

Bartlett Respect Awards, established by the Bartlett family in memory of Anne and Charles Bartlett–Vera and Spencer Bartlett, are presented yearly to men and women graduates who have shown the greatest respect for God, the United States, and their fellowman. Two first-place and two-second place winners have been chosen for most years with individual cash awards of $500 and $300 respectively, though the amount can vary.

APPENDIX 7

Homecoming Queens, 1940–1992

Year	Name	Year	Name
1940	Victoria Evans*	1966	Christy Gladden
1941	Patty Lacy*	1967	Judy Repplinger
1942	Peggy Elliott*	1968	Judy McMillan
1943	None	1969	Nancy Anderson
1944	None	1970	Christie Reed
1945	None	1971	Janet Gladwin
1946	Mary Alice Dabbs**	1972	Kreta Cable Gladden
1947	Kathleen Cearnal***	1973	Nancy Tyler
1948	Kathryn Tipping	1974	Kathy Walker
1949	Norma Long	1975	Kim Moore
1950	Lorraine Miller	1976	Lori Bresnahan
1951	Mary Lou Gullette	1977	Nancy Hubbard
1952	Jo Ann Holman	1978	Cherrie Dickerman
1953	Diana Martin	1979	Beverly Edwards
1954	Janice Hargis	1980	Debbie Gibson
1955	Madalyn Gustafson	1981	Kimberly Ann Hillenburg
1956	Wanda Gibb	1982	Marcia Hennessy
1957	Donna Finley	1983	Mindy Woodfill
1958	Pam Spenny	1984	Michelle Patrick
1959	Barbara Arehart	1985	Marsha Bishop
1960	Sally Burress	1986	Robin Reed
1961	Margee Webb	1987	Katrina Todd
1962	Cheryl Martin	1988	Leigh Sligar
1963	Kay Baker	1989	Emma Jo Walker
1964	Judy Thompson	1990	Elivette Alvarez
1965	Sharon Campbell	1991	Emily Casavecchia; Greg Banks****
		1992	Lori Fausett; Keith Allen****

*   *Known as "Pigskin Princess"*
**   *Known as "Football Queen"*
***   *First to be identified as "Homecoming Queen"*
**** *Queen and king; now known as "Homecoming Royalty"*

APPENDIX 8

Crossroads *Queens, 1938–1974*

Year	Name	Year	Name
1938	Edith Lundien*	1957	Maureen Vincent
1939	Joan Epperson**	1958	Linda Miles
1940	Billye Grattis	1959	Nancy Smith
1941	Jane Marshall	1960	Nancy Robson
1942	Martha Kassab	1961	Sue Winchester
1943	Geraldine Benge	1962	Lois Ramsey
1944	Nina Geisert	1963	Suzanne Jameson
1945	Ruby Granger	1964	Sherry Howard
1946	Carolyn Johnson	1965	Joyce Miller
1947	Nancy Braeckel and Jean Gillie, Co-Queens	1966	Sally Anderson
1948	Nancy Moss	1967	Beverly Baum
1949	Jeanne Hansford	1968	Christy Heisten
1950	Berna Jean Taylor	1969	Jane Bettebenner
1951	Jane McWethy	1970	Not available
1952	Donna Ackerman	1971	Leslie Scott
1953	Patty Gray	1972	None
1954	Patty Deatherage	1973	Debbie Hough
1955	Wylene Waggener	1974	Julia Hudson
1956	Jane Medcalf		

Crowned queen at the Coronation Ball held at the Sagmount Inn in the spring of 1938. There was no Crossroads *at this time.*

**The first* Crossroads *Queen.*

APPENDIX 9

The Chart *Editors, 1937–1992*

Year	Editors
1937–38	A column in the J.H.S. *Spyglass*
1938–39	Charles L. Davis (*The Challenge*), one issue
1939–40	Kenneth McCaleb, First *Chart* (November 10, 1939)
1940–41	Hildred Bebee and Doris Ransom
1941–42	Hildred Bebee (first semester); Jean Paschall (second semester)
1942–43	Jean Paschall
1943–44	Wilma Hardin
1944–45	None
1945–46	Paula Costley and Rob Roy Ratliff
1946–47	Mary Ellen Butler
1947–48	Milo Harris
1948–49	Marilyn Land and Helen Hough
1949–50	June Sillaway
1950–51	Leslie Pearson
1951–52	Billie Blankenship
1952–53	Henry Heckert
1953–54	Rosemary Mense and Marion Smith
1954–55	Charles Garde
1955–56	JoAnn Williams and Helen Barbee
1956–57	Ron Martin
1957–58	Rayma Hammer and Nancy Hopkins
1958–59	Marion Ellis
1959–60	Jan Austin and Allene Strecker
1960–61	Sue Winchester
1961–62	Mary Blankenship and Leroy Tiberghein
1962–63	Marilyn Blatter and Helen Coombs
1963–64	Karen Anderson and Karalee Pearson
1964–65	Ron Hiser and Richard Hood
1965–66	John Beydler and Cheryl Dines
1966–67	Kay Ann Floyd and Carol Reinhart
1967–68	Linda Brown and Peggy Chew
1968–69	Peggy Chew and Kathleen Bagby
1969–70	Larry White

Year	Editors
1970–71	Larry White
1971–72	Jim Price
1972–73	Rick Davenport (first semester) / Rich Nielsen (second semester)
1973–74	Phil Clark
1974–75	Donna Lonchar
1975–76	Steve Smith
1976–77	Tim Dry
1977–78	Liz DeMerice
1978–79	Clark Swanson
1979–80	Clark Swanson
1980–81	Clark Swanson
1981–82	Chad Stebbins
1982–83	A. John Baker
1983–84	A. John Baker
1984–85	Daphne Massa
1985–86	Martin Oetting
1986–87	Pat Halverson
1987–88	Mark Ernstmann
1988–89	Robert J. Smith
1989–90	Christopher A. Clark
1990–91	Christopher A. Clark
1991–92	Angie Stevensen (first semester) / T. R. Hanrahan (second semester)
1992–93	T. R. Hanrahan (first semester) / John Hacker (second semester)

APPENDIX 10

Crossroads (Yearbook) Editors, 1937–1992

Year	Editors
1937–38	Enos Currey, supplement to J.H.S. yearbook
1938–39	Mary Laird, first Crossroads editor
1939–40	Dorothy Friend
1940–41	Maxine Edmondson
1941–42	Lorraine White
1942–43	Kathleen Hight and Lois Avery
1943–44	Nancy McKee and Betsy Balsley
1944–45	Peggy Davison and Margaret Ann Rawdon
1945–46	Margaret Ann Boyd and Kathlee Crane
1946–47	Margaret Ann Boyd
1947–48	Beauford Zumwalt
1948–49	Milo Harris
1949–50	Sara Lou Wells, Loretta Gullette, and Mary Walker
1950–51	Mickey Bauer and Eddy Vaughan
1951–52	John Edwards and Tom Tipping
1952–53	Paulina Tuggle and Patricia Croley
1953–54	Charlene Dale and Patty Deatherage
1954–55	Betty Jarvis and Patty Deatherage
1955–56	Sara Belden and Betty Board
1956–57	Jane Kirk and Kay O'Bryant
1957–58	Margaret Kenney and Carol Klimpt
1958–59	Janice Felker and Roberta Lamb
1959–60	Judy Griffis and Nelly Ann Trewyn
1960–61	Judy Griffis and Nancy Mapes
1961–62	Gayleen McKenzie and Janice Fickle
1962–63	Gayleen McKenzie
1963–64	Vicki Vernatti and Linda Yokley
1964–65	Patti Smith and Barbara Coombs
1965–66	Larry Strong and Sharon Ritzman
1966–67	Ray Mathis
1967–68	Ray Mathis
1968–69	Ray Mathis
1969–70	Jim Burrell and Kathy Bailey
1970–71	Audrey Gray

(Appendix 10 continued)

Year	Editors
1971–72	Cancelled
1972–73	Patti Storm
1973–74	Don Sill and Phil Steed
1974–75	Gayla Neumeyer
1975–76	Gharon Plummer
1976–77	Sharon Klein and Rebecca Spracklen
1977–78	Carolyn Spracklen
1978–79	Sue Hulett
1979–80	Not available
1980–81	Joyce Cole
1981–82	Joyce Cole
1982–83	Richard Williams
1983–84	Cancelled
1984–85	Richard Williams and Ed Hill
1985–86	Jean Campbell
1986–87	JoAnn Hollis
1987–88	Teresa Merrill and Melanie Hicks
1988–89	Teresa Merrill
1989–90	Lisa Clark and Bobbie Severs
1990–91	Margaretha Lodin
1991–92	T. Rob Brown
1992–93	Suzanne LeJeune

Missouri Southern Football Games
Total Wins, Losses, Ties, 1937–1938 to 1992–1993

Junior College Era				Senior College Era			
Year	Wins	Losses	Ties	Year	Wins	Losses	Ties
1937–38	0	5	0	1968–69	2	8	0
1938–39	1	6	0	1969–70	2	8	0
1939–40	6	2	0	1970–71	2	7	1
1940–41	3	5	1	1971–72	4	6	0
1941–42	0	5	0	1972–73	12	0	0
1942–43	4	3	0	1973–74	4	6	0
1943–44	No	Games		1974–75	6	3	0
1944–45	No	Games		1975–76	7	3	1
1945–46	No	Games		1976–77	8	2	0
1946–47	4	5	0	1977–78	5	5	0
1947–48	2	7	1	1978–79	6	3	1
1948–49	3	5	1	1979–80	5	6	0
1949–50	7	2	0	1980–81	6	3	1
1950–51	5	3	0	1981–82	6	4	1
1951–52	0	6	0	1982–83	7	2	1
1952–53	1	6	0	1983–84	9	2	0
1953–54	4	4	0	1984–85	6	3	0
1954–55	6	3	0	1985–86	6	4	0
1955–56	5	3	0	1986–87	2	7	0
1956–57	6	1	1	1987–88	3	7	0
1957–58	7	1	0	1988–89	3	7	0
1958–59	5	1	1	1989–90	6	4	0
1959–60	7	1	0	1990–91	4	5	0
1960–61	5	3	0	1991–92	8	3	0
1961–62	5	3	0	1992–93	4	6	0
1962–63	3	5	0				
1963–64	5	2	2				
1964–65	6	3	0				
1965–66	10	0	0				
1966–67	6	3	0				
1967–68	8	1	0				

APPENDIX 12

MSSC Men's Basketball Games
total wins and losses, 1937–1938 to 1992–1993

Junior College Era			Senior College Era		
Year	Wins	Losses	Year	Wins	Losses
1937–38	8	7	1968–69	16	16
1938–39	7	6*	1969–70	21	8
1939–40	16	4	1970–71	18	6
1940–41	11	6	1971–72	21	10
1941–42	12	7	1972–73	18	10
1942–43	9	7	1973–74	12	16
1943–44	No Games		1974–75	11	15
1944–45	6	5	1975–76	14	15
1945–46	7	6	1976–77	15	15
1946–47	9	8	1977–78	27	9
1947–48	6	13	1978–79	11	18
1948–49	8	11	1979–80	12	19
1949–50	6	12	1980–81	23	10
1950–51	4	11	1981–82	15	15
1951–52	1	11	1982–83	20	9
1952–53	8	12	1983–84	15	14
1953–54	14	5	1984–85	10	18
1954–55	9	11	1985–86	20	11
1955–56	20	2	1986–87	20	13
1956–57	16	7	1987–88	5	22
1957–58	7	17	1988–89	4	22
1958–59	14	8	1989–90	12	15
1959–60	11	13	1990–91	11	17
1960–61	14	11	1991–92	21	8
1961–62	8	13	1992–93	21	10
1962–63	14	7			
1963–64	10	13			
1964–65	8	13			
1965–66	7	14			
1966–67	1	20			
1967–68	9	18			

1938–39—also one tie for a total of 14 games

APPENDIX 13

Baseball Games: Total Wins, Losses, Ties, 1971–1972 to 1992–1993

Year	Wins	Losses	Ties
1971–72	11	13	0
1972–73	13	13	0
1973–74	33	19	0
1974–75	33	15	0
1975–76	28	10	1
1976–77	15	29	0
1977–78	24	16	0
1978–79	29	24	0
1979–80	29	30	0
1980–81	32	28	0
1981–82	26	26	0
1982–83	16	23	0
1983–84	22	22	0
1984–85	33	25	0
1985–86	36	27	0
1986–87	38	22	0
1987–88	23	26	0
1988–89	36	22	0
1989–90	25	15	0
1990–91	48	13	0
1991–92	44	13	0
1992–93	19	21	1

APPENDIX 14

Soccer Games; Total Wins, Losses, Ties, 1972–1973 to 1992–1993

Year	Wins	Losses	Ties
1972–73*	1	9	3
1973–74*	5	8	3
1974–75*	13	4	3
1975–76*	14	2	0
1976–77	11	5	2
1977–78	9	6	3
1978–79	11	6	1
1979–80	16	3	1
1980–81	15	4	1
1981–82	12	5	2
1982–83	11	6	3
1983–84	11	6	1
1984–85	10	8	2
1985–86	7	9	3
1986–87	12	7	1
1987–88	10	7	2
1988–89	14	4	3
1989–90	11	6	2
1990–91	7	9	2
1991–92	6	11	2
1992–93	3	13	0

Played as a club team.

APPENDIX 15

Women's Basketball Games; Total Wins
and Losses, 1974–1975 to 1992-1993

Year	Wins	Losses
1974–75	9	2
1975–76	15	6
1976–77	11	13
1977–78	16	12
1978–79	21	11
1979–80	15	16
1980–81	10	19
1981–82	23	12
1982–83	12	14
1983–84	22	6
1984–85	24	5
1985–86	25	7
1986–87	15	10
1987–88	8	18
1988–89	17	12
1989–90	9	18
1990–91	12	15
1991–92	18	10
1992–93	27	4

APPENDIX 16

Women's Softball Games; Total Wins
and Losses. 1974–1975 to 1992-1993

Year	Wins	Losses
1974–75	3	9
1975–76	Unknown	
1976–77	Unknown	
1977–78	10	14
1978–79	22	13
1979–80	20	23
1980–81	19	20
1981–82	14	20
1982–83	18	17
1983–84	19	16
1984–85	29	17
1985–86	44	13
1986–87	40	16
1987–88	29	18
1988–89	31	22
1989–90	36	9
1990–91	36	8
1991–92	50	7
1992–93	38	12

APPENDIX 17

Women's Volleyball Games; Total Wins,
Losses, Ties, 1975–1976 to 1992–1993

Year	Wins	Losses	Ties
1975–76	12	9	3
1976–77	23	14	1
1977–78	25	16	1
1978–79	16	17	3
1979–80	17	17	0
1980–81	20	18	1
1981–82	22	18	5
1982–83	33	11	5
1983–84	42	10	1
1984–85	42	6	0
1985–86	40	18	0
1986–87	47	10	0
1987–88	38	17	0
1988–89	19	31	0
1989–90	9	25	0
1990–91	14	19	0
1991–92	32	11	0
1992–93	20	17	0

APPENDIX 18

Jim Talbot MSSC Letterman's Alumni Association Hall of Fame Awards, 1984–1993*

1984 Glen Wills (deceased), football

1985 Terron Jackson, football
       John Thomas, basketball

1986 Jim Frazier, football coach,
       men's athletic director

1987 Ray Harding, football

1988 Tom Cox, football
       Alan Potter, football

1989 Rusty Shelley, football

1990 Dean Collins, football
       Don Gross, sports announcer

1991 Kerry Anders, football
       Russell Bland, basketball
       Wendell Redden,
       Joplin Globe Sports Editor

1992 Sallie Beard, women's sports coach,
          women's athletic director
       Mike Hagedorn, baseball player,
          assistant baseball coach
       Bernie Busken, football
       Ken Howard, football
       Willie Williams, football

1993 Dudley Stegge (deceased)
          Joplin Junior College football,
          track coach
       Pam (Brisby) Laughlin,
          women's basketball
       Barbara (Lawson) Cowherd,
          women's basketball, volleyball,
          track, softball
       Patty Vavra, women's basketball, track

Hall of Fame awards are given in memory of Dr. Jim Talbot, a noted Lionbacker and a Joplin dentist.

APPENDIX 19

E. O. and Virginia Humphrey Awards, 1972–1993

1972 John Thomas, basketball

1973 Terron Jackson, football

1974 Robert Hall, basketball

1975 Kerry Anders, football

1976 Mark Flanegin, basketball

1977 Willie Williams, football

1978 Russell Bland, basketball

1979 Scott Schulte, basketball

1980 Vincent Featherson, football

1981 George Major, soccer

1982 Pam Brisby, basketball

1983 Joel Tupper, football

1984 Glen Baker, football

1985 Darin McClure, football

1986 Margaret Womack, basketball

1987 Rick Berg, baseball

1988 Anita Rank, basketball

1989 Jim Baranoski, baseball

1990 Alan Brown, football

1991 Diane Miller, softball

1992 Kenny Simpson, basketball

1993 Jason Riddle, Cross Country
       and Track

Established in 1972, the annual E. O. and Virginia Humphrey Award is "named in honor of E. O. Humphrey, who was the first football coach at Joplin Junior College in 1937, and his wife Virginia. It honors the student-athlete who best exemplifies highest respect for MSSC, athletic ability, leadership, and respect for fellow teammates and students."

APPENDIX 20

Silver Anniversary Commemorative Basketball Team, 1968–1969 to 1992–1993

Name	Years played
Russell Bland	1976–78
Greg Garton	1982–86
Reggie Grantham	1985–87
Fred Hatfield	1969–71
Willie Rogers	1980–83
Kenny Simpson	1990–91
Kenn Stoehner	1979–81
John Thomas	1969–73
Marvin Townsend	1985–87
Chris Tuggle	1985–87
Carl Tyler	1980–84
Bill Wagner	1969–72

APPENDIX 21

Silver Anniversary Commemorative Football Team, 1968–1969 to 1992–1993

Name	Years Played	Position
Defense		
Kenric Conway	1974–77	End
Jack Varns	1969–72	End
Marty O'Brien	1975–79	Tackle
Jay Pride	1989–92	Tackle
Kelly Saxten	1980–81	Tackle
Stan Gardner	1978–81	Linebacker
Barry Korner	1971–73	Linebacker
Glen Baker	1980–83	Back
Lamonte Blanford	1989–90	Back
Jack Duda	1969–72	Back
Ozzie Harrell	1979–80	Back
Offense		
Kerry Anders	1972–75	Wide Receiver
Rod Smith	1988–92	Wide Receiver
Brent Cook	1977–79	Tight End
Terron Jackson	1971–72	Tackle
Billy Jack Smith	1980–83	Tackle
Gary Embry	1974–78	Guard
Willie Williams	1973–76	Guard
Joel Tupper	1979–82	Center
Ray Harding	1970–72	Quarterback
Larry Barnes	1975–78	Running Back
Harold Noirfalise	1981–84	Running Back
Specialists		
Terry Joyce	1975	Punter
Harvey Derrick	1974–77	Place Kicker
Vincent Featherson	1976–79	Kick Returner

APPENDIX 22

Faculty Senate Presidents 1969–1970 to 1992–1993

Year	Name
1969–70	B. W. "Woody" Mason
1970–71	E. Sam Gibson
1971–72	Sam J. Starkey
1972–73	Rochelle L. Boehning
1973–74	Carl A. Finke
1974–75	Henry L. Harder
1975–76	Roger Adams
1976–77	Richard W. Massa
1977–78	Richard W. Massa
1978–79	J. Larry Martin
1979–80	Vonnie R. Prentice
1980–81	J. Merrell Junkins
1981–82	Robert P. Markman, first semester William L. Ferron, second semester
1982–83	Judith L. Conboy
1983–84	Joseph P. Lambert
1984–85	Marilyn J. Jacobs
1985–86	Donald L. Seneker
1986–87	Lanny Ackiss
1987–88	Betsy Q. Griffin
1988–89	Paul Teverow
1989–90	Retha L. Ketchum
1990–91	Bruce K. Kelley
1991–92	Duane O. Eberhardt
1992–93	Franklyn W. Adams

APPENDIX 23

Outstanding Teacher Awards, 1979–1980 to 1992–1993

Year	Outstanding Teacher
1979–80	J. Larry Martin
1980–81	Vonnie R. Prentice
1981–82	Donald L. Seneker
1982–83	J. Merrell Junkins
1983–84	Charles E. Leitle
1984–85	Robert P. Markman
1985–86	Larry W. Goode
1886–87	Milton W. Brietzke
1987–88	G. Joyce Bowman
1988–89	Joseph J. Shields
1989–90	Rosanne S. Joyner
1989–90	Brian C. Babbitt
1990–91	D. David Tate
1991–92	Gwendolyn K. Murdock Arthur M. Saltzman
1992–93	Judith L. Conboy James H. Shaver

Year	*Outstanding Teacher of a Freshman Class*
1979–80	Grace C. Mitchell
1980–81	Marilyn J. Jacobs
1981–82	Richard W. Massa
1982–83	James R. Jackson
1983–84	Carmen M. Carney
1984–85	Samuel L. Claussen
1985–86	Henry G. Morgan
1986–87	Doris T. Elgin
1987–88	Marion E. Sloan
1988–89	Jack G. Spurlin
1989–90	Terry D. Marion
1990–91	Dale W. Simpson

APPENDIX 24

Emeritus Faculty

Year Employed	Name	Year Emeritus Status Granted
1938	Harry C. Gockel (Deceased)	1973
1937	Martha Ann McCormick (Deceased)	1973
1939	Dorothy A. Stone	1977
1950	Dr. Lloyd L. Dryer (Deceased)	1978
1946	Cleetis Headlee	1978
1965	Fred Cinotto (Deceased)	1980
1963	Julie S. Hughes	1982
1958	Grace C. Mitchell	1983
1966	E. Enid Blevins	1985

APPENDIX 25

Jasper County Junior College District Board of Trustees, 1964–1986

Trustees Name	Residence	Year Elected	Term Expired
Fred G. Hughes	Joplin	1964*	1986**
Norval M. Matthews (Deceased)	Webb City	1964*	1974
Lauren R. Reynolds (Deceased)	Joplin	1964*	1968
Gene Taylor	Sarcoxie	1964*	1972
Thomas E. Taylor (Deceased)	Carthage	1964*	1975
Elvin Ummel	Jasper	1964*	1986**
Arthur Kungle (Deceased)	Joplin	1972	1986**
Donald Patterson	Joplin	1974	1986**
Carolyn Rodgers McKee (Deceased)	Carthage	1976	1986**

* Original Trustees

** The Board of Trustees ceased to function in 1986. The last election of Trustees was April 1976. At that time Carolyn Rodgers McKee and Fred Hughes were reelected. McKee had been appointed in January 1976 to fill the unexpired term of Thomas E. Taylor.

APPENDIX 26

MSSC Board of Regents, 1965–1992

Regents Name	Residence	Year Appointed	Term Expired
Lauren R. Reynolds (Deceased)	Joplin	1965*	1968
Thomas E. Taylor (Deceased)	Carthage	1965*	1974
Mills Anderson	Carthage	1965*	1977
Norval M. Matthews (Deceased)	Webb City	1965*	1977
Fred G. Hughes	Joplin	1965*	1981
Jerry E. Wells	Joplin	1968	1985
Carolyn Rodgers McKee (Deceased)	Carthage	1974	1979
Donald Roderique (Deceased)	Webb City	1977	1978
William S. Schwab, Jr.	Joplin	1977	1981
Ray W. Grace	Carthage	1977	1982
Glenn D. Wilson	Joplin	1978	1983
Loren Olson	Sarcoxie	1979	1985
Anthony Kassab	Joplin	1981	1986
William C. Putnam	Carthage	1981	1987
W. Terry James	Webb City	1982	1988
Robert Higgins	Joplin	1983	1989
Russell G. Smith	Joplin	1985	1990
John O. "Pat" Phelps	Carthage	1985	1991
Gilbert Roper	Joplin	1986	1992**
Frank S. Dunaway	Carthage	1987	1993**
Douglas K. Crandall	Carthage	1989	1994**
Cynthia H. Schwab	Joplin	1990	1995**
D. Keith Adams	Joplin	1991	1996**
Elvin Ummel	Jasper	1991	1997**

* Original Regents; five-member board.

** Members of the Board of Regents as of January 1, 1993. Though by state statute members serve six-year terms, the actual length of service may vary due to death, resignations, or delays in the appointment and confirmation process. Retiring members continue to serve until their replacements are officially installed.

APPENDIX 27

Major New Campus Buildings, or Additions Completed 1967–1992

Buildings or Additions	Approximate Square Feet	Completion Date	Approximate Cost
George A. Spiva Library	22,234	1967	$ 580,207
L. R. Reynolds Science-Math Building	36,975	1967	577,181
Hearnes Hall	40,390	1967	630,705
Fine Arts Center (Art and Music)	21,060	1967	487,719
Mansion Annex	6,554	1967	125,990
Barn Theatre	4,609	1967	29,000
Robert Ellis Young Gymnasium	33,320	1968	461,200
Leon C. Billingsly Student Center	34,230	1969	649,374
Kuhn Hall	14,500	1969	302,250
Ummel Technology Building	19,900	1970	219,767
Residence Hall (South)	20,808	1970	620,250
Residence Hall (North)	34,200	1970	620,250
Mills Anderson Police Academy	7,037	1971	128,200
George A. Spiva Library Addition	33,680	1973	925,415
Fine Arts Center Addition	16,492	1974	607,483
Maintenance Building	12,950	1974	165,000
Fred G. Hughes Stadium		1975	1,702,953
Thomas E. Taylor Performing Arts Center	53,358	1975	2,935,241
Robert Ellis Young Gymnasium Addition	1,435	1976	90,751
Modular Residence Halls (2)	10,167	1976	65,000
Mills Anderson Police Academy Addition	10,161	1977	231,046
Gene Taylor Hall	20,205	1977	640,000
Leon C. Billingsly Student Center Addition	27,123	1979	1,176,167
Norvall M. Matthews Hall	32,550	1980	1,463,764
Residence Apartment A	7,994	1980	400,986
Residence Apartment B	11,991	1980	400,986
Residence Apartment C	11,991	1980	400,986
Residence Apartment D	7,994	1980	400,986
Residence Apartment E	7,994	1980	$ 400,986
Television Studio Addition	2,000	1981	96,970
Robert Ellis Young Gymnasium Addition	24,116	1982	1,798,725
Norval M. Matthews Hall Addition	43,000	1986	2,731,236
Gene Taylor Hall Addition (Child Care Center)	11,000	1986	637,506
Residence Apartment F	7,994	1987	402,173
Residence Apartment G	7,994	1987	402,173
L. R. Reynolds Science and Mathematics Hall Addition	26,000	1988	1,900,000
Residence Apartment H	7,994	1991	452,000
Richard M. Webster Communications and Social Science Hall	69,090	1992	7,000,000

ANNOTATED BIBLIOGRAPHY

College Catalogs:

Published in 1938–1939 through 1993–1995 editions, except for 1944–1945, these catalogs provide a complete record of Southern's curriculum and degree offerings as well as other general information. Complete sets are maintained in the Archives and in the Registrar's Office.

Southern Perspectives:

"Perspectives" is a series of more than one hundred videotaped interviews conducted by the Communications Department. Most of the interviews were just prior to or during Southern's fiftieth anniversary celebration. Included are veteran faculty, administrators, and students, many of whom were important in Southern's development and some of whom are deceased.

Personal Interviews:

Interviews are an important source of information on Southern's history. A number of MSSC employees, and others associated with the college, have experiences that span most of the college's history and whose perspectives cannot be matched by any written sources. The Acknowledgement section lists many of these.

Joplin R-8 School District Administrative Records:

These records, consisting of minutes of board meetings, news clippings, and miscellaneous items, provide a rich mine of information on Southern's early history. The Joplin Junior College was a part of the public school system, 1937–1964.

Fred G. Hughes Papers:

These papers, consisting of correspondence, minutes of board meetings, copies of official documents, and miscellaneous items, principally cover the period, 1964–1981, when Hughes served on Southern's Board of Trustees and Regents. Hughes' position as president of these boards during most of this period and as a driving force in the creation of MSSC, make these files one of the richest sources of information on Southern's development into a four-year college.

MSSC Archives:

The major depository of Southern's history, the Archives contain most issues of MSSC's major publications, photographs, programs, news clippings, and miscellaneous memorabilia, including many of the items listed in this bibliography.

Registrar's Office:

The official depository of student records, the Registrar's Office has extensive information on students' academic progress. While grades are confidential, much other information is available.

Minutes of Boards of Trustees and Regents Meetings:

These minutes are an important source on MSSC's administrative history and are maintained in the administrative offices.

Minutes of Faculty Senate and subsidiary faculty organizations:

These minutes provide an important source of information on curriculum development and faculty matters.

The Chart:

Southern's official student newspaper, The Chart, has been published since 1939. The Chart office and the MSSC Archives contain the most complete files, but a number of the early issues are missing. The Archives has complete files from the 1949–1950 academic year to the present, except for an occasional missing issue.

Crossroads:

Southern's official student yearbook, the Crossroads has been published since the 1939 edition with an unnamed issue for the 1937–1938 school year. None were produced in 1972 or 1984. The Crossroads provides the most extensive pictorial account of MSSC's history and features much information on student activities.

Southern! and earlier alumni newsletters:

Published as the Alumni Newsletter, 1969–1978 and as the Lion's Alum, 1978–1981, this alumni news organ has used the name Southern! since 1981. It provides much information on current student and faculty activities and honors, as well as notes on developments among the alumni. The Archives has a complete file except for scattered missing issues.

The Joplin Globe and News-Herald:

The Joplin Globe, now the city's only newspaper, and earlier its afternoon edition, the News-Herald, have always been strong supporters of the college and their issues are a rich source on MSSC administrative developments, sports, and student activities. The News-Herald ceased publication in 1970.

North Central Association of Colleges and Schools (North Central) and National Council for Accreditation of Teacher Education (NCATE) Self Studies:

These studies, made to gain or retain North Central or NCATE accreditation, provide excellent profiles of the college on the specified dates as to student body, curriculum, faculty, facilities, missions, and administrative policies.

The North Central Self Studies for 1949, 1964, 1966, 1970, 1980, and 1987 and the NCATE Self Studies for 1973, 1983, 1984, and 1990 can be found in the MSSC Archives.

Sports Information Center:

This center is a depository of sports programs, guides, photographs, video tapes, miscellaneous statistics, and bulletins. Very complete for the period 1968 forward, the center has little on the junior college era.

Career Planning and Placement Center Reports:

The center has issued these reports annually since the 1968–1969 academic year. They provide an analysis of enrollment and of degrees granted. The MSSC Archives has a complete file.

Public Information Office files:

This office has extensive files of photographs, biographical data on faculty/staff and records of student activities.

Southern Accents:

This Public Information Office newsletter has been published since 1985. It lists upcoming college activities and provides notes on faculty/staff and student activities. The MSSC Archives has copies.

ABOUT THE AUTHOR

G. K. Renner retired from Missouri Southern State College in 1990 where he served in the Social Science Department for twenty-five years, teaching principally American history and holding the position of department head for two years.

Renner has a bachelor's degree from Southwest Missouri State University, Springfield, a master's degree in education from the University of Missouri, Kansas City, and a master's in history from the University of Missouri, Columbia. He also has a doctor of philosophy degree in history from the latter institution, and has done postgraduate work at the University of California, Berkeley, and at the United States Military Academy, West Point.

The author has written a number of articles published in professional journals and one book, *Joplin: From Mining Town to Urban Center*, published in 1985. He has been active in civic affairs, serving on public boards and as a member of the Silver Creek Village Board of Trustees for eight years where he held various posts including that of chairman.